POSTCARD HISTORY SERIES

Watertown

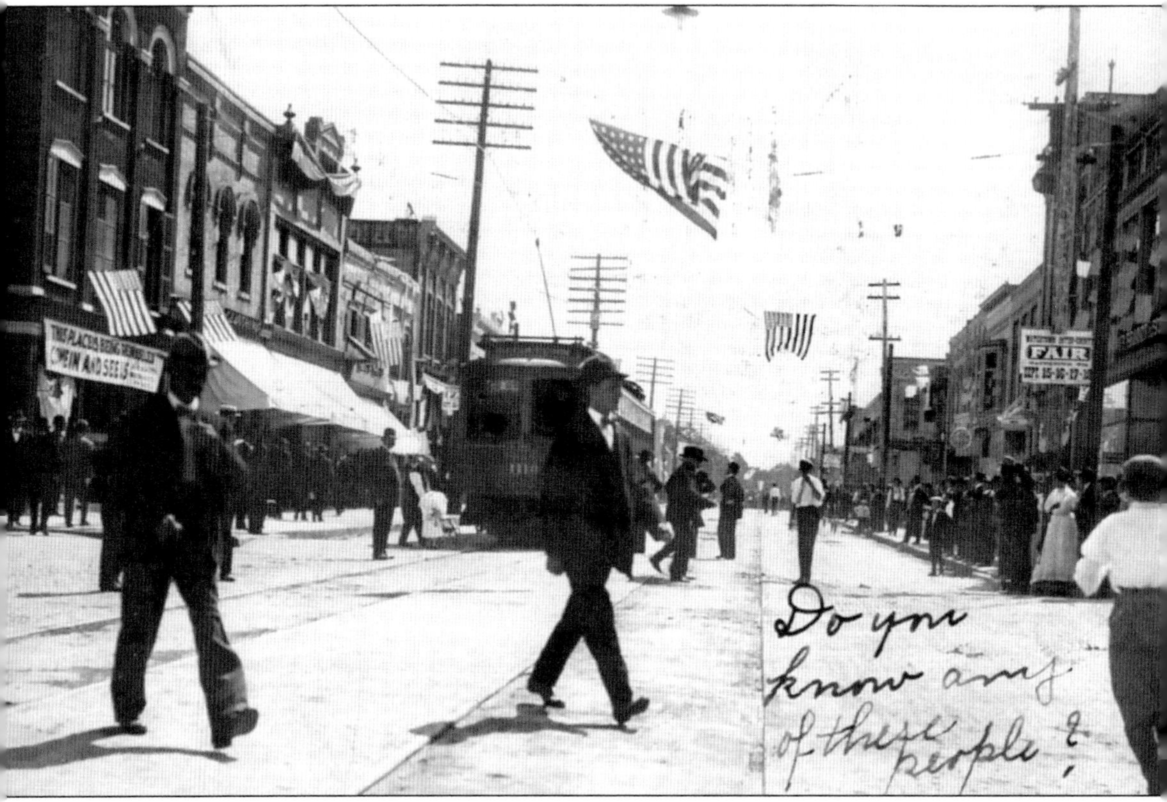

The Inter-County Fair was held in Watertown for many years. This view shows a throng of fairgoers assembled on Main Street in 1908.

POSTCARD HISTORY SERIES

Watertown

W. F. Jannke III

ARCADIA
PUBLISHING

ISBN 978-0-7385-3998-0

Published by Arcadia Publishing
Charleston, South Carolina

Printed in the United States of America

Library of Congress Catalog Card Number: 2005932196

For all general information contact Arcadia Publishing at:
Telephone 843-853-2070
Fax 843-853-0044
E-mail sales@arcadiapublishing.com
For customer service and orders:
Toll-Free 1-888-313-2665

Visit us on the Internet at www.arcadiapublishing.com

Contents

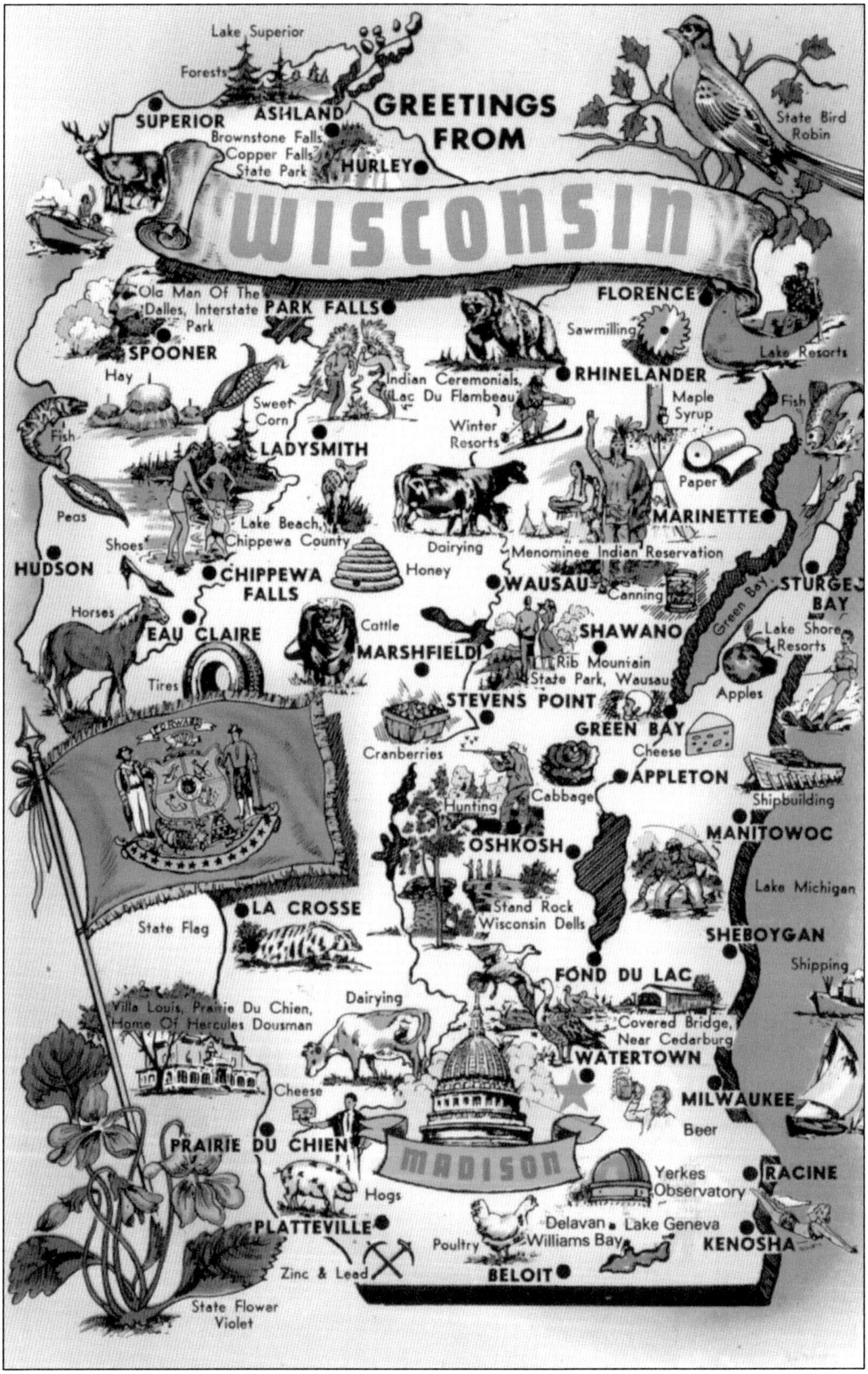

Watertown is located in the southeastern corner of Wisconsin, halfway between Milwaukee, the state's largest city, and Madison, the state capital.

Introduction

I began to collect Watertown postcards in the mid-1980s. It began as an outgrowth of my interest in the city's history. There were only a few people who were collecting at that time, and it was possible to still find rare views cheaply. But by the 1990s, it seemed as though the entire population of Watertown was collecting postal views of the city, and suddenly these delicate pieces of ephemera became harder and harder to find, their values rising dramatically.

People began to hoard postcards and became very secretive about their collections. But, really, what good is a collection of anything if it is not shown and shared with others? It is with that thought in mind that I set out to compile this book. This was not my first foray into book publishing—far from it. But this book was surely the hardest to assemble because of the wealth of images that exist of Watertown. What to choose? What to choose?

Let me tell you a little about my hometown. Watertown is located in the southeastern corner of Wisconsin, midway between Milwaukee, the state's largest city, and Madison, the state capital. It was founded in 1836 by Timothy Johnson, a Connecticut Yankee. Our chief claim to fame is the fact that the first kindergarten in America was founded here in 1856. Watertown is also the birthplace of Joseph E. Davies, ambassador to Russia during the administration of Franklin Delano Roosevelt; Edwin S. Witte, the creator of the Social Security Act; and Daniel Brandenstein, a NASA astronaut. We are a city of rich and diverse ethnicity, made up chiefly of German and Irish settlers, with smatterings of Bohemian and Welsh immigrants. We also have a rising Hispanic population. With a population of over 22,000 and diverse industries, not to mention a large public park system, the quality of life here is good. We are a big city with a small-town feel.

That said, allow me to mention something about the views you will encounter in this book. Who would have imagined that a city the size of Watertown, with a mere 10,000 or so residents during the so-called golden era of postal views (1900–1950), would have generated so many postcards? There are at least 10 to 15 variations of certain views, such as Veteran's Park, the library, or Riverside Park. The sheer number of cards is staggering.

The oldest postcard I have seen, not counting private mailing cards, which date to the 1870s, is a card from the Harvest Jubilee in 1899. Most cards date from between 1905 and 1961, with a few views coming out into the present time. These cards were available at drugstores, bookstores, and ice-cream parlors—in short, anywhere one could look. Some were done in bright colors, others were hand tinted, and some were cheaply done.

The subjects covered were extraordinary, from industry to Main Street to hospitals and calamitous events. Nothing seemed too trivial not to warrant a postcard. Many were produced by the L. L. Cook Company, while others were put out by various independent publishers and private individuals.

Thus, I was drawn to collecting these images of old Watertown, and, in turn, I present them to you, the reader. Most of the cards contained in this work come from my personal collection. However, I have also had the good fortune to be able to have access to the collections of a few others—namely, Gerald Kreitzman and Frank Lindemann. I would like to thank them for their kindness in allowing me to publish images from their collections. I would like to dedicate this book to collectors of Watertown memorabilia everywhere.

If you have never been to Watertown, or if you are new to the city, then let this book be a sort of introduction to you. Allow me to be your guide through the many changing faces of Watertown, Wisconsin, a very untypical, typical Midwestern city.

—W. F. Jannke III

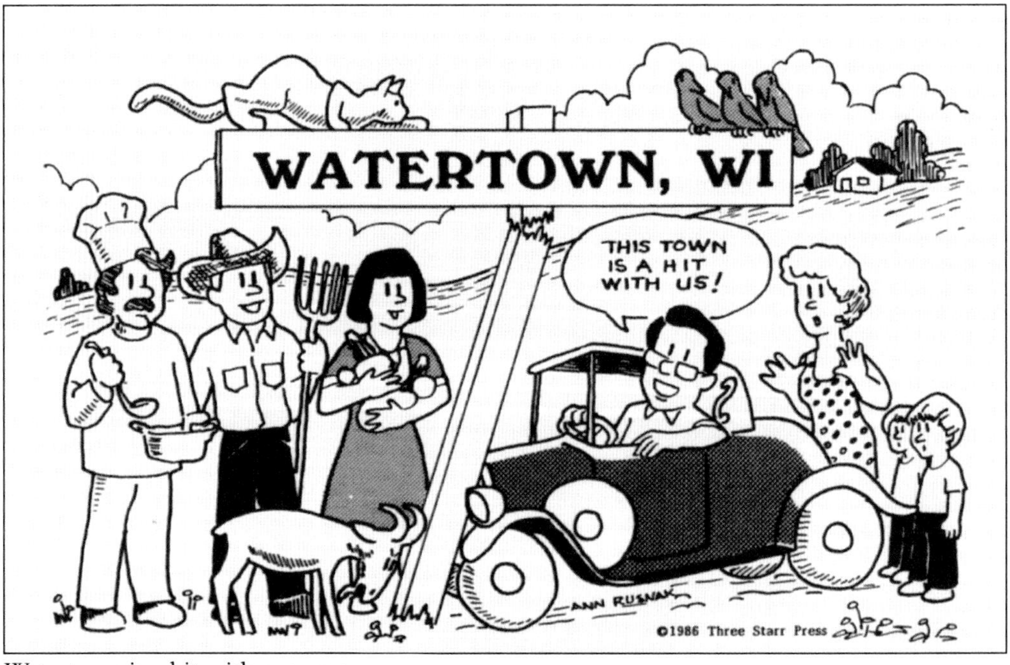

Watertown is a hit with everyone.

One

A Tour of Watertown

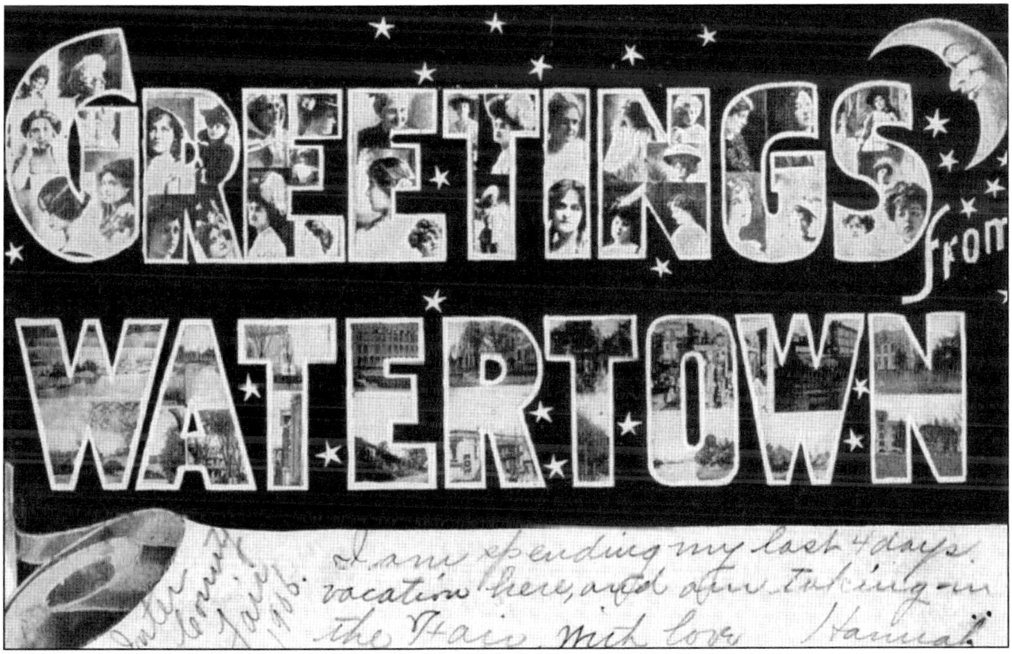

This nostalgic look back at the history of this little town starts by acquainting the reader with some of Watertown's features. On the next few pages, readers will travel down the same streets people have been traversing for more than 160 years. This postcard, reading, "Greetings from Watertown," dates to around 1908.

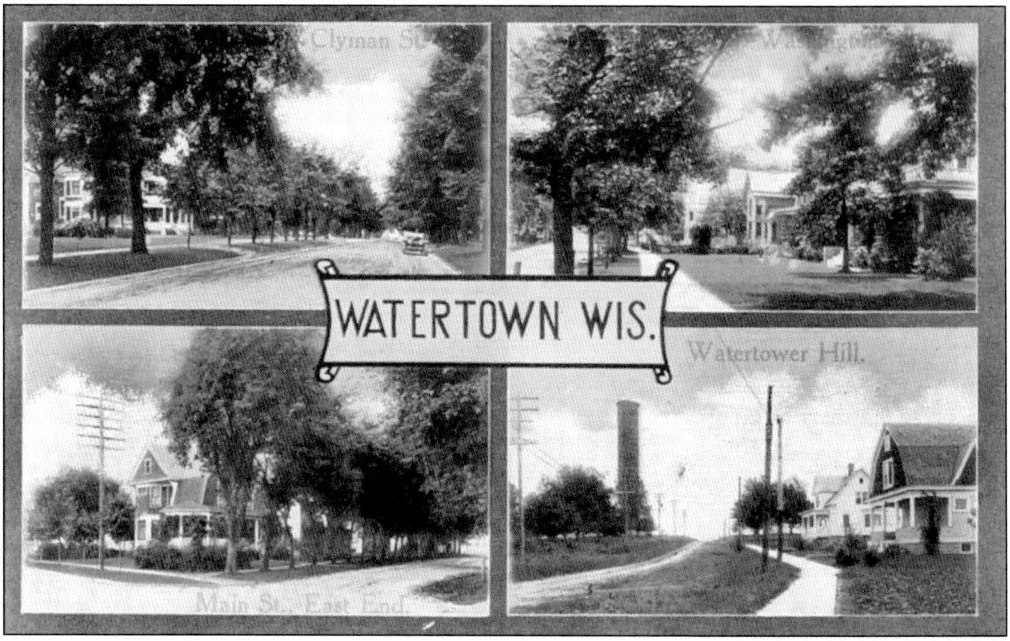

Some of the many areas of the city are featured on this *c.* 1910 card, including Clyman Street, where the rich lived; Washington Street, where the professionals made their homes; East Main Street, which for many years was almost rural; and Western Avenue.

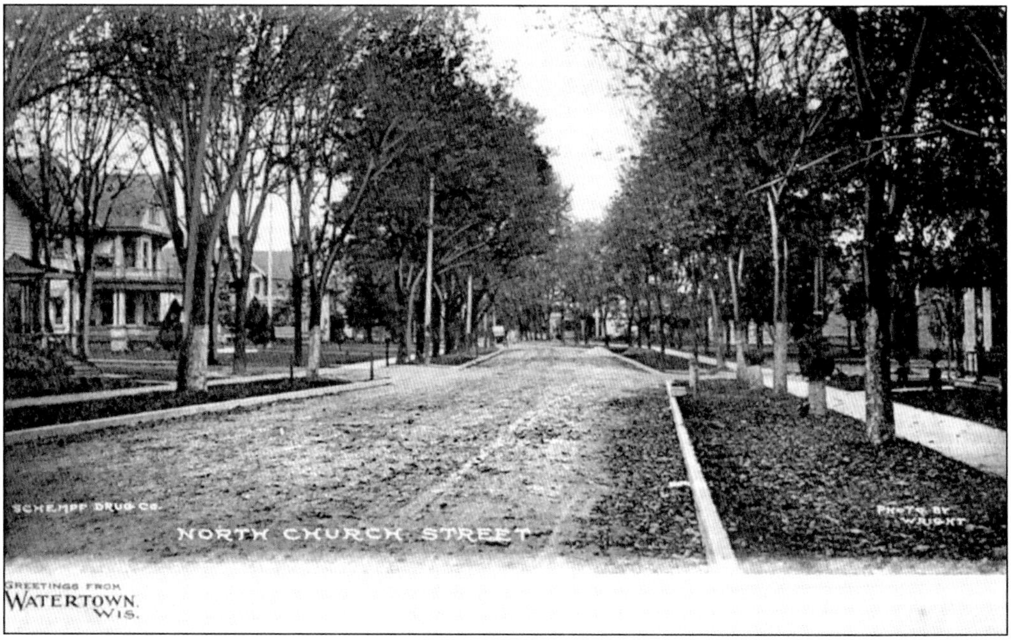

North Church Street, seen here about 1910, was originally called Main Street. When the name of the street was changed is not known precisely, but the fact that one of its chief landmarks is St. Bernard's Catholic Church probably had something to do with it. Most of the homes seen here still line the street, though today it is a much wider street, and some of the trees seen here no longer exist.

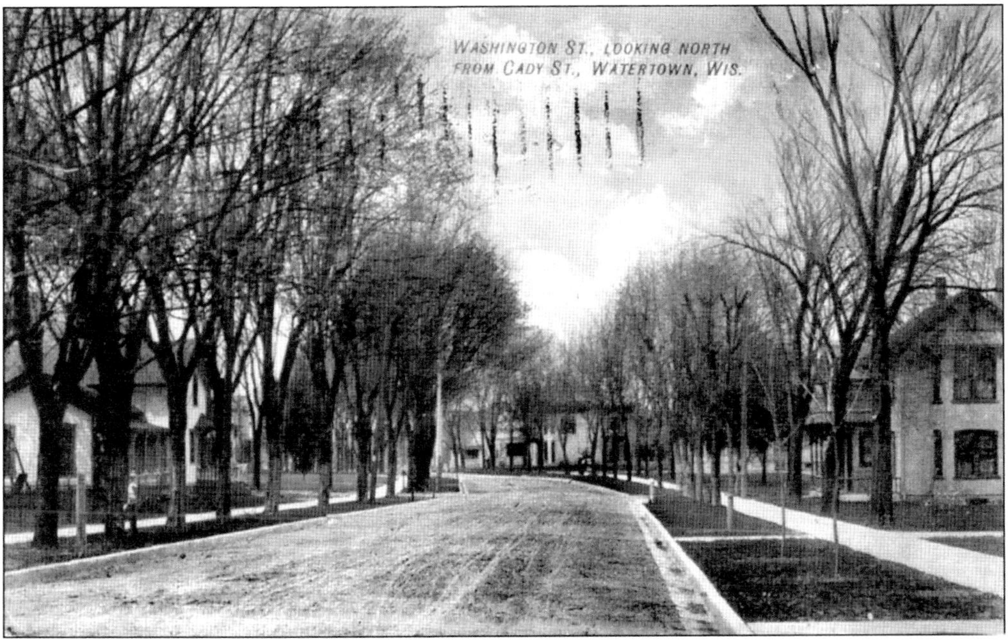

North Washington Street, seen here about 1908, makes a graceful curve as it wends its way northward. The street maintains its quiet elegance, and many of the city's professionals made their homes along here, such as Dr. Martin Barber, known locally as "the children's doctor," since he had a winning way when treating children.

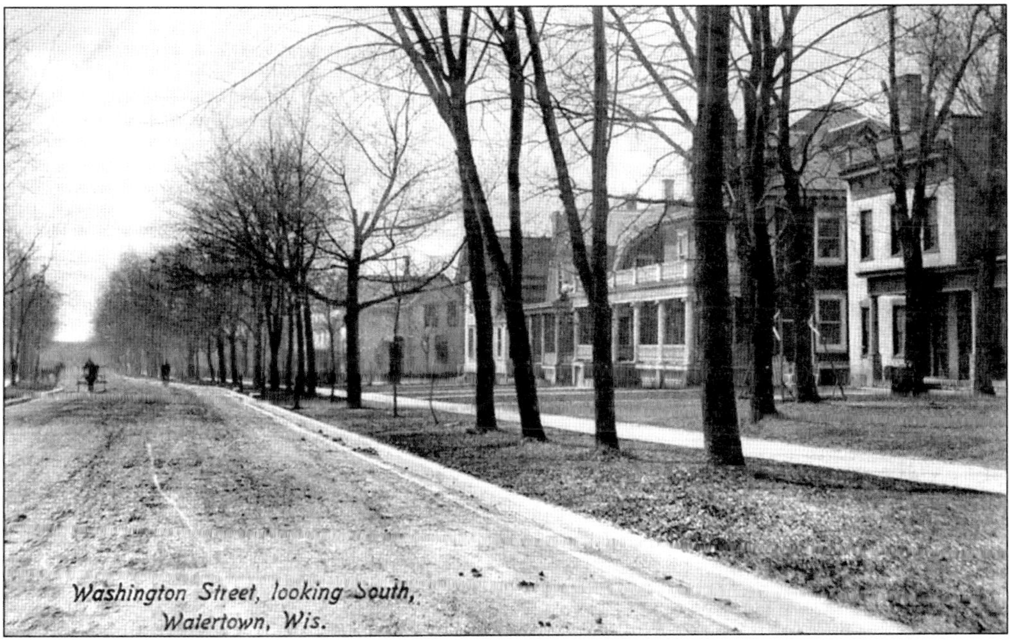

South Washington Street is shown here, also in a 1908 view. Though it may appear to be a rather bucolic setting, in reality South Washington was and still is in the heart of a commercial area, with busy South Church Street a block to the west and South Water Street, also a scene of commerce and industry, a block to the east. Many of the homes located along this street are considered architectural gems and belonged to men with ties to commerce.

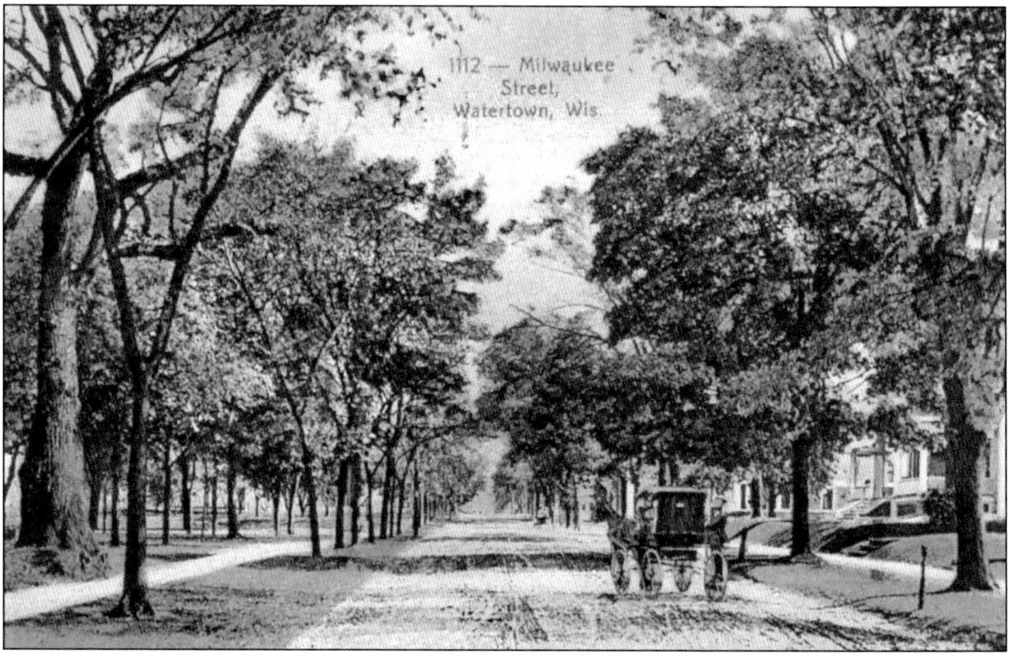

Milwaukee Street bisects South Church, South Washington, and South Water Streets, running east and west. Seen here in 1911, the street runs along the south of a large public square known today as Veteran's Park. A portion of the park can be seen on the left of the image shown here.

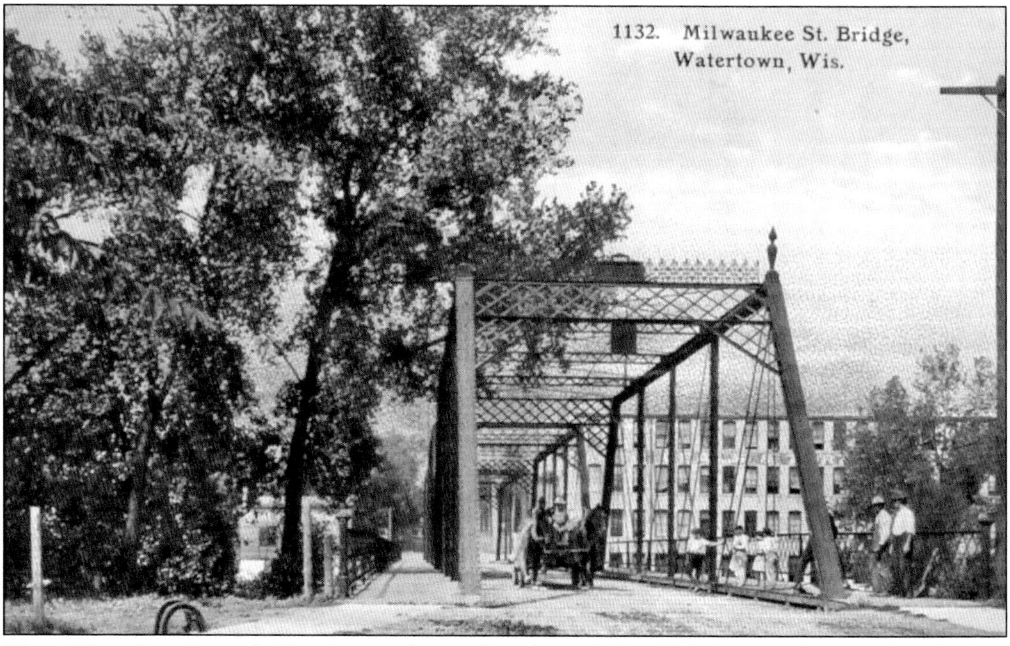

The Milwaukee Street bridge is seen here, also about 1911. This is a good example of a box girder bridge, the kind that was seen in the city and in many of the outlying areas. A new bridge replaced this one about 1930.

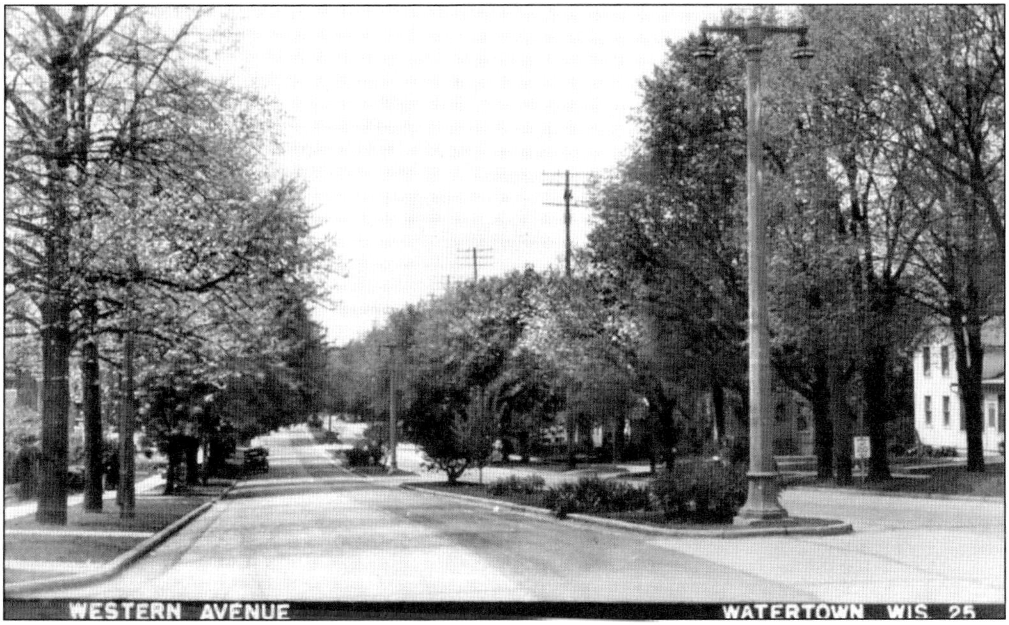

This is Western Avenue about 1944. Despite its name, this street is located on the eastern side of the Rock River and runs to the east. There was some talk at one time about connecting this street by bridge to the west side, but apart from an artist's rendering on a bird's-eye view map of 1867, nothing ever came of it.

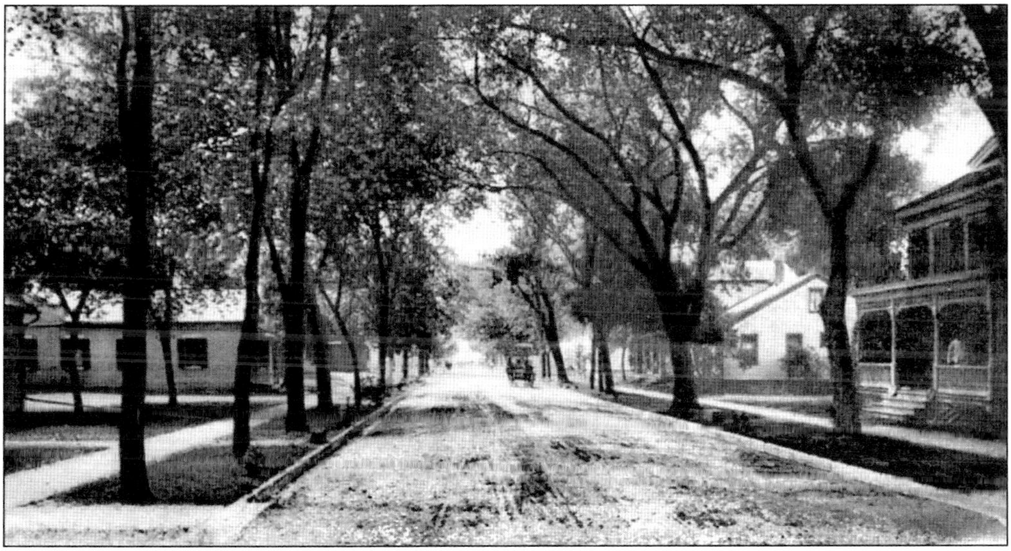
This image of Second Street dates to about 1908. This quiet street is made up chiefly of small, brick homes that once belonged to German residents. Stores and saloons at one time peppered the corners of the street. Shown on the right of the image is the home of Dr. William F. Whyte, one of the city's most beloved physicians.

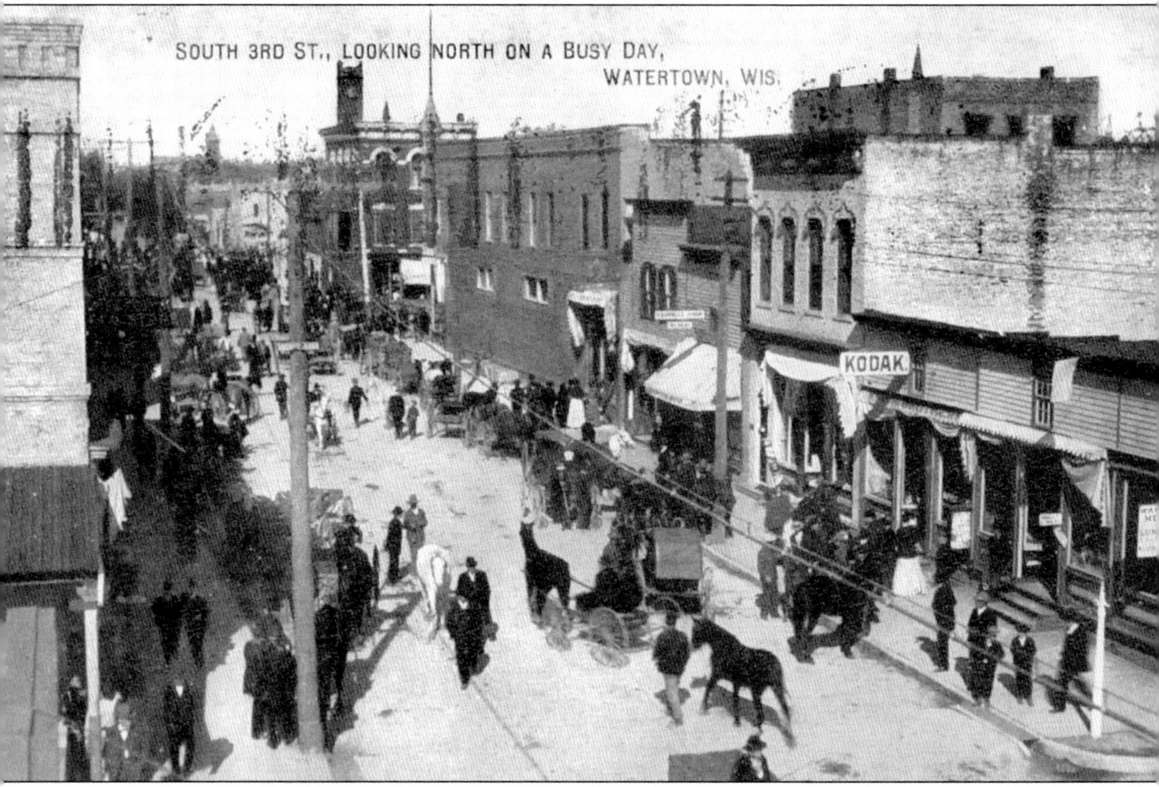

This image of South Third Street, taken about 1909, shows one of the busier thoroughfares in the city. This picture was taken during one of the city's cattle fairs, or "Viehmarkt," a monthly event held in the city since 1860. The buildings shown here, for the most part, still stand and are still used as retail and commercial enterprises.

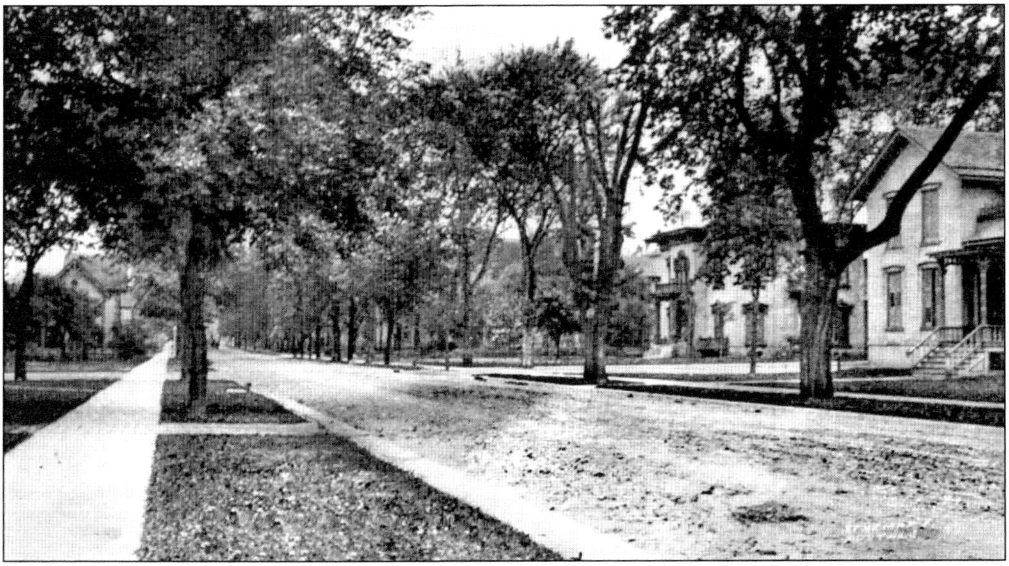

This is South Fourth Street, once a very quiet street with the Congregational church being the major landmark of the area. Today this is a very busy thoroughfare, with the city's post office and Turner Hall located along this stretch of street. The home seen here on the right, about 1910, was originally built by Christian Schmutzler, a pioneer builder of homes in Watertown, for David Pugh, a dealer in boots and shoes, in the 1880s. The home still stands.

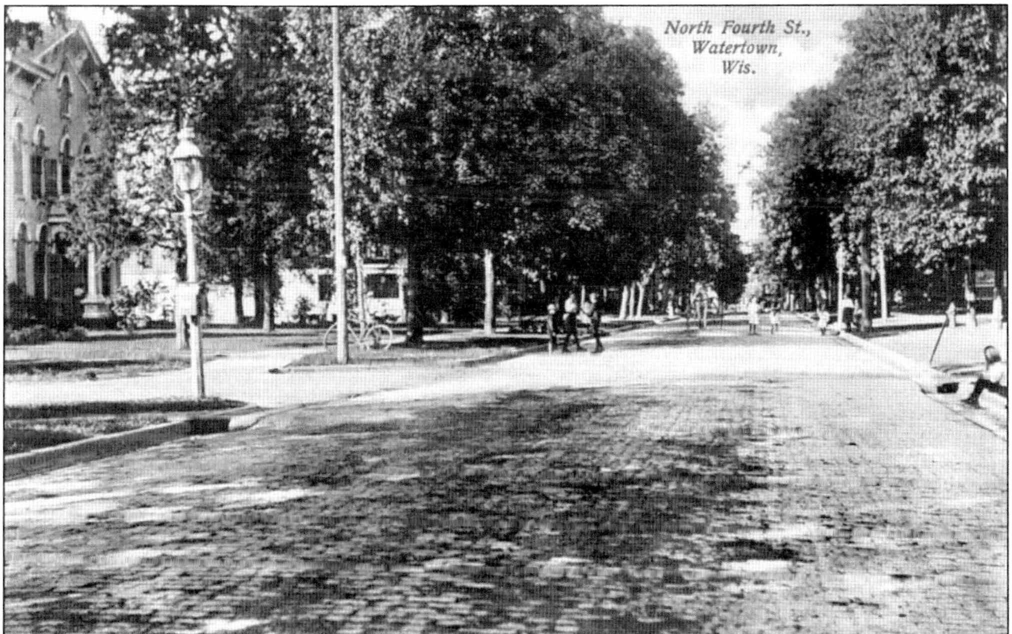

North Fourth Street, seen here about 1912, has never been a terribly quiet street, located on a direct route to the town of Hustisford, which lies to the north of Watertown. The home of John W. Cole, built in the mid-1850s, can be seen on the left-hand side of the picture. Cole was a pioneer resident and city benefactor.

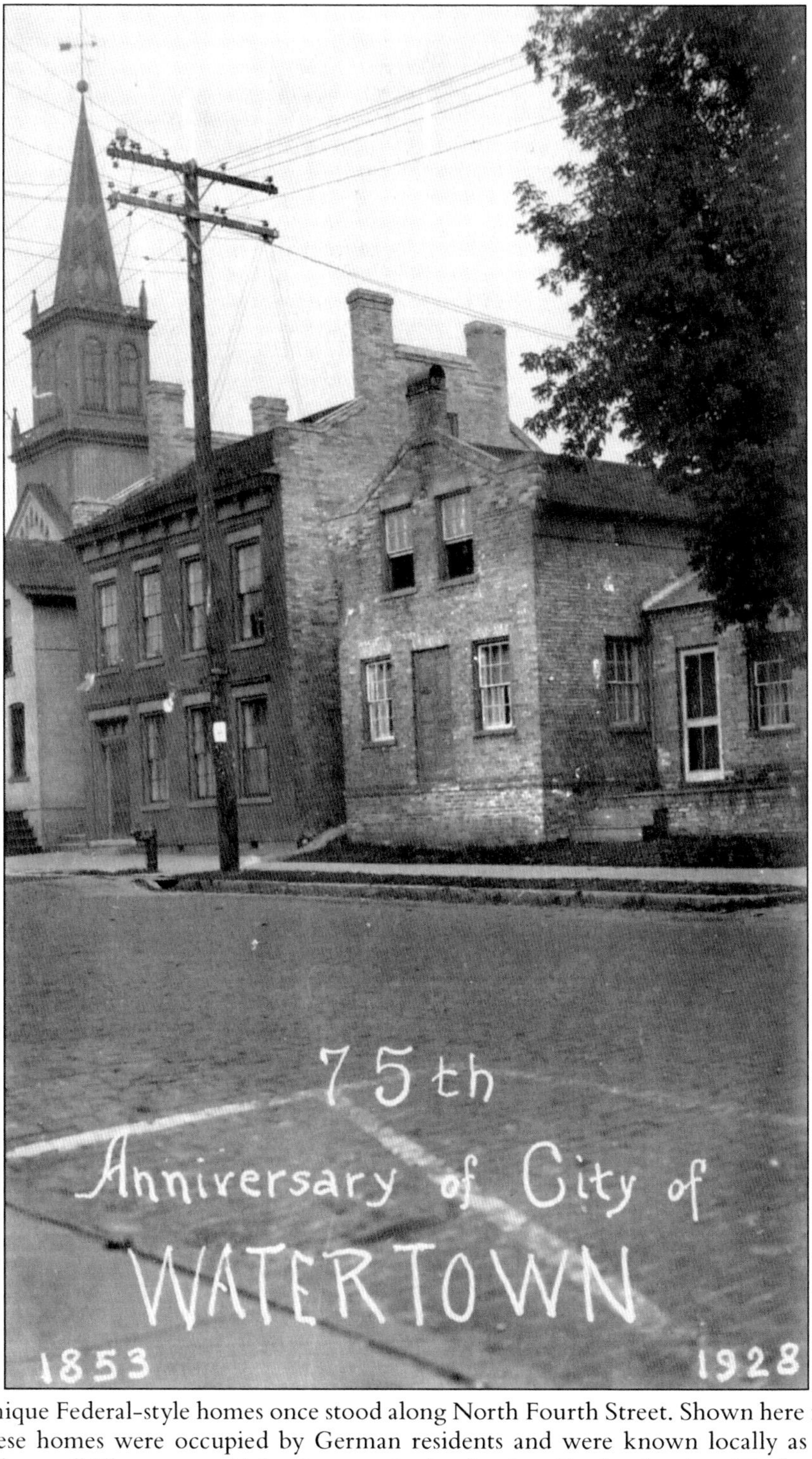

These unique Federal-style homes once stood along North Fourth Street. Shown here in a 1928 view, these homes were occupied by German residents and were known locally as the "old German homes." They were widely photographed and painted by local artists. The homes were demolished in the 1960s to allow for East Madison Street to be extended. Today all that exists of these once distinctive homes is a parking lot.

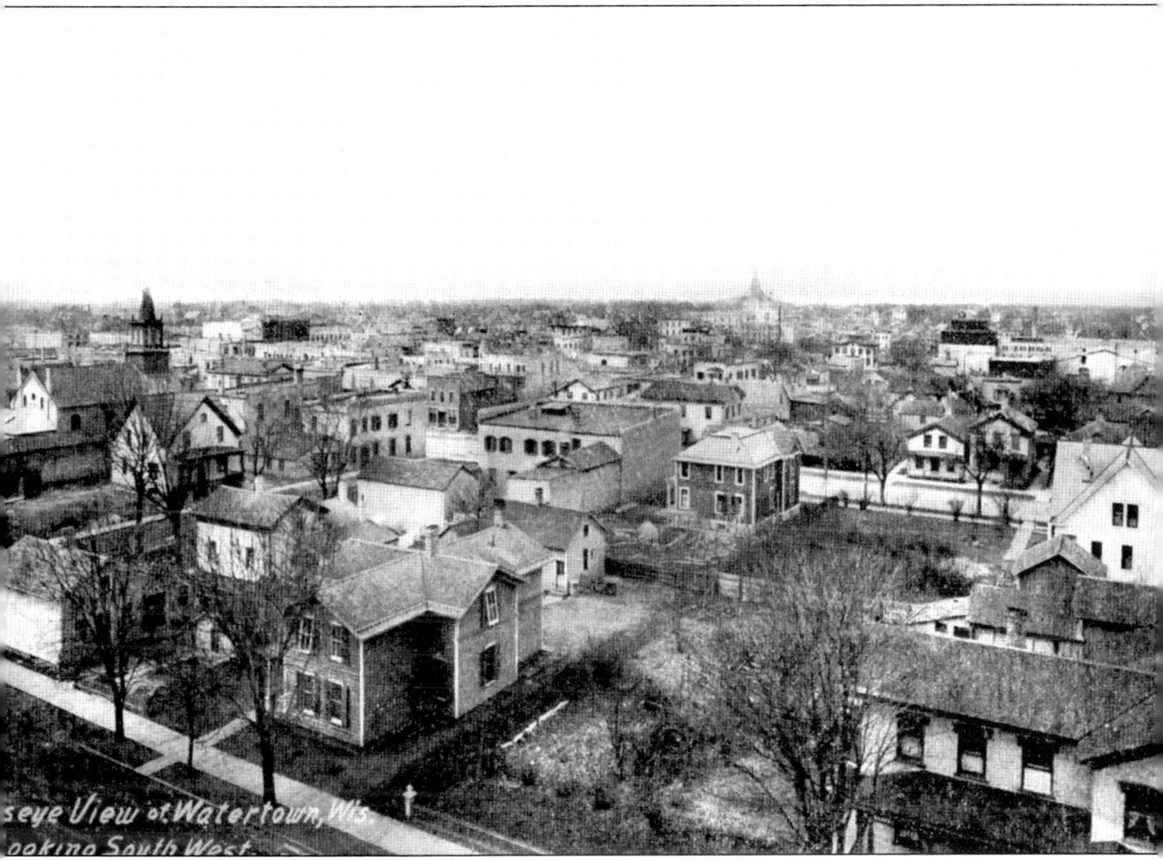

Here is a bird's-eye view of North Fourth Street, in the background, and North Fifth Street, in the foreground. Most, if not all, of the buildings seen still stand in the city, with the exception of St. Luke's Lutheran Church, which was demolished in the early 1960s, and the city's first high school, which can just be seen on the extreme left of the image. This image dates from about 1908.

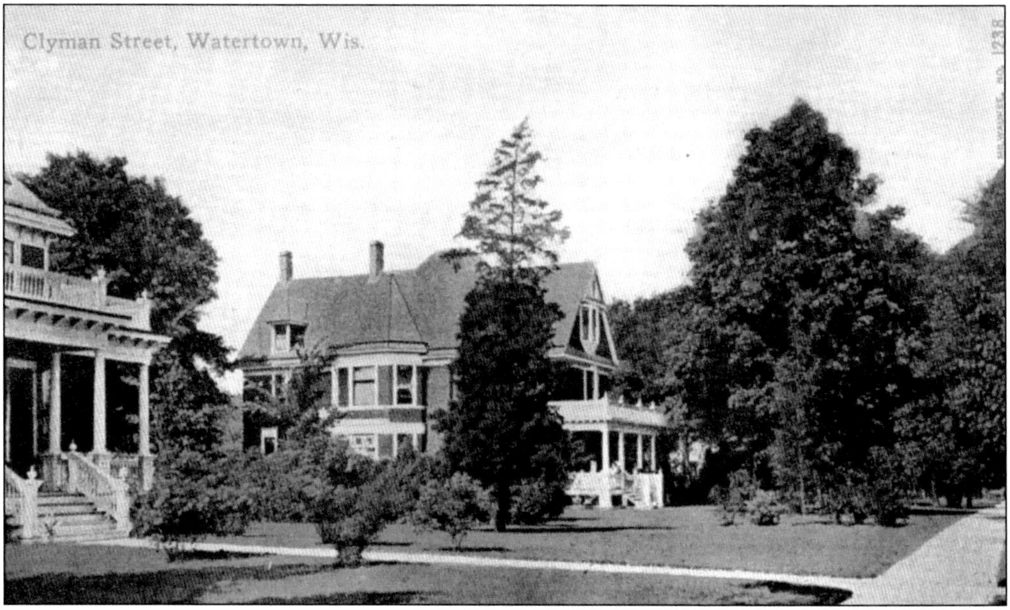

The second largest collection of historic architectural styles can be found along Clyman Street, located in the southern part of the city. Many of the homes here date to the 1890s and are in the Queen Anne style, though there are a few that date to the 1850s and 1860s. The street was known as the home of the city's well-to-do, and many prominent personages lived along here, such as the Kading family, all of whom were in the legal profession, the Wiggenhorns, prominent cigar manufacturers, and Theodore Prentiss, the city's first mayor.

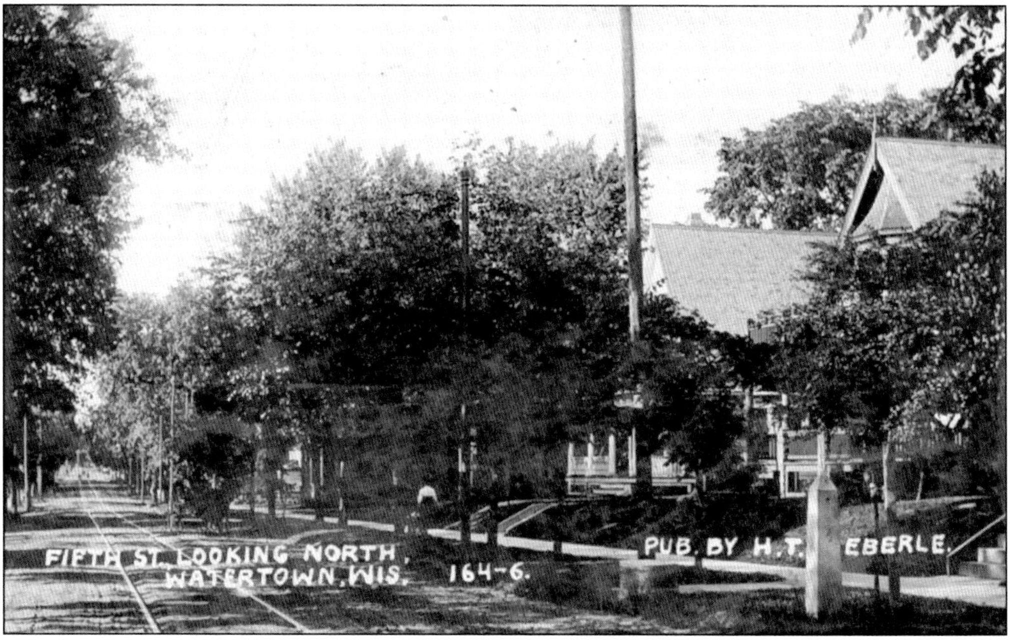

Looking north in 1909, this view shows Fifth Street, which was heavily tree lined at one time. Note the trolley tracks running along the street and the hitching post, a quaint reminder of the past. If you look hard, you can still find a few hitching posts and carriage steps located along the city streets.

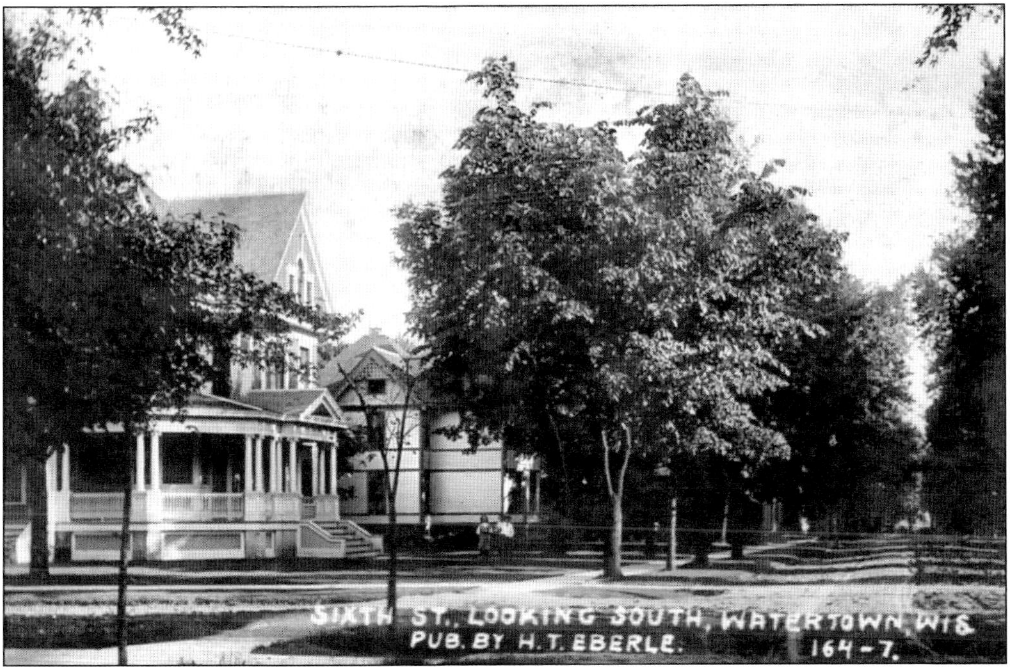

Taken about 1909, this view of Sixth Street shows a few of the large homes located along the right of way. The Andrew Hoffmann home, 601 Sixth Street, can be seen on the left. Hoffmann was a partner in the firm of Hertel and Hoffmann, a tailoring and clothing firm.

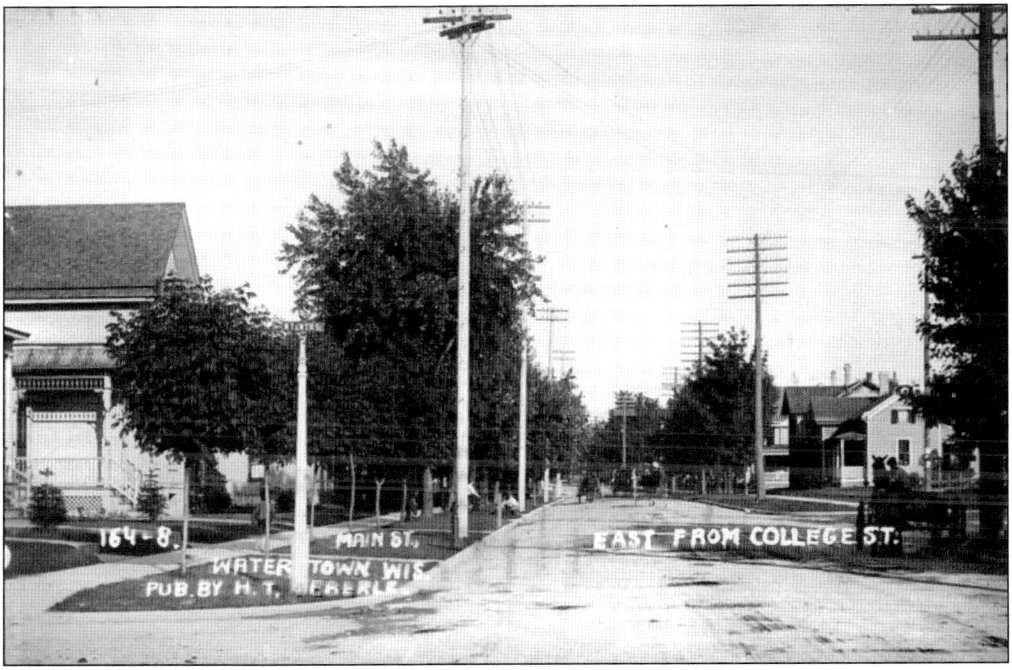

Though identified as East Main Street from College Street, this is, in fact, East Main Street and Tenth Street. Many of the homes seen here still stand. East Main Street was for many years almost rural in its look, with St. Mary's Hospital, a gas station, and a tavern being the sole commercial structures located along the street.

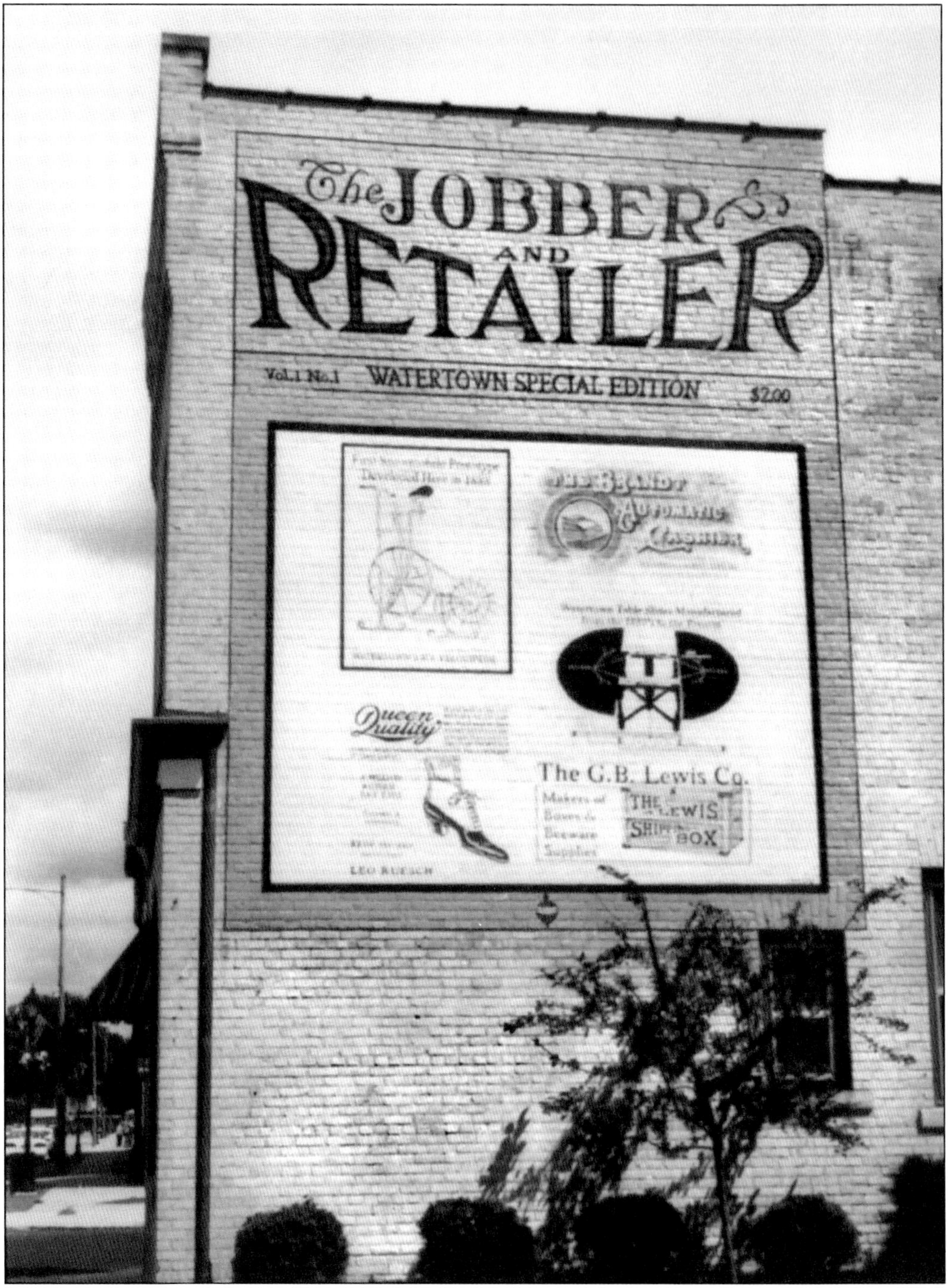

Beginning in the late 1990s, the Watertown Tourism Board, the Watertown Arts Council, and the Watertown Main Street Program began to fund a series of murals depicting aspects of the city's history. This mural, which highlights various goods once manufactured here, appears on the side of the chamber of commerce building. Built in 1901, the building originally housed a saloon, then a doctor's office, and later a karate studio before becoming the headquarters of the chamber. It is amazing to note how many buildings in Watertown were once saloons.

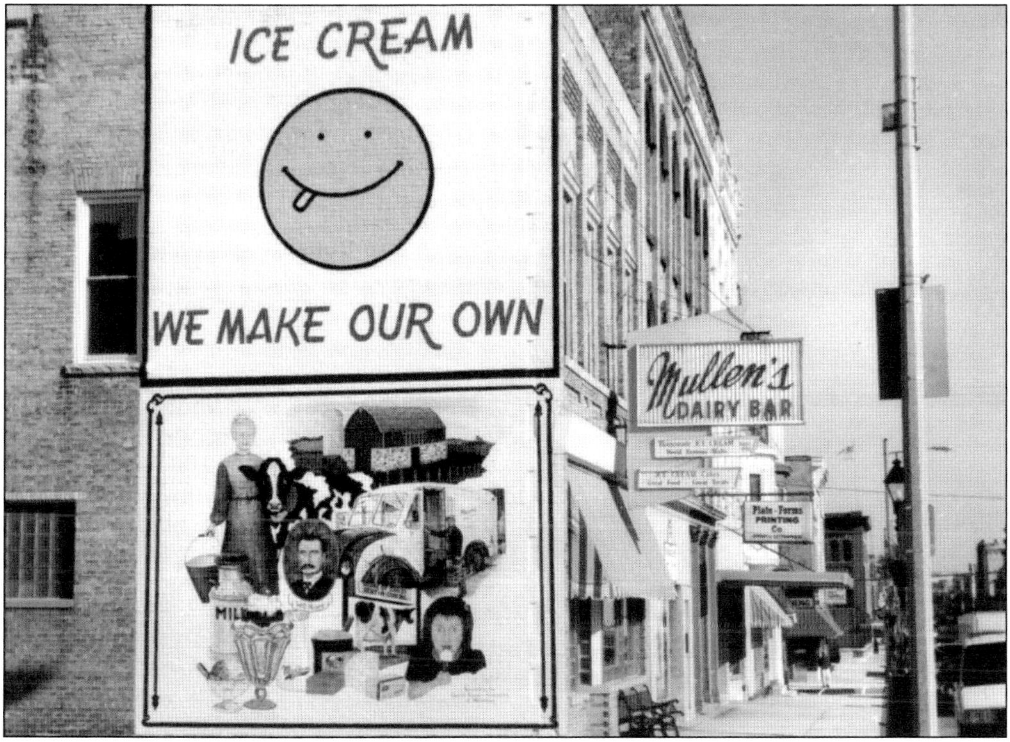

Another of the city's colorful murals can be seen on the side of Mullen's Dairy Bar on West Main Street. This mural depicts various aspects of the history of the dairy industry. William Dempster Hoard, the father of modern dairying practices, is seen prominently in this mural.

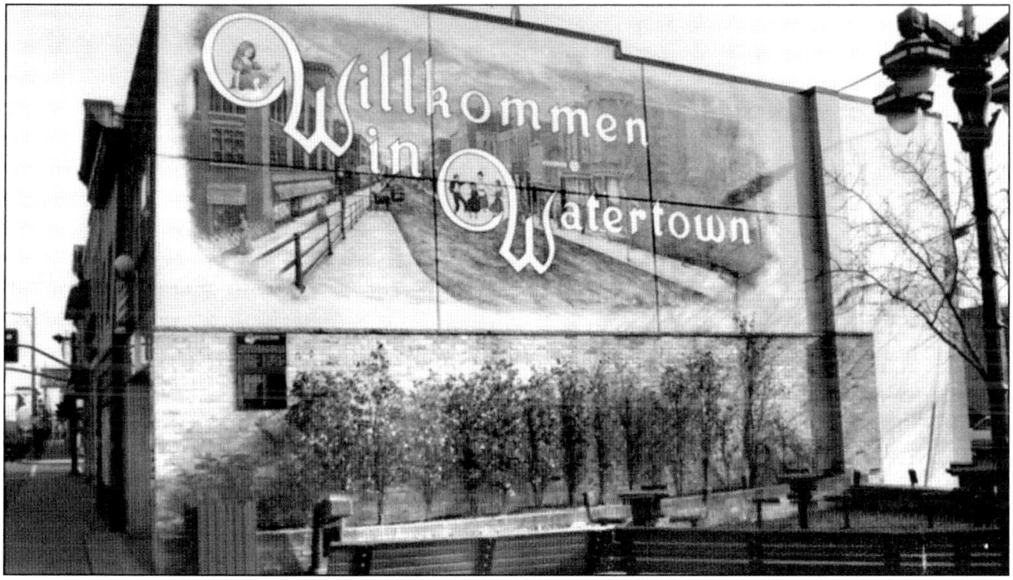

One of the most spectacular murals painted to date would have to be this one, which depicts Watertown's German heritage. The mural can be seen by anyone entering the city from the west. It is visible on the side of Jim's Downtown Barber Shop, located along the river walkway. It shows Watertown's Main Street as it looked in the 1880s.

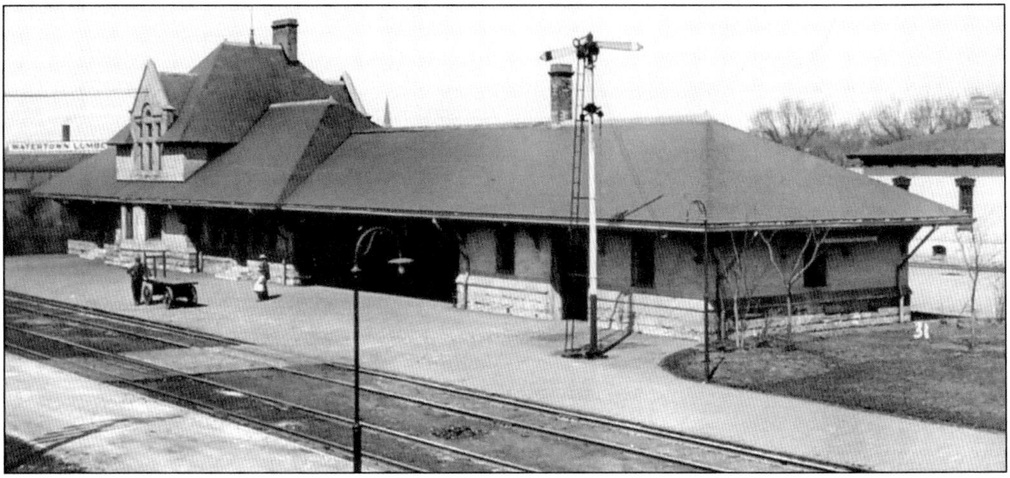

The railroad first entered Watertown in September 1855, bringing prosperity and a certain amount of woe to the city. Here is the Chicago, Milwaukee and St. Paul depot, once located below South Fifth Street, in an image taken about 1915. This is one of three depots that once stood in the city. Only one currently remains—the old Northwestern depot located along West Main Street, today a florist. (Kreitzman Collection.)

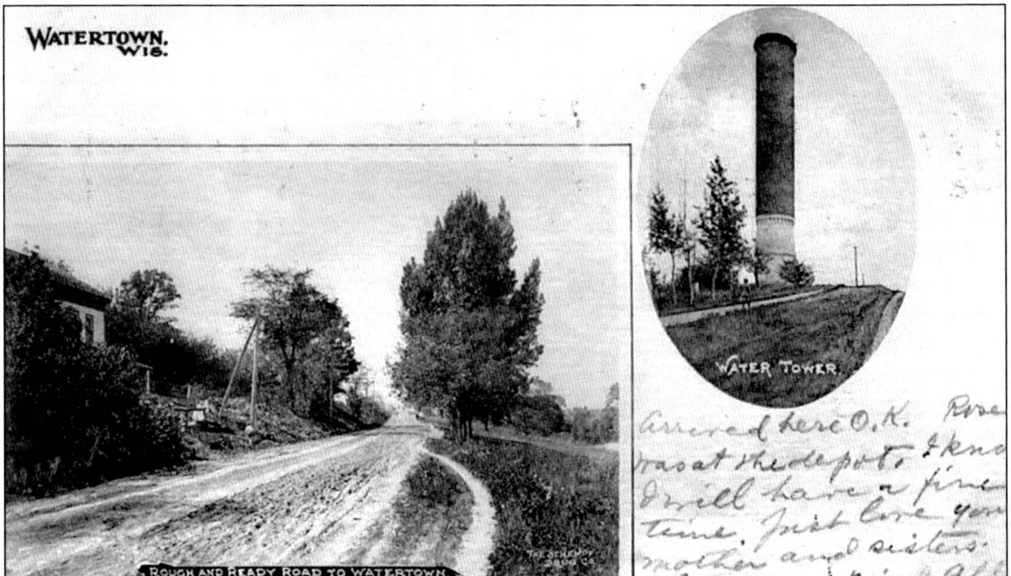

The old Rough and Ready Road is one of the roads leading into the city and is known today as South Concord Avenue. The state of the roads leading into the city, and in the city proper, were often terrible and during certain seasons almost impassable. Improvements in the form of a plank road, which reached the city in 1853, and the railroad, which reached the city in 1855, and later paving of the streets with bricks, which began in 1899, helped travelers reach Watertown and aided in the exporting and importing of goods. Note the home pictured on the left. This house, once believed to have been a tavern, still stands in roughly the same condition as it is pictured here. The water tower on the right was erected in 1895 along Western Avenue and replaced in the 1960s. This road took its name from the Rough and Ready Mill, which stood on the right side of the road until fire destroyed it in 1888.

Two

The River

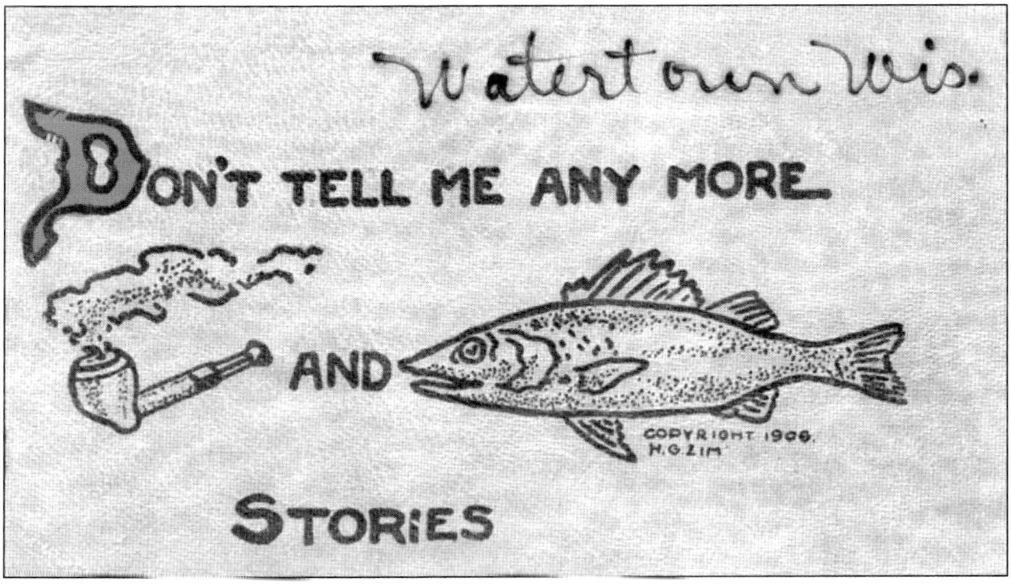

Flowing majestically through the heart of Watertown and forming a graceful loop, or oxbow, is the Rock River. Many businesses were once located along the river, making use of its current to turn their turbines and power their machinery. Homes built by the earliest settlers were also located within easy walking distance from the river to allow for its pure water to be used for drinking and washing and to propel settlers via canoe. Fish were once in abundance as well, and according to one account, there were spots that so teemed with fish that a wagon could cross without fear of dropping in. The river is still fished, people still live near it, and boats and canoes can still be found there today. Thanks to a lovely river walk constructed in 1987 in downtown Watertown, the Rock River and its many beauties can be enjoyed by everyone. The rebus joke slogan on this leather card from 1906, "Don't tell me any more smoke and fish stories," could well describe the stories of early settlers who were fond of spinning yarns about their life in this wild area. One such story told of how much fish the early settlers of Watertown ate. It was claimed that they ate so much fish that no one could take off their clothes and wash them because the fish bones stuck out of their bodies and held their clothes tight to them.

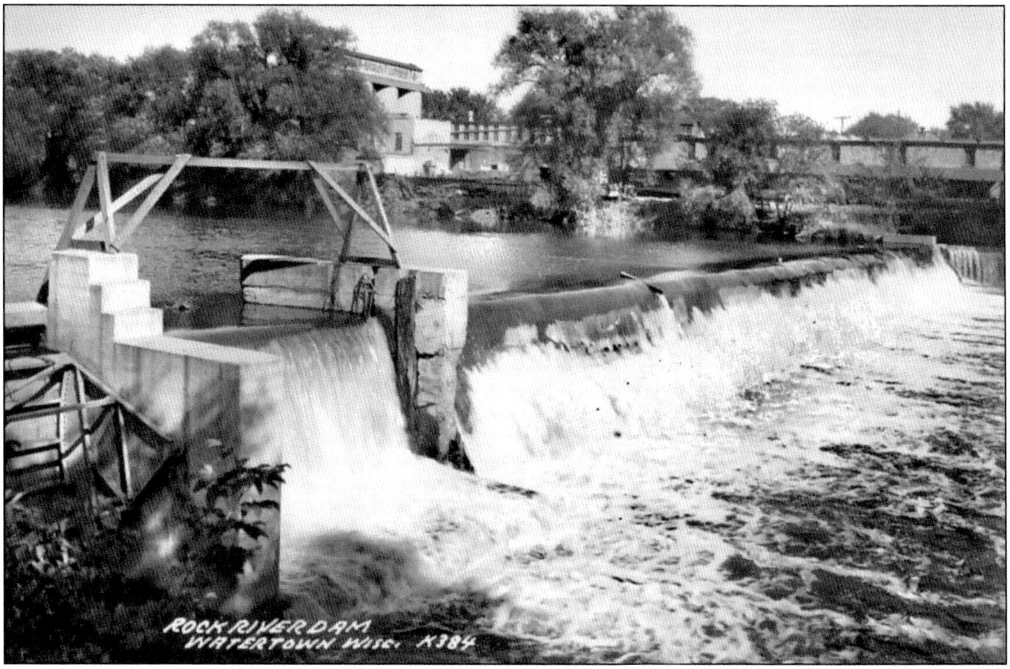

The dam below Main Street along the Rock River is shown about 1950. The first dam ever laid across the river in what is now Wisconsin was laid here in 1837 by Charles Goodhue in connection with the building of a sawmill. Before it was dammed, the Rock River was a raging torrent with dangerous rapids and falls. Native Americans termed this area "Grand Rapids" due to the state of the Rock River here.

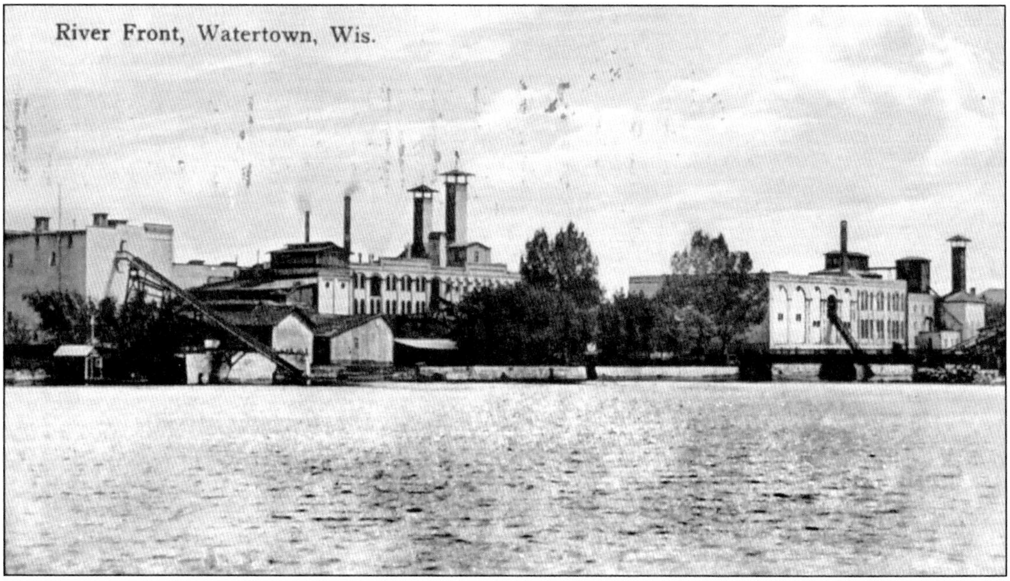

This evocative image shows the Rock River, viewed from the west bank looking east at the Hartig Brewery about 1915. The William Hartig Brewing Company was the city's major brewery, in existence from 1884 to 1947. At one time, breweries such as this used the water in the river for cooling purposes. Each January, teams would go out onto the frozen river and cut ice for the icehouses. The chutes from the icehouse can be seen on the building on the left.

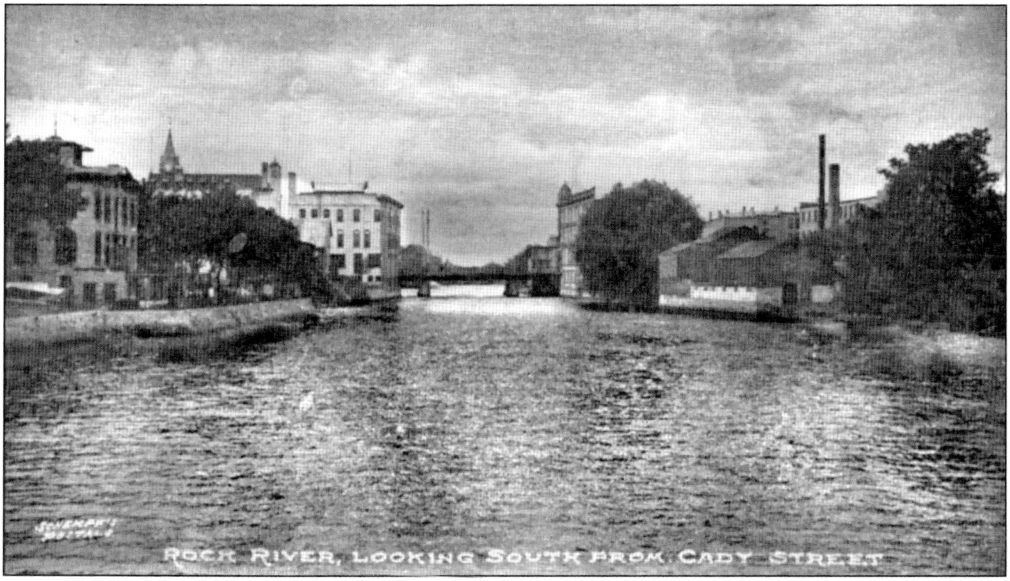

This view of the river is taken from Cady Street bridge looking south about 1910. This charming scene shows the old Fuermann Brewery buildings on the far left. On the right side of the bridge, the Wiggenhorn Cigar Factory can be seen. Today the only buildings left that one could identify using this image as a guide would be the building on the left of the bridge, which was the Masonic temple but is today a department store. The rest of the sites are now, for the most part, parking lots.

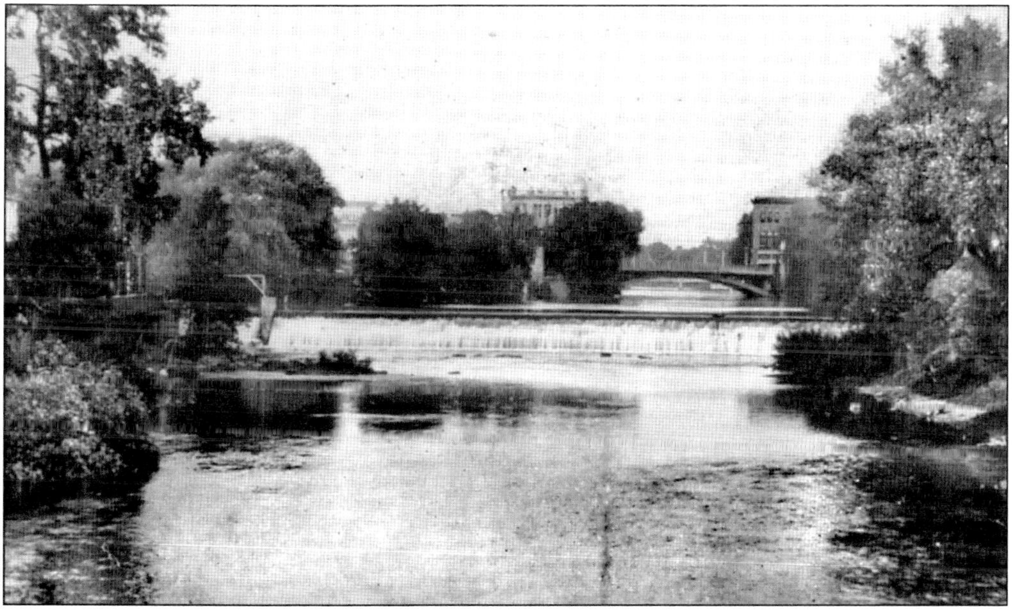

This is the Rock River looking north from the Milwaukee Street bridge around 1938.

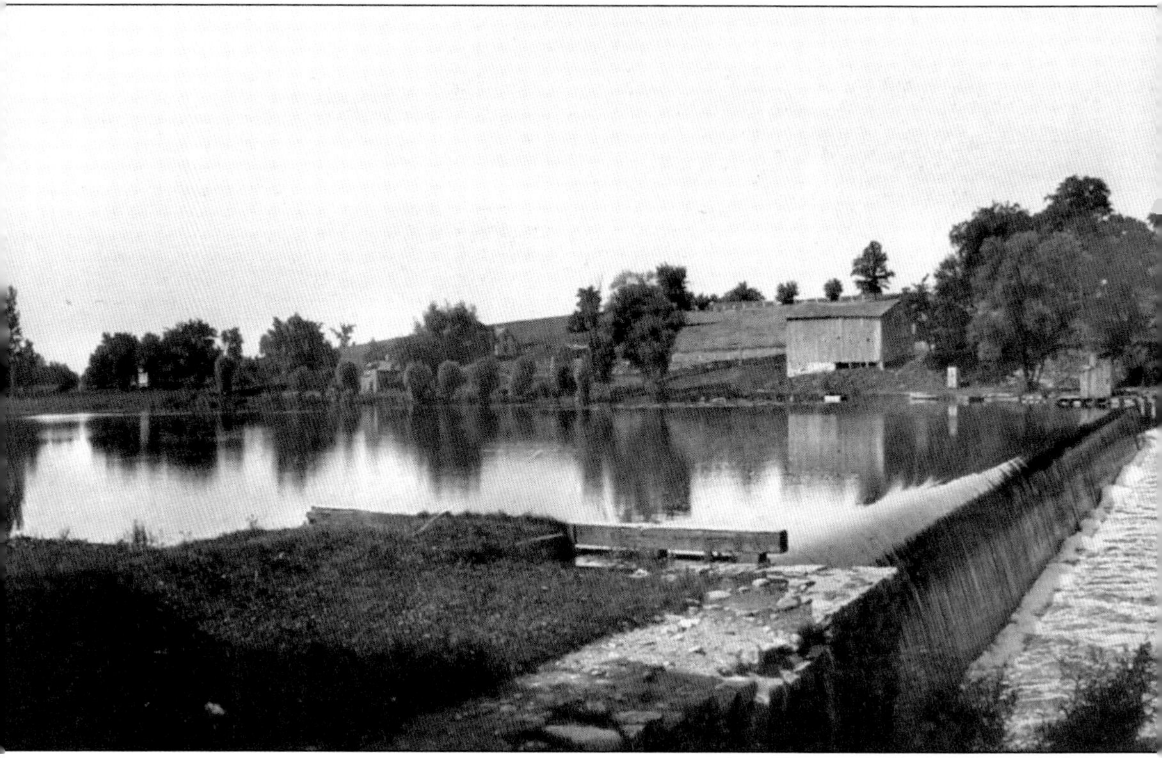

This panoramic view of the old Rough and Ready Dam was taken about 1905. The dam was erected in the mid-1840s by pioneer mill owner John Richards (who built the famous Octagon House, which can be seen in the distance), Heber Smith, and others. There was originally a

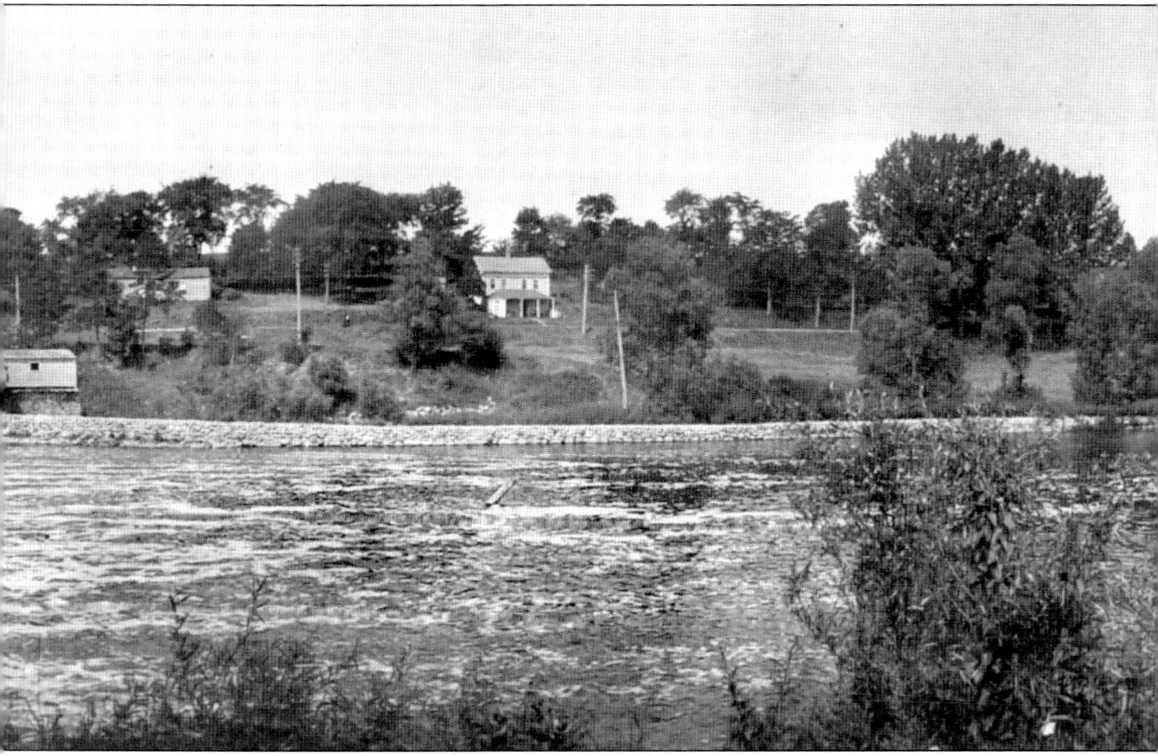

gristmill associated with the dam, but it was destroyed by fire in 1888. In 1909, a power station was built along the river, and a new dam was erected as well.

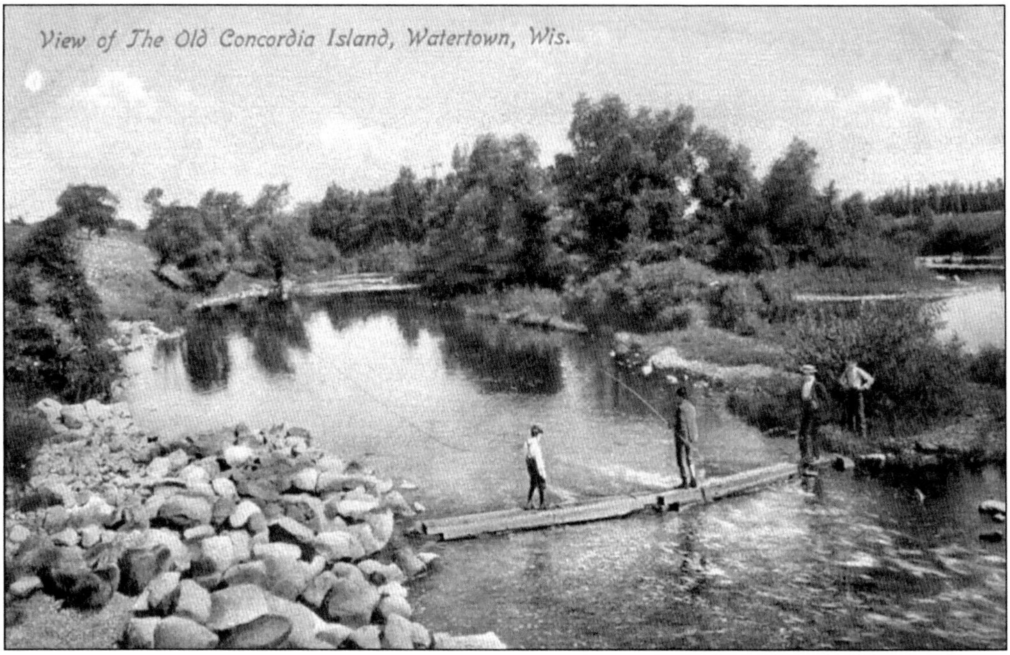

This is Concordia Island about 1908. Located just to the north of the Rough and Ready Dam, this island, now known as Tivoli Island, was a popular haven for picnickers and others seeking recreation from the mid-19th century to the 1920s. Today it is a nature preserve. Fishermen are seen here in a shallow spot on the river along the former millrace.

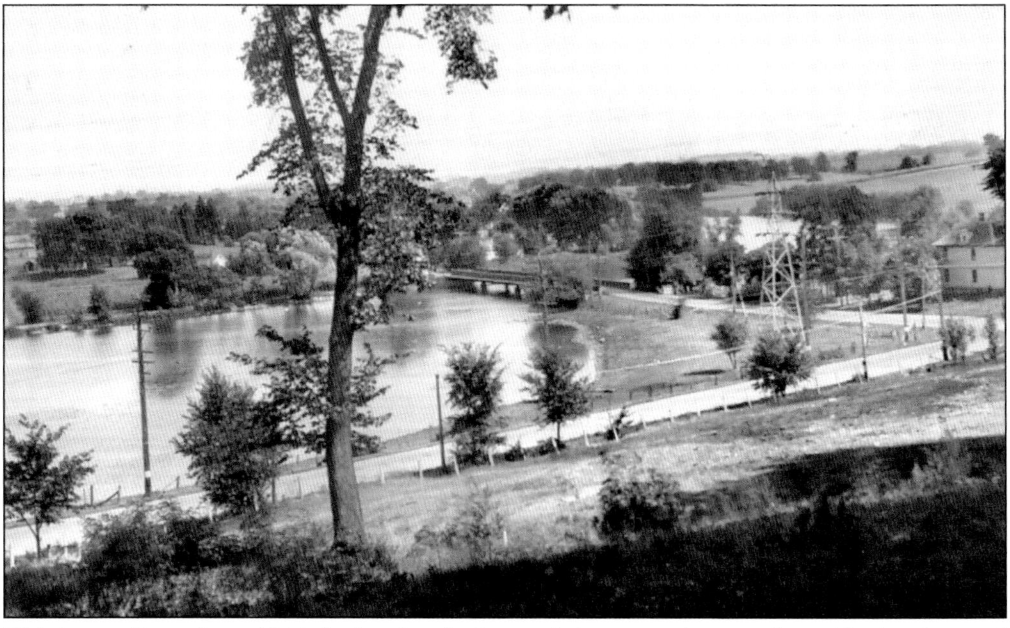

This image from about 1944 depicts South Concord Avenue as it runs alongside the river and Oconomowoc Avenue, which intersects it. This area was known at one time as the Bohemian Settlement due to the abundance of settlers from the former Czech and Slovak Republics who populated this area in the 1850s.

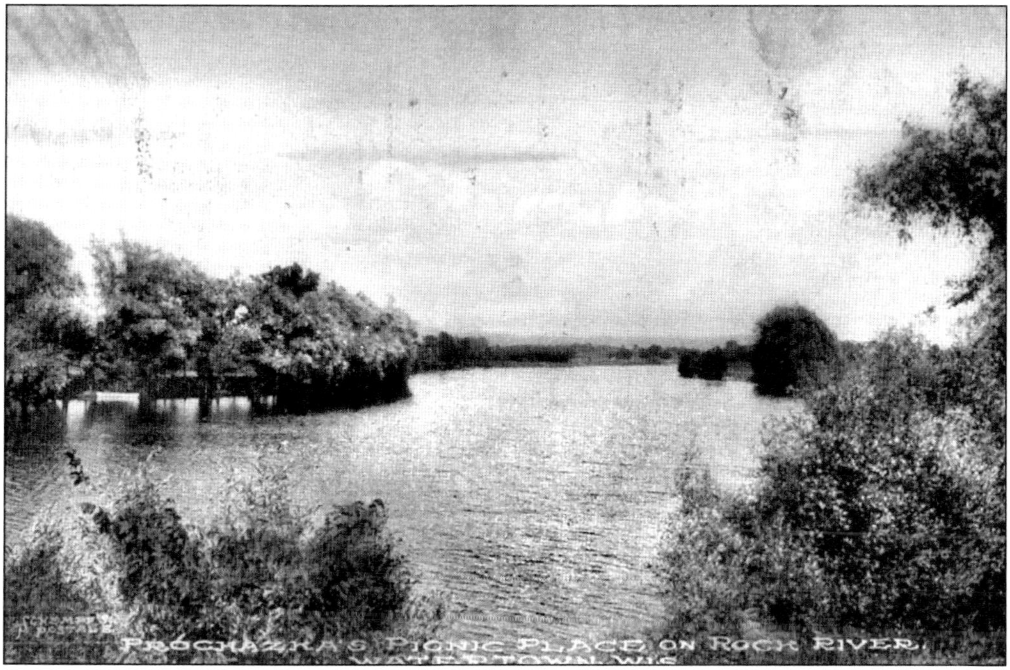

This is Prochazka's Picnic Place, a popular spot for Sunday afternoon picnics and swimming. The Prochazkas were early Bohemian settlers who ran a thriving truck garden business and later left a sizeable fortune to the city that was used to build the band shell at Riverside Park in the 1950s.

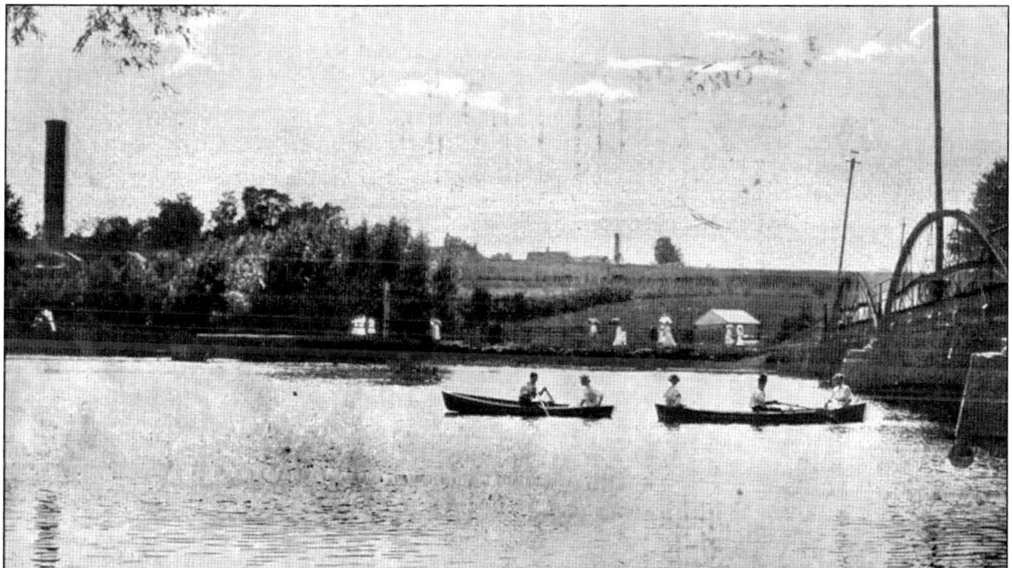

Boating on the Rock River has always been practiced, first as a means of transportation, now as a means of sport. This image shows pleasure seekers making their way over to Tivoli Island to enjoy a day dancing and taking in the beauties of the island.

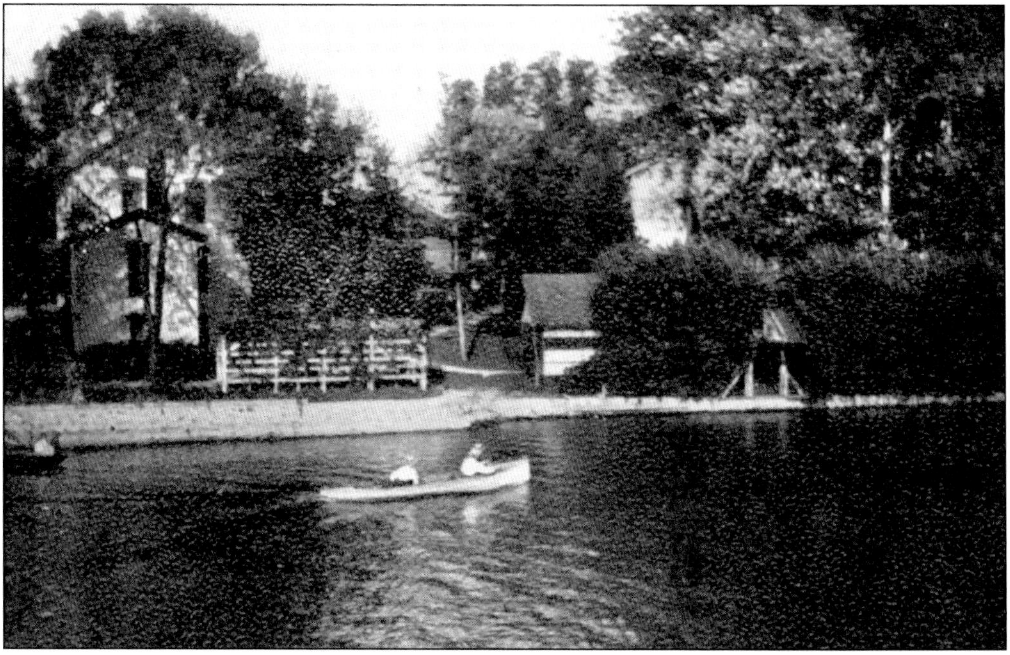

At one time, boaters could paddle along the river and dock not only at Tivoli Island but also at several *sommergartens*, or German pleasure spots. One such place was Habbhegger's Sommergarten, located along North Fourth Street. Today this is the Dew Drop Inn. Sommergartens boasted various amenities, such as outdoor dining, archery ranges, music under the stars, and, of course, good German *bier.*

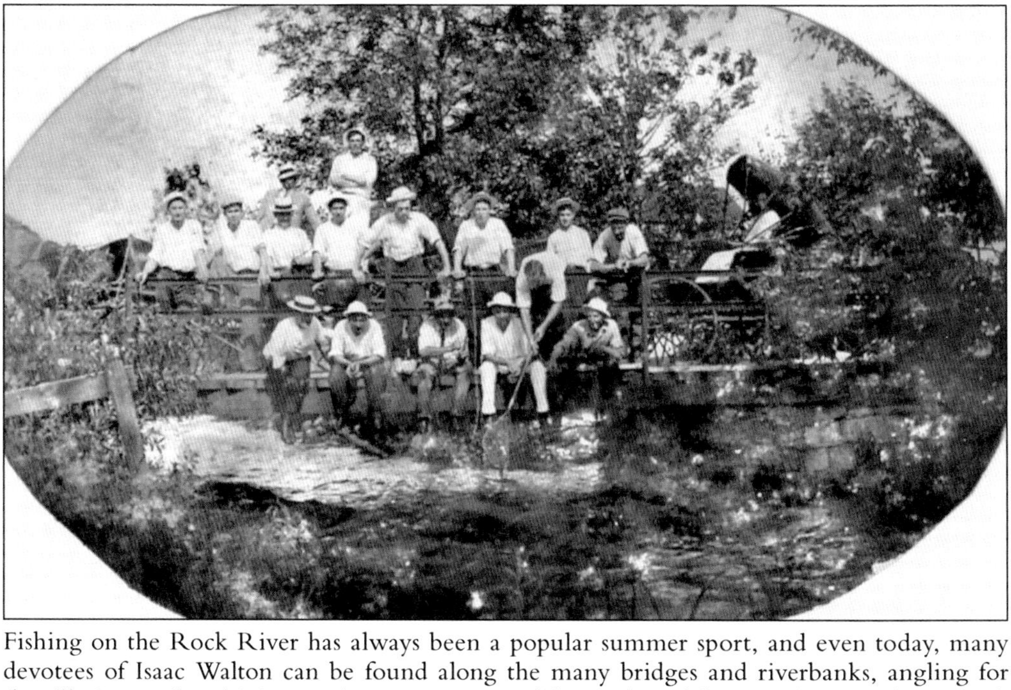

Fishing on the Rock River has always been a popular summer sport, and even today, many devotees of Isaac Walton can be found along the many bridges and riverbanks, angling for that illusive catch. This image shows an outing of the Eagles Club around 1910. The author's grandfather William Jannke Sr. can be seen standing on the bridge, second from the right.

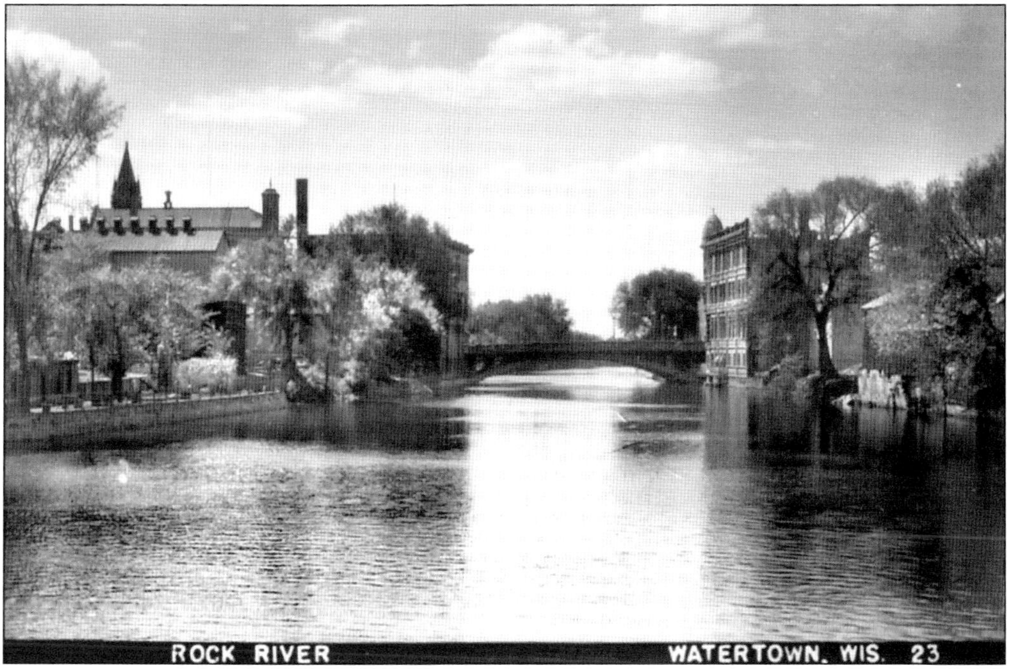

This was and is Watertown, a city built along the Rock River. This image was taken about 1944 from the Cady Street bridge looking southward.

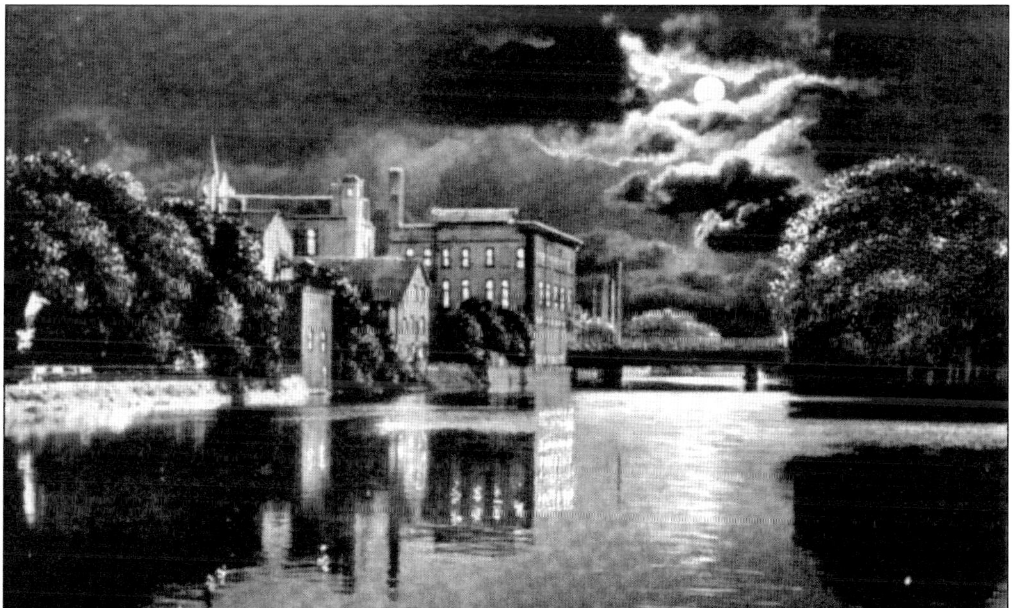

As night falls, a farewell is bid to the majestic Rock River, haven for animals, friend to the Native Americans, and source of power and delight to the early settlers. This image dates to about 1908.

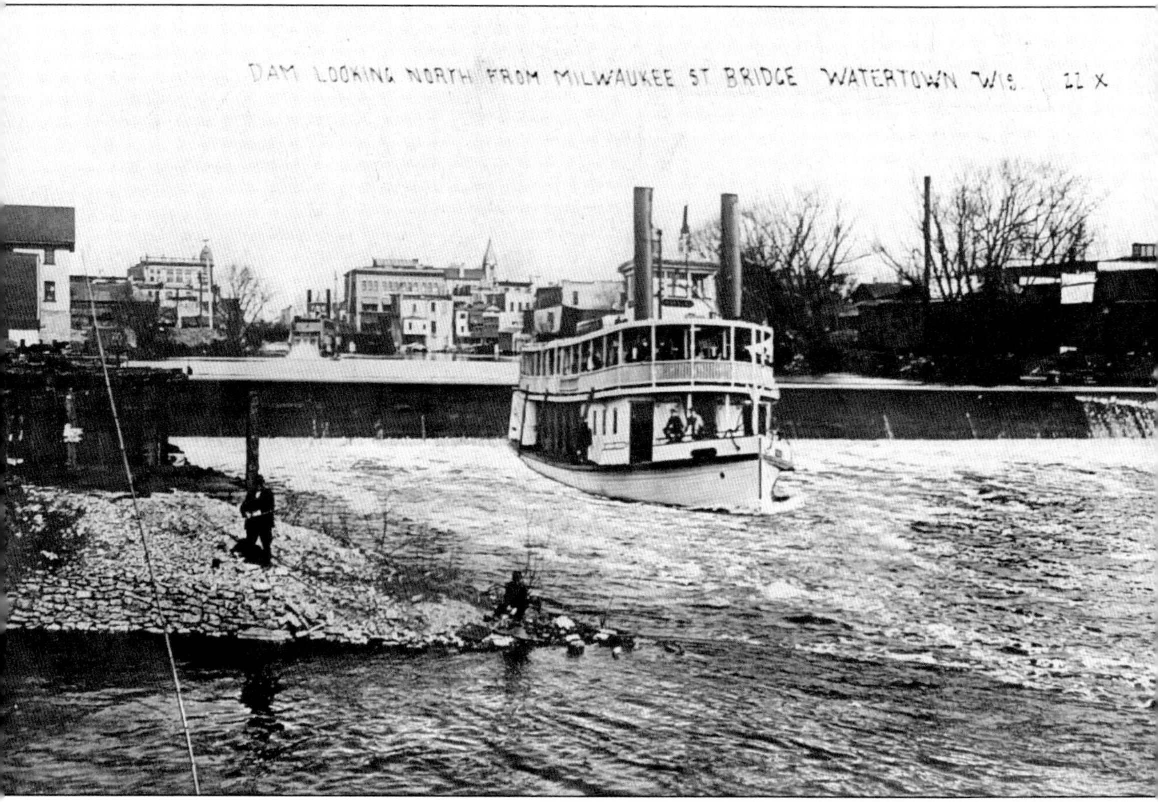

Presenting an exaggerated view of the dam along the Rock River about 1912, this postcard shows something that could never have happened in Watertown—namely, a paddle wheeler coming down the river from the dam. Though there were sporadic attempts in the 1830s and 1840s to make the river navigable, there was no way to combat the shallow areas and the many dams that began to appear; thus, a potential system of shipping was never realized.

Three

BUSINESS, INDUSTRY, AND A TRIP DOWN MAIN STREET

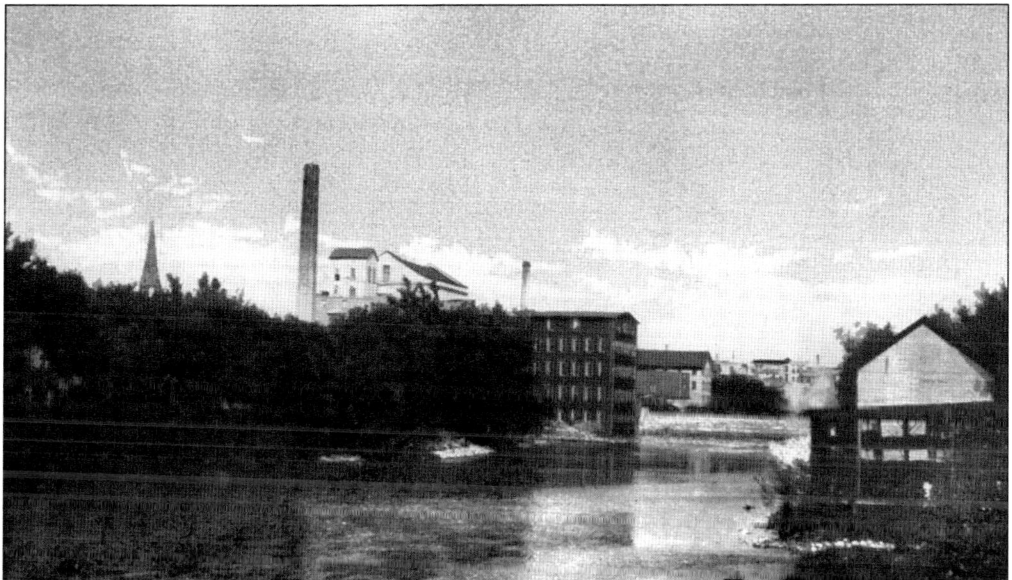

Watertown has always enjoyed a history of diverse industries, from milling to barrel making, tanning, and furniture making, to name but a few. Thanks to this, the city has never been dependent upon one major industry for its collective livelihood. The tradition still carries on today with various firms making everything from metal products to currency counters. The next few pages feature a sampling of some of the area's old-time industries. This is the G. B. Lewis Company around 1907. The Lewis Company made boxes and wooden products in Watertown and was one of the many industries to be found in Watertown at one time.

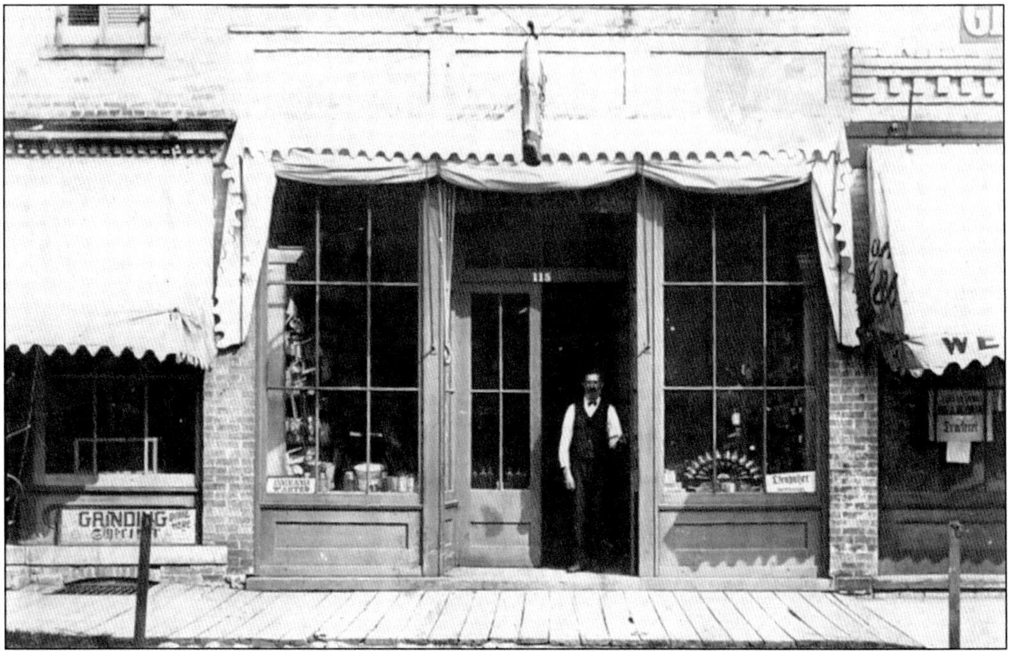

Richard Geschke, seen here, opened a stove and tinware store located at 115 South Second Street sometime in the 1860s and ran it through the 1920s. This image is from about 1910. The first hardware or tinware store in Watertown was opened in 1849 by Daniel Kusel, a native of Germany and a founding member of St. Mark's Lutheran Church. His shop carried on until the early 1980s. Today the Plattdeutscher Verein hall is on the site of the former Geschke hardware store.

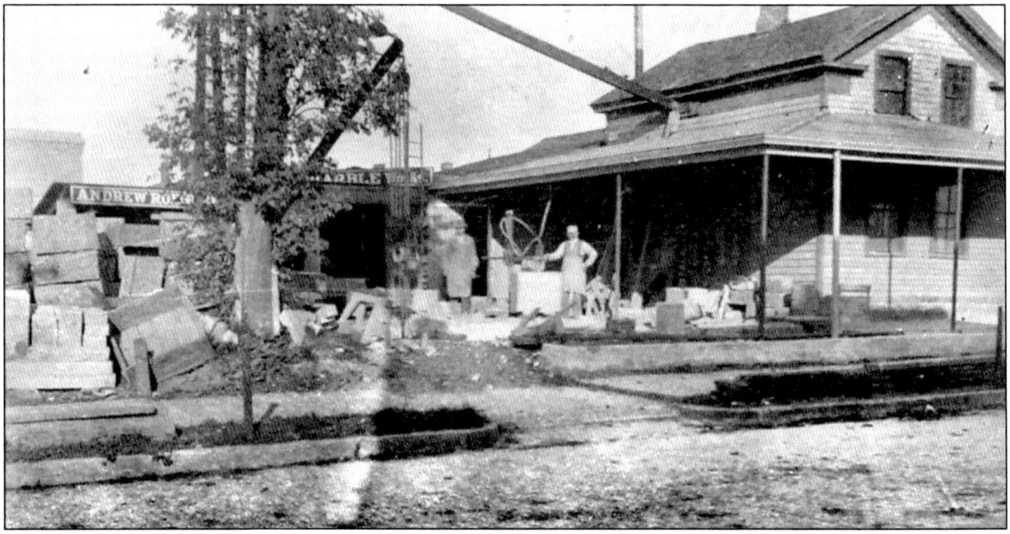

The Roegner Stone and Marble Works, located at 116 North Fourth Street, was one of many marble and stone works once located in the city. Andrew Roegner and his partner John Block opened a small marble works at 208 North Fourth Street in the 1890s. They later split up. Roegner opened his own concern in the late 1890s and moved to 116 North Fourth Street about 1905. His shop was later bought out by John Block, and today this is the site of the Block Monument Company. This image was taken in 1907.

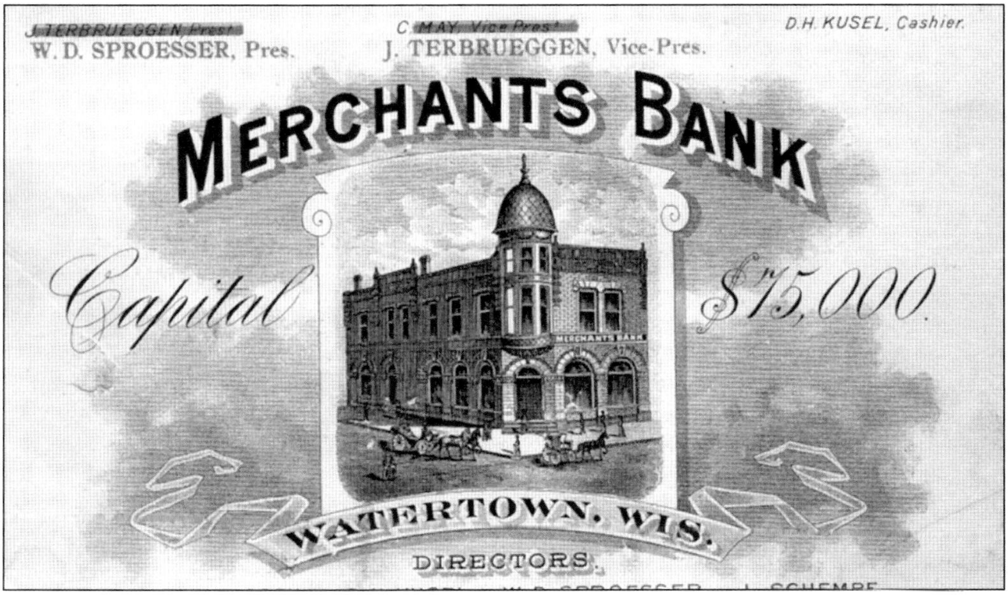

Banking began in Watertown in a small way in the early 1850s, when the Jefferson County Bank opened. From that meager beginning, banking grew to become one of the most important commercial resources in the city. At last count, there were over seven banking establishments in Watertown. This image shows the Merchants Bank, built in 1892 on the corner of North First and Main Streets. This image, which appeared on a trade card from 1900, shows the bank's original, distinctive Moorish tower that was removed sometime in the early 1940s. The Merchants Bank was later absorbed by Bank One. The old Merchants Bank building is currently undergoing a restoration and houses a music store.

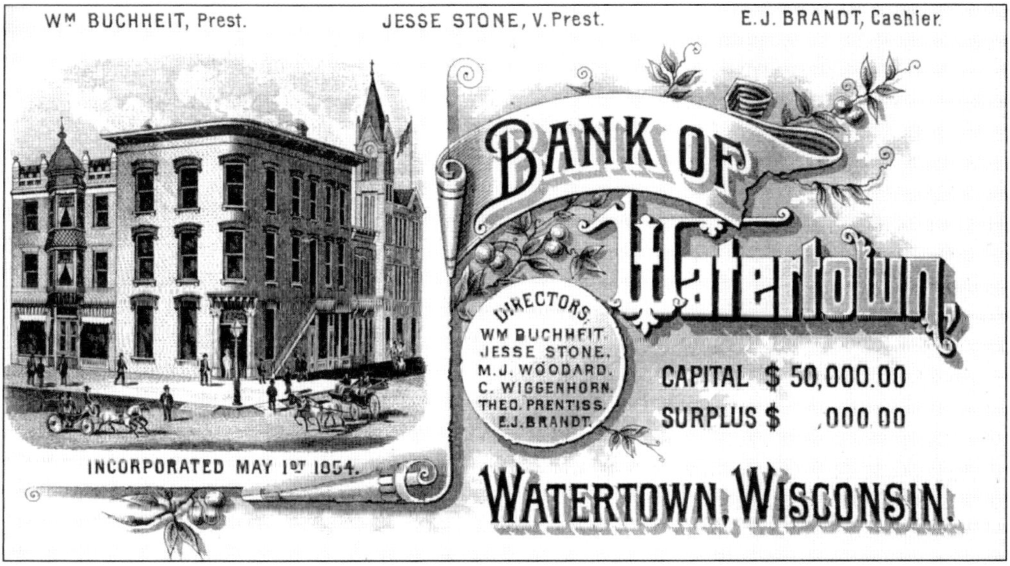

Across the street from the Merchants Bank was the Bank of Watertown, which was organized in 1854 by A. L. Pritchard. This building, known locally as "Pritchard's Block," stood on the western corner of North First and Main Streets until 1916, when it was demolished and a new two-story bank building was erected. The Bank of Watertown is now known as the M&I Bank. The old Bank of Watertown building is currently a tanning salon.

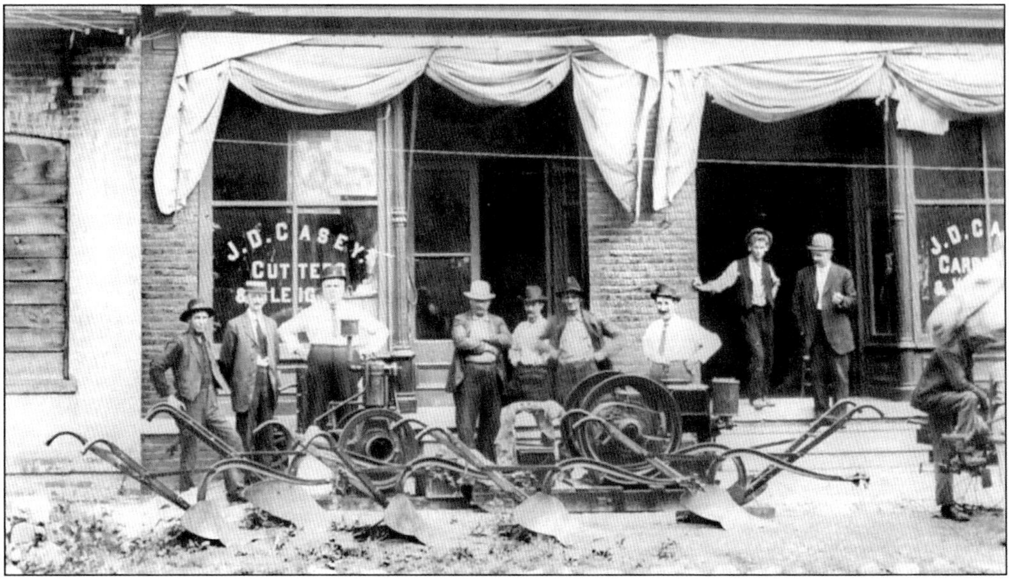

This image shows the James Casey Farm Implement Company on South Water Street about 1910. James D. Casey began his career as a blacksmith in Watertown in the 1870s. By the early 1880s, he had established himself as a wagon maker, and his fame grew until, by the turn of the century, he was dealing in not only wagons but agricultural implements of all kinds. When automobiles became the standard mode of transportation, the Casey Company began to deal in them. The company lasted well into the 1950s. Today a beauty parlor is on the site of the former Casey Company. (Lindemann Collection.)

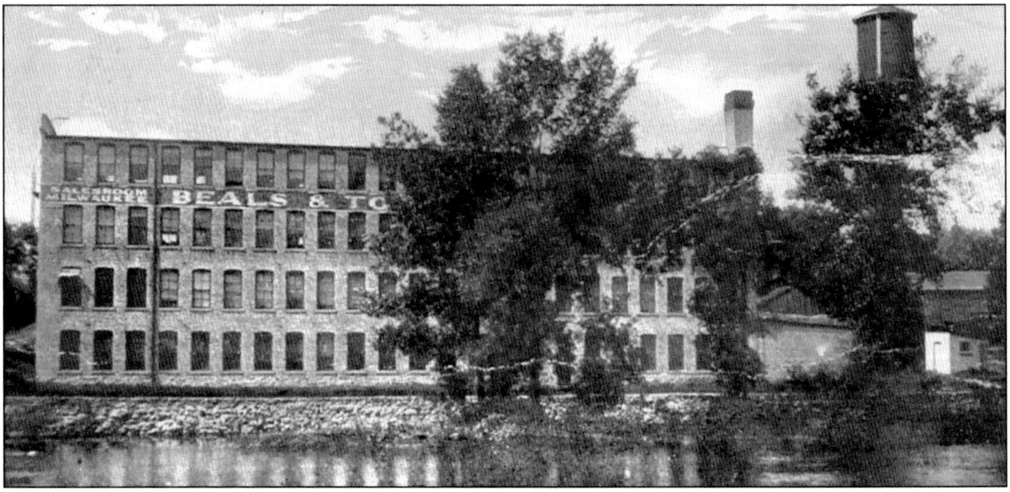

Shoes were first made in Watertown in the 1840s. At first there were small commercial enterprises usually run by cobblers and leather workers. By the turn of the century, large shoe factories began to open in Watertown. One of the first was the Beals and Torrey Shoe Factory, located at 100 West Milwaukee Street. Built in 1904, this large brick factory employed over 125 workers and had a daily output of 800 pairs of shoes. In 1918, the plant moved to 316 Hart Street in the industrial park district of Watertown. After the shoe factory left, this building, seen here about 1912, became the home of the Kusel Dairy Equipment Company until 1978, when that plant moved to West Street in Watertown. In 1987, the former Beals and Torrey Shoe Factory became an apartment building known as Riverview Terrace.

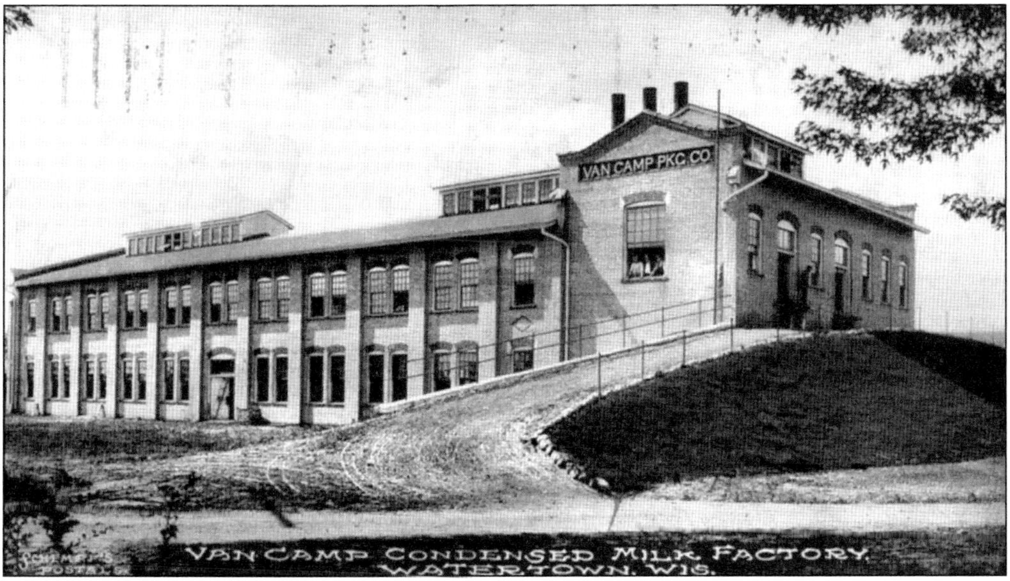

Watertown is in the heart of the dairy country, and at one time many dairies were operating in the area. One of the biggest was the Van Camp Company, which operated here at 500 Milford Street from 1907 to 1946. In 1946, the plant became the Pet Milk Company, and later this served as a satellite office for Brandt Incorporated. Today this is Karma, a firm that makes, among other things, vending machines.

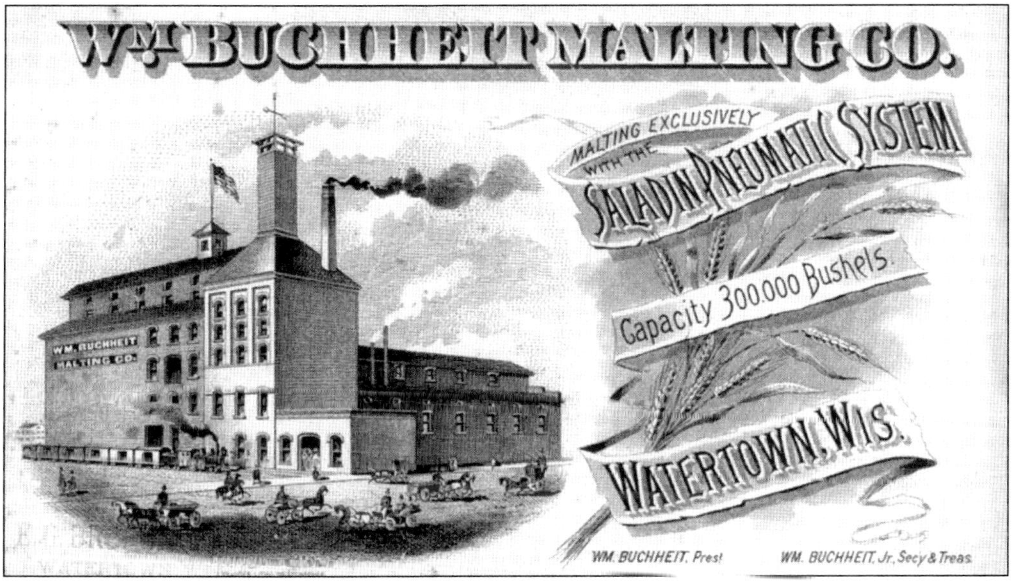

The William Buchheit malting company is featured here in an image from a trade card in 1895. Buchheit was a failed brewer and grocer who turned his sights toward the processing of malt for brewing purposes in 1888. The firm was located at 110 South Ninth Street. In 1897, the company produced 750,00 bushels of malt. In 1900, the firm became the American Malting Company, and in 1920, it was purchased by the Fleischmann Malting Company. This firm suffered two disastrous fires, one in 1946 and one in 1959, when it was known as the Old Elm Mills. Today this is the site of a carpeting and floor-covering firm. As for Buchheit, he later went on to become mayor of Watertown.

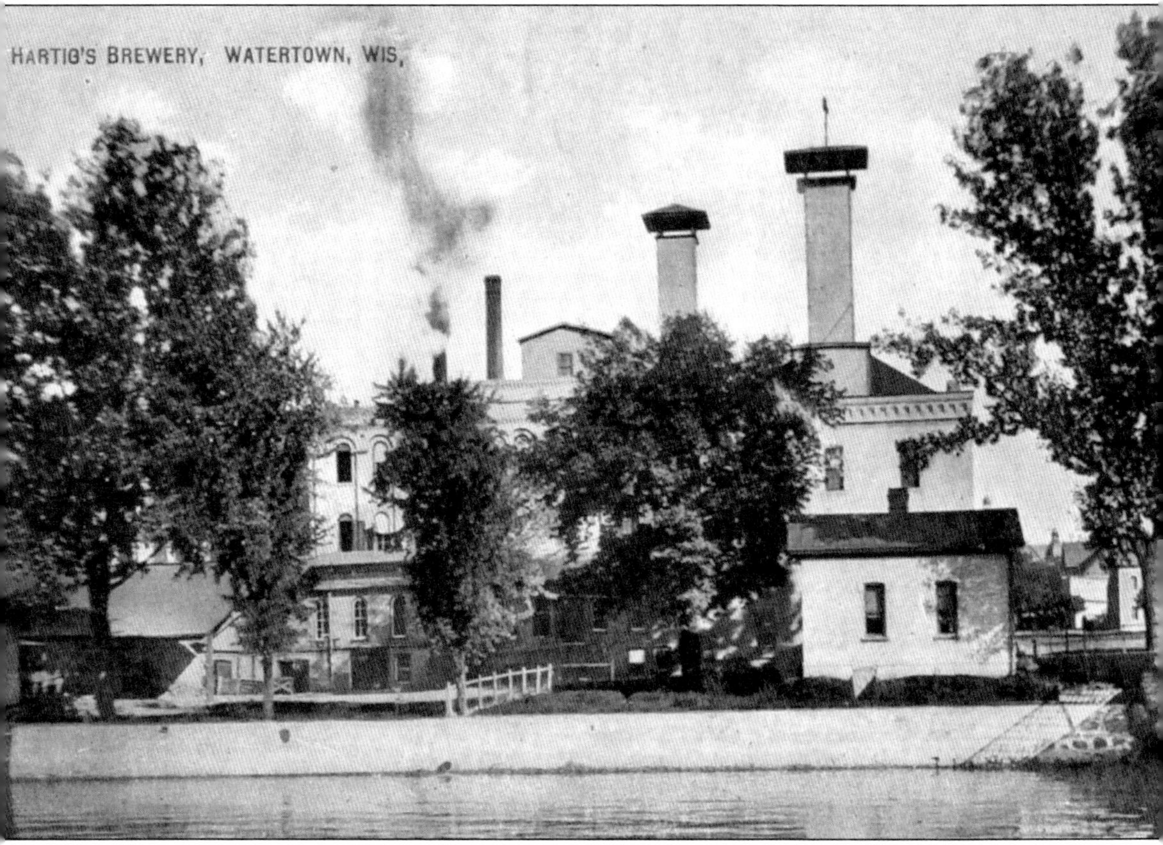

The William Hartig Brewery, seen here in 1915, was Watertown's major brewery, in existence from 1884 (known at that time as Hartig and Manz) to 1946. Brewing began in the city about 1846 with the arrival of William Anson, who opened an ale brewery. In the next year, 1847, Johann Jacob Hoeffner opened a larger brewery on the site of the Hartig plant and thus began the tradition of brewing good German beer in Watertown. His brewery was sold in 1854 to Joseph Bursinger, who, in turn, sold out to William Hartig and his cousin Carl Manz, both related to the Schiltz family of Milwaukee, celebrated brewers. A supermarket is on this site today.

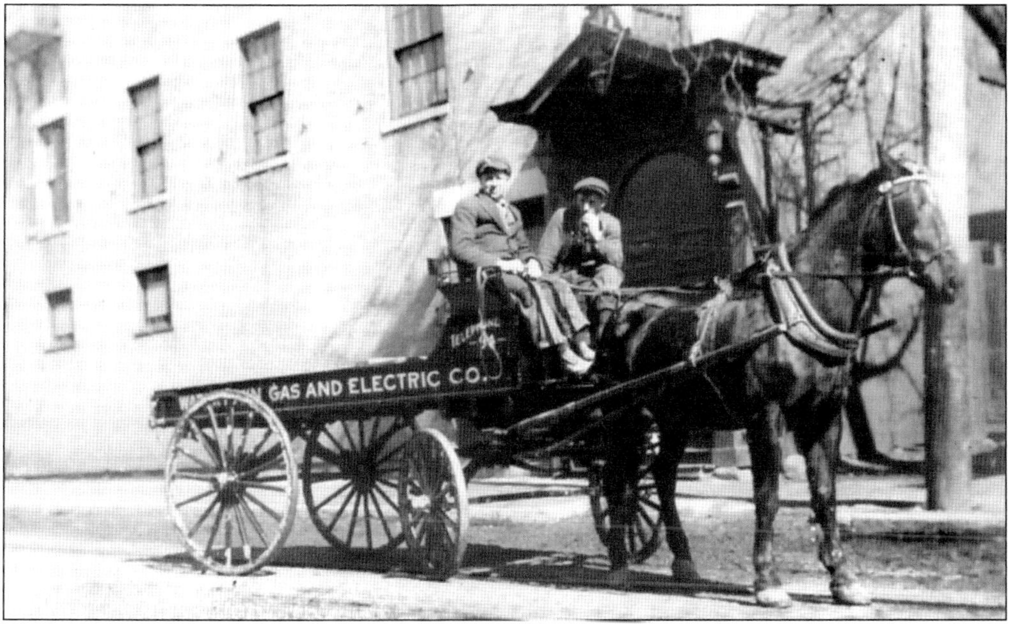

This image shows a horse-drawn wagon and drivers for the Watertown Gas and Electric Company about 1912. The gas company was formed in Watertown in 1856 and reorganized in 1864. By 1903, more than 900 customers in the city were connected to gas lines. It became known as the Watertown Gas and Electric Company in 1905, and in 1928, the local plant closed down, and the entire firm became a part of the Wisconsin Gas and Electric Company, today known as WeEnergies. (Krietzman Collection.)

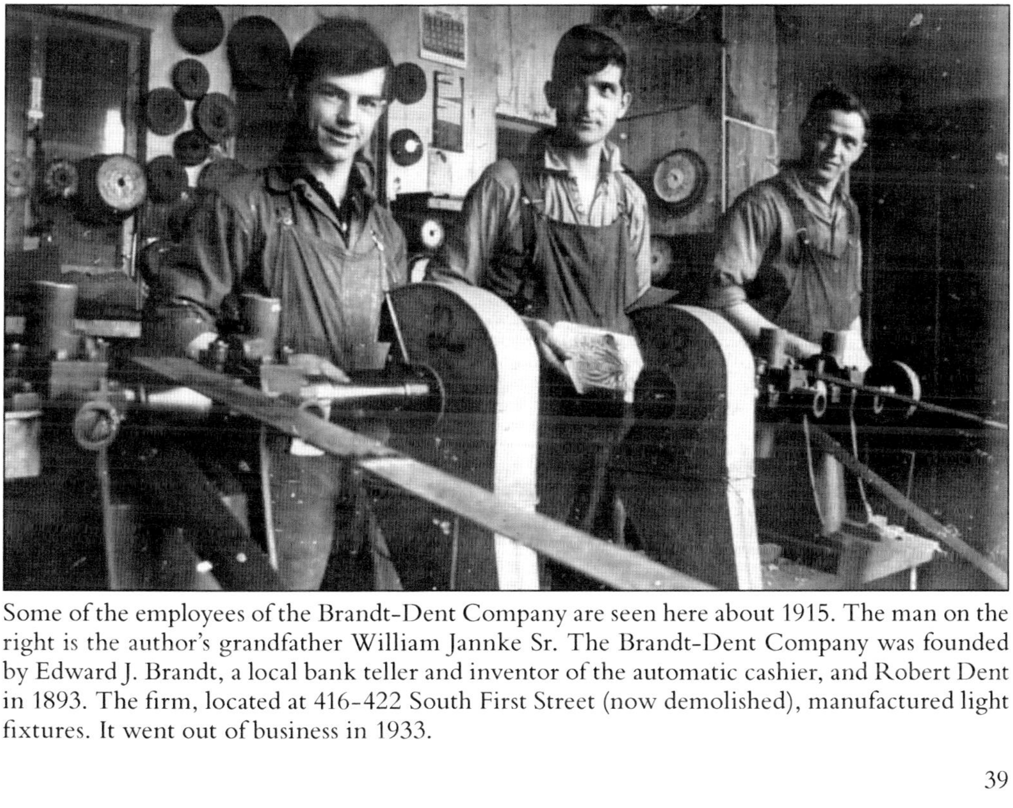

Some of the employees of the Brandt-Dent Company are seen here about 1915. The man on the right is the author's grandfather William Jannke Sr. The Brandt-Dent Company was founded by Edward J. Brandt, a local bank teller and inventor of the automatic cashier, and Robert Dent in 1893. The firm, located at 416–422 South First Street (now demolished), manufactured light fixtures. It went out of business in 1933.

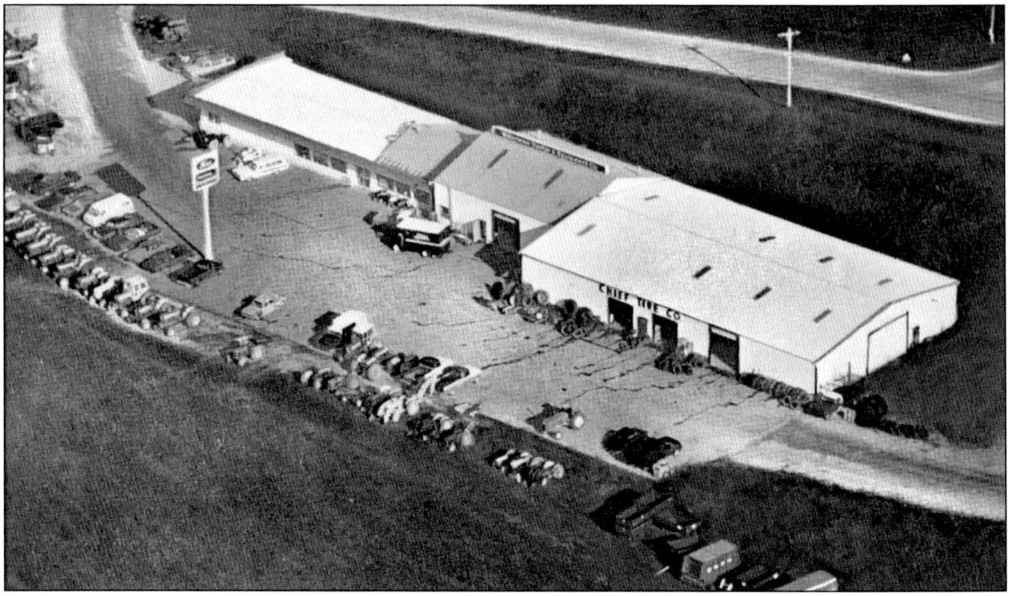

This is the Watertown Tractor and Equipment Company, located at one time along the Highway 16 bypass north of the city. The firm dealt, as its name implies, in tractors and other types of farming equipment. Today this is the site of Spuncast, a firm that makes centrifugal castings. The tractor company was in existence from about 1968 to 1976.

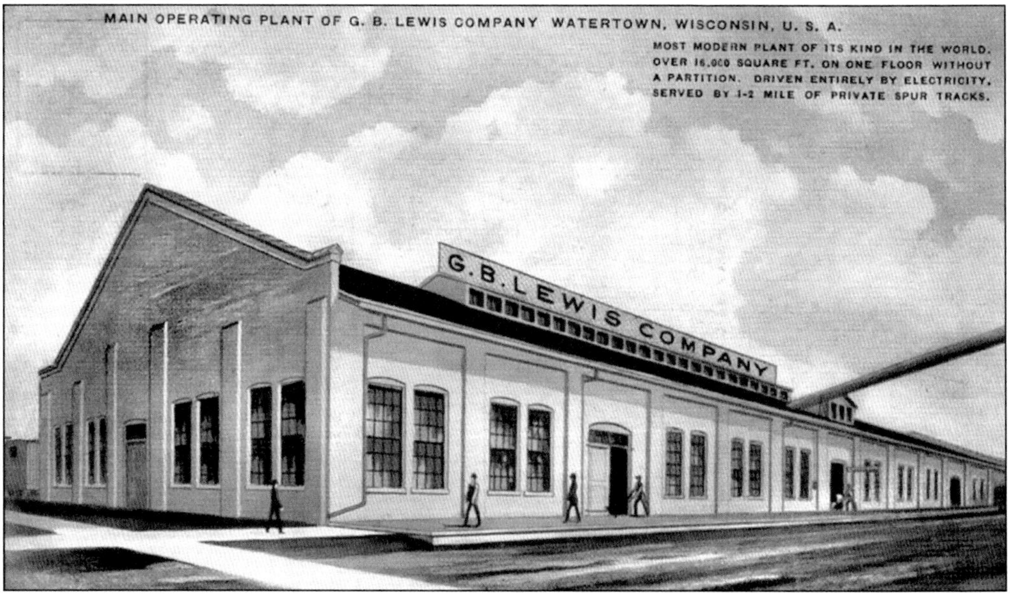

Located along South Montgomery Street, this is the G. B. Lewis Plant about 1920. The firm was founded in 1863 and at one time was located on South Water Street along the Rock River. Its output was wood products, such as boxes and sash and door frames. The factory sustained two disastrous fires and, after the last one, decided to pull up stakes and relocate to a modern brick factory building, shown here, at 426 South Montgomery Street. In the 1920s, the Lewis Company began to make and manufacture bee-raising supplies, and in the 1930s, it introduced a line of wooden toys and airplane propellers. In the late 1940s, the factory became a pioneer in the making of fiberglass products. This firm ceased to exist in 2000.

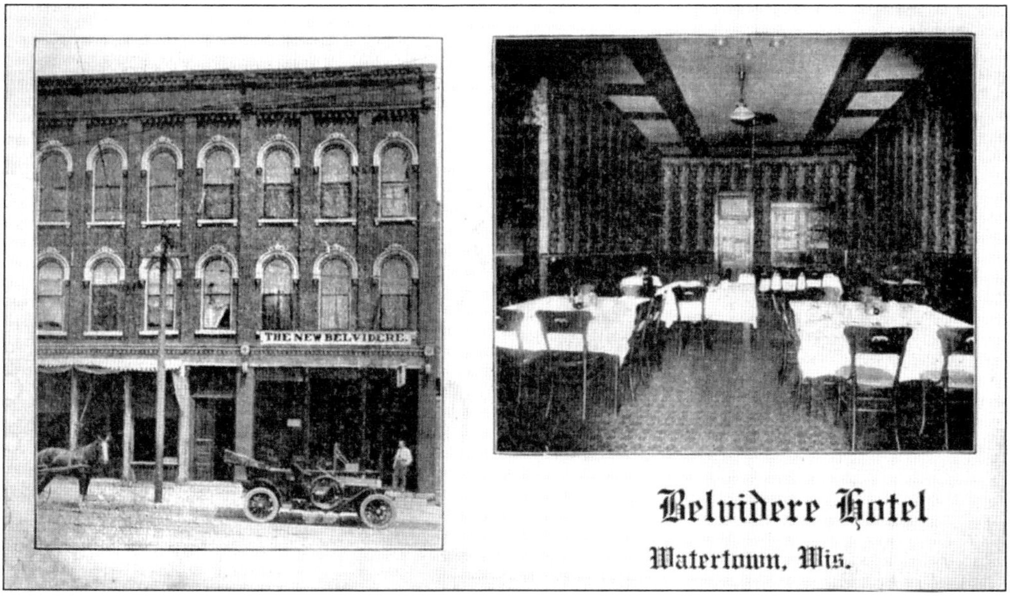

The field of hospitality services has been a part of the Watertown scene since the first hotel opened its doors to weary travelers in 1840. At one time, there were about 10 hotels in the city, which were almost always filled to capacity. This is the New Belevidere Hotel, originally known as the West Avenue House and later known as the Grand Hotel. This hostelry was located along West Main Street, and it flourished in the early days of the 20th century. Today this building is a plumbing firm.

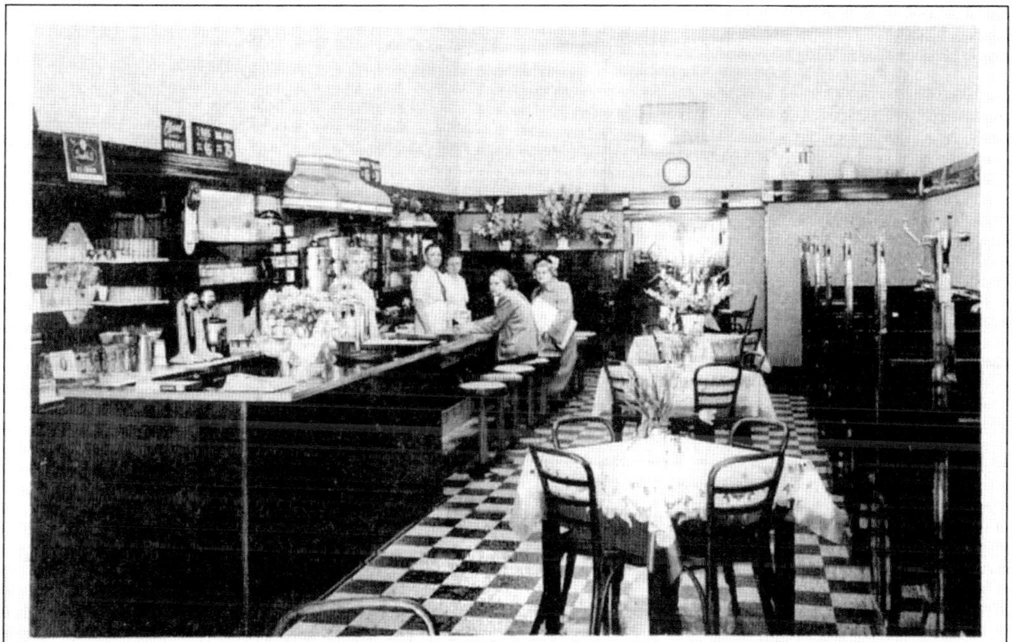

The Main Café, shown here about 1938, is one of a number of fine restaurants that have dotted the Watertown area. Opened in 1925, the Main Café still exists today under the name of Bismarck's, and it is known for its chili and hamburgers.

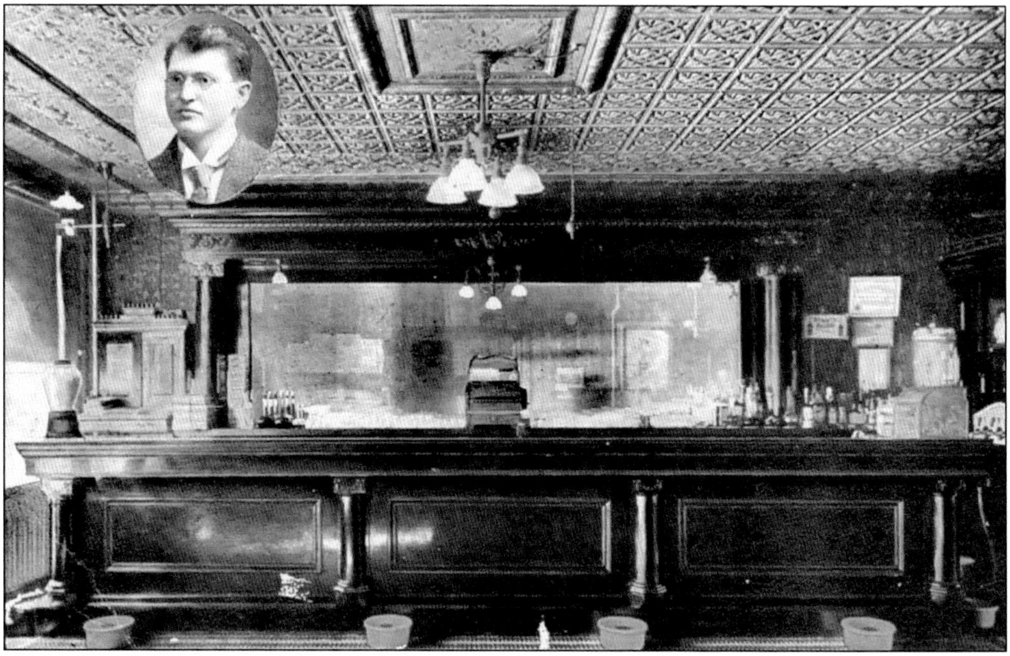

Another type of business that has long roots in the city is the saloon. One of the best was Otto's Inn, shown here about 1905. Opened in the late 1800s by Carl Otto, this saloon and restaurant was located along East Madison Street. Carl Otto, the genial proprietor, is pictured in the upper left-hand corner. The specialty of the house, which many people in the city remember with great fondness, was sauerbraten. Today this is a Chinese restaurant.

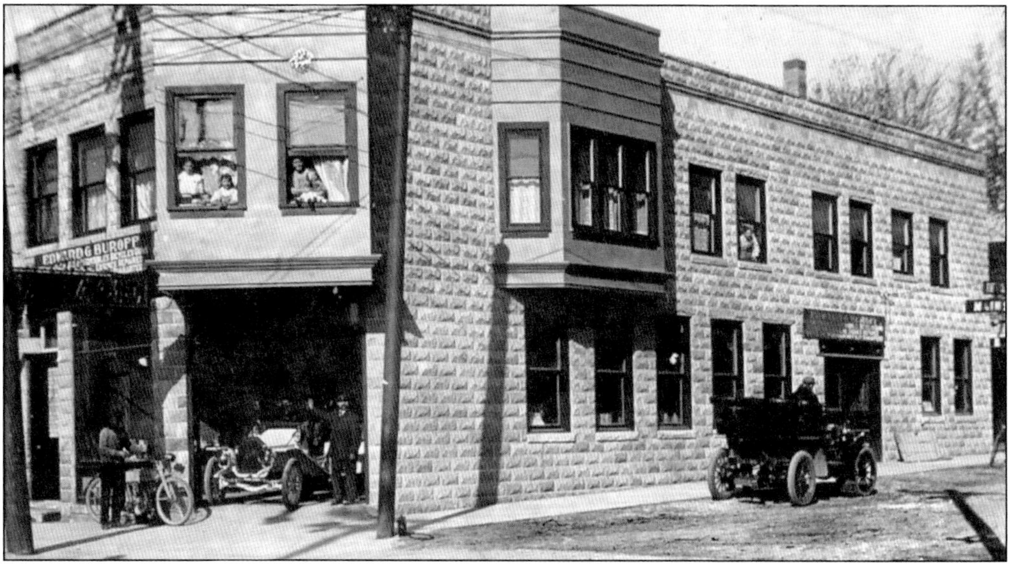

The first automobiles to be seen in Watertown arrived early in the 20th century. By 1910, it was clear that they were here to stay, and enterprising men began to open garages and filling stations to accommodate drivers and car owners. This is the Edward G. Buroff garage, located at one time at 418 East Main Street. The garage operated from 1913 to the early 1920s and was taken over by several other owners until the early 1960s, when a street-widening project caused this building to be demolished.

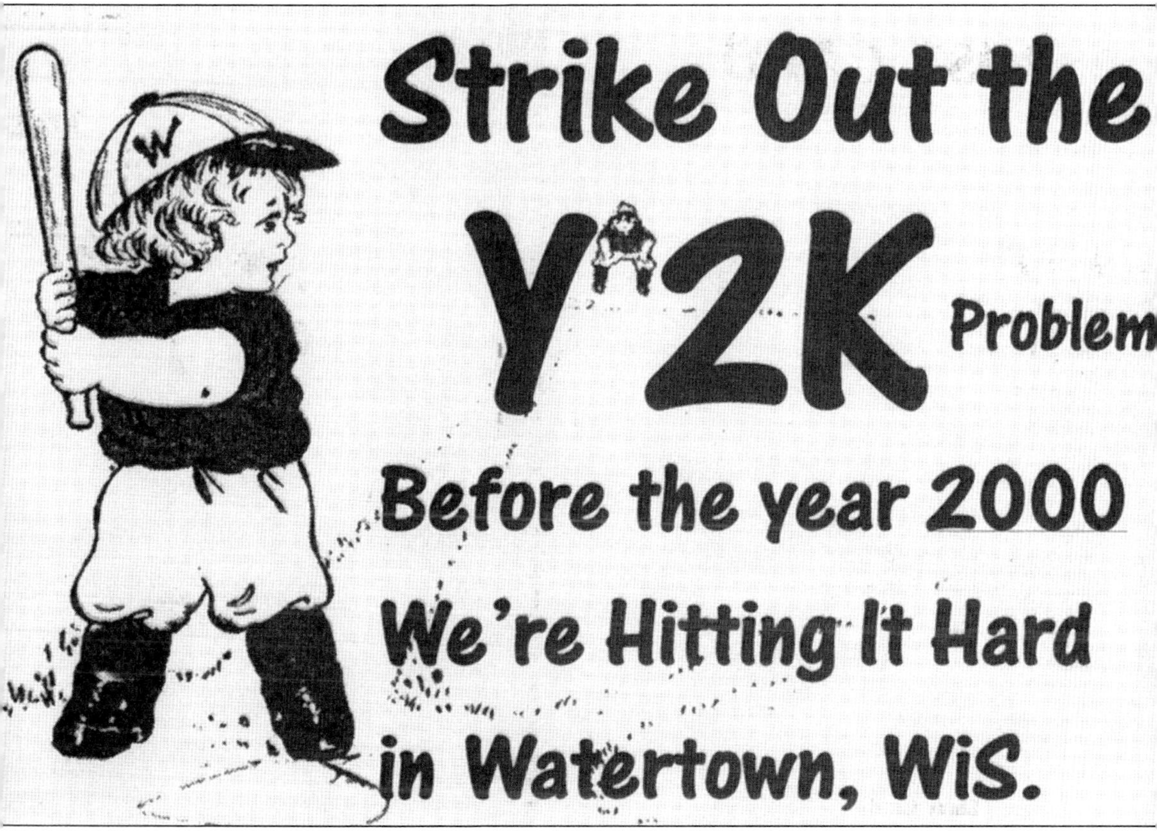

Every town has a main street, that area where retail stores opened and proliferated. In Watertown, Main Street was and still is the hub of commerce, and people from the surrounding areas made it a destination for their weekly shopping. When the city was originally plotted out into streets and blocks in the 1840s, the business district was supposed to have been Western Avenue, but things just did not work out. In 1841, the first retail store, owned by the enterprising Cole brothers (John and Luther), opened and the historic downtown was born. Many changes have taken place in business in the past 160 years, and there were times that it seemed like Main Street would become a ghost town. But through it all, Main Street has continued to hold its own with large commercial strip malls and the introduction of megastores and still maintains a certain charm and pull. Main Street has always risen to the occasion and met the many challenges with grit and determination. It is small wonder that Watertown has one of the largest historic downtown districts in Wisconsin. This Y2K postcard was created by local postcard collector Frank Lindemann. Watertown weathered the storm and fury just like every other city. On the next few pages, the reader will be given a tour of Watertown's historic Main Street.

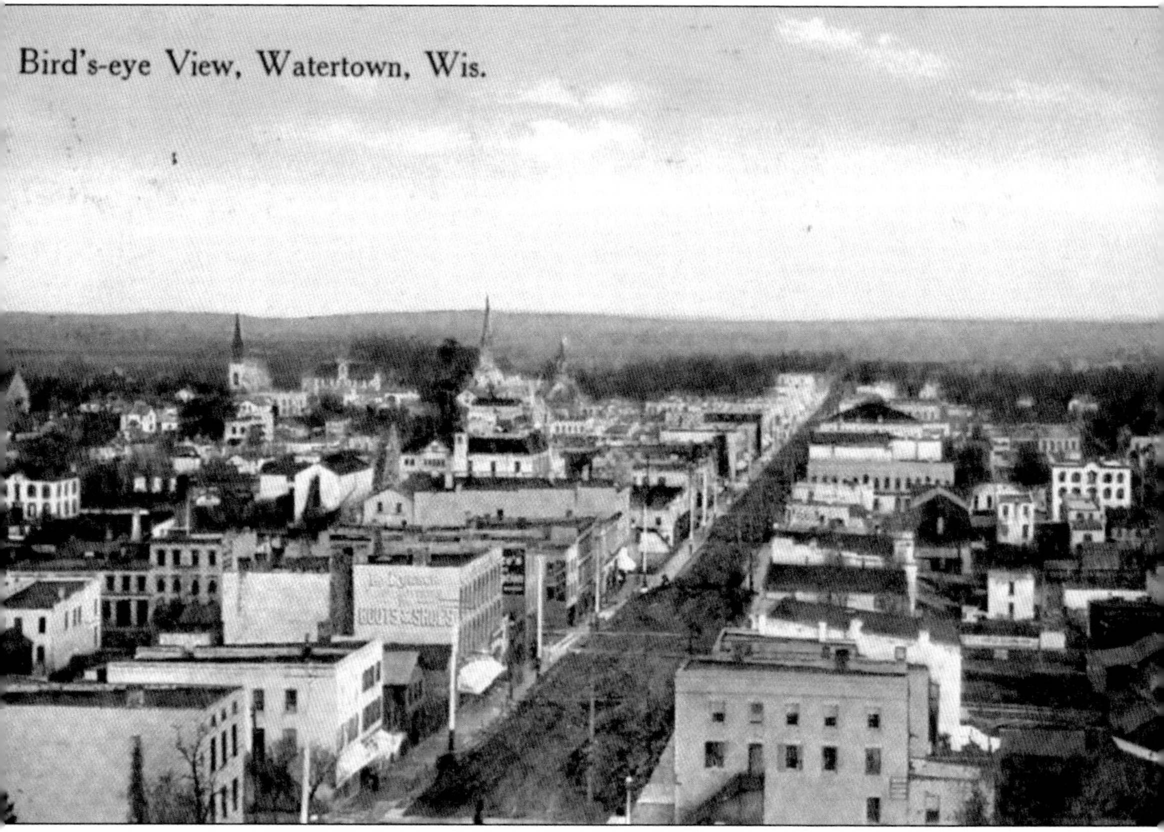

This is Main Street about 1908. Many of the buildings pictured here still line the street and date, in some cases, to the 1850s. Watertown residents are proud to say that their historic downtown is one of the largest historic districts in Wisconsin.

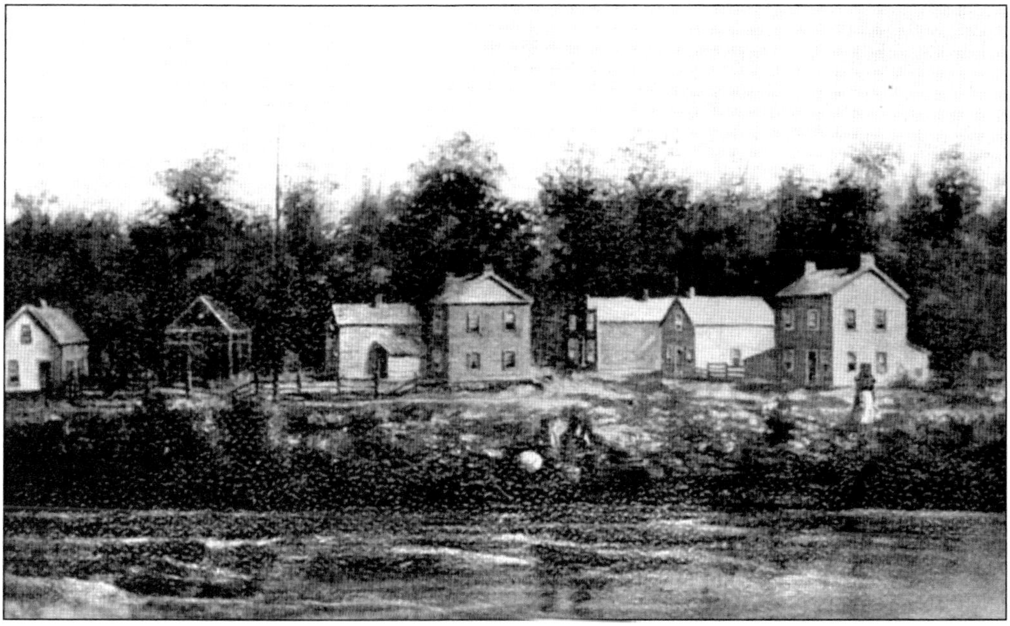

This is Main Street as it appeared in 1842. The large building in the center is the Exchange Hotel, built in 1840, and the building to the right of the hotel is the Cole Brothers store, which opened in the fall of 1841.

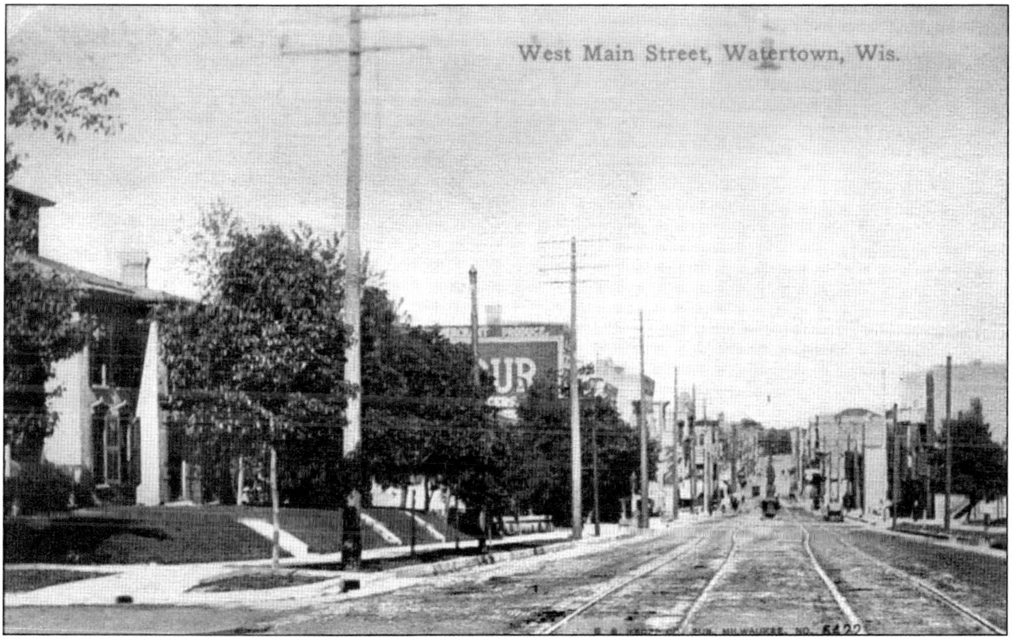

Starting at the intersection of West Main and Church Streets, shown here about 1908, the trip down Main Street journeys eastward. The home on the left was built in the 1860s by pioneer Irish settler Patrick Rogan. Today this is a professional building.

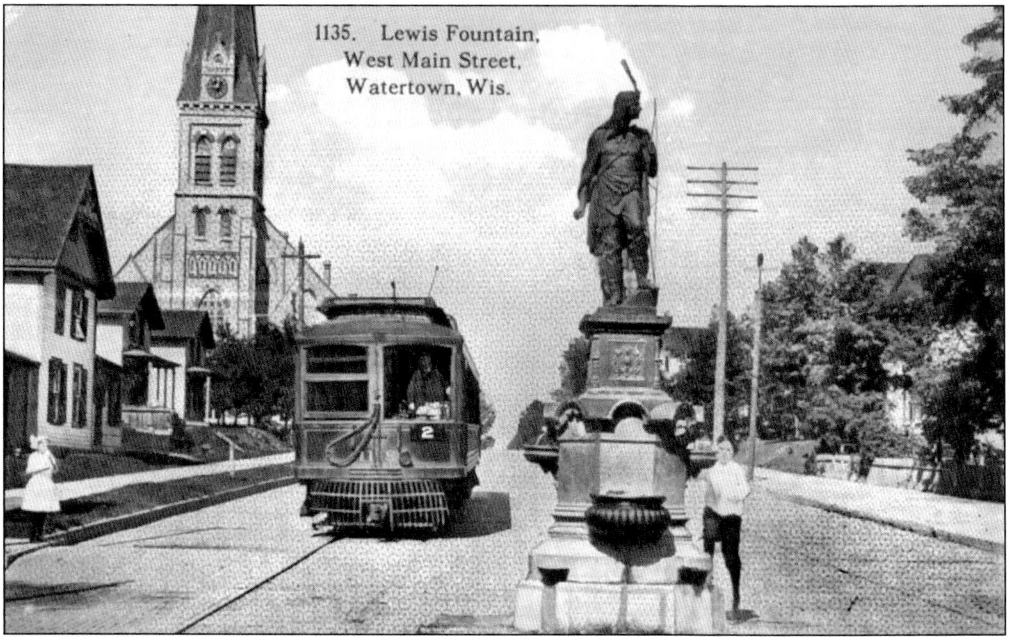

At the intersection of West Main and Washington Streets, shown here about 1910, stood this fountain, presented to the city by Mr. and Mrs. G. B. Lewis in 1896. The statue stood here until the mid-1920s, when it was destroyed in an auto accident. The statue was damaged beyond repair, so an exact duplicate was purchased and placed in a city park, where it stood until 1964. At that time, the Lewis Fountain, as it was known, was placed on the grounds of the Octagon House Museum, where visitors can see it today.

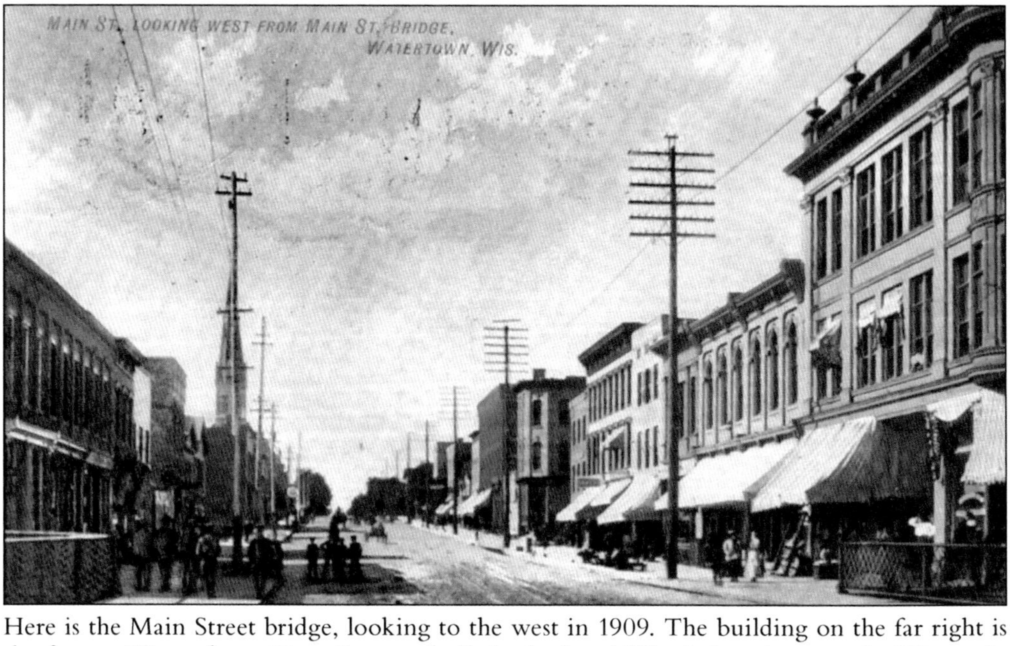

Here is the Main Street bridge, looking to the west in 1909. The building on the far right is the former Wiggenhorn Cigar Factory, built in the late 1890s. It later became the Wisconsin National Bank and was finally demolished in 1985. Next to it was the D&F Kusel hardware store, which was in existence from 1849 to 1985.

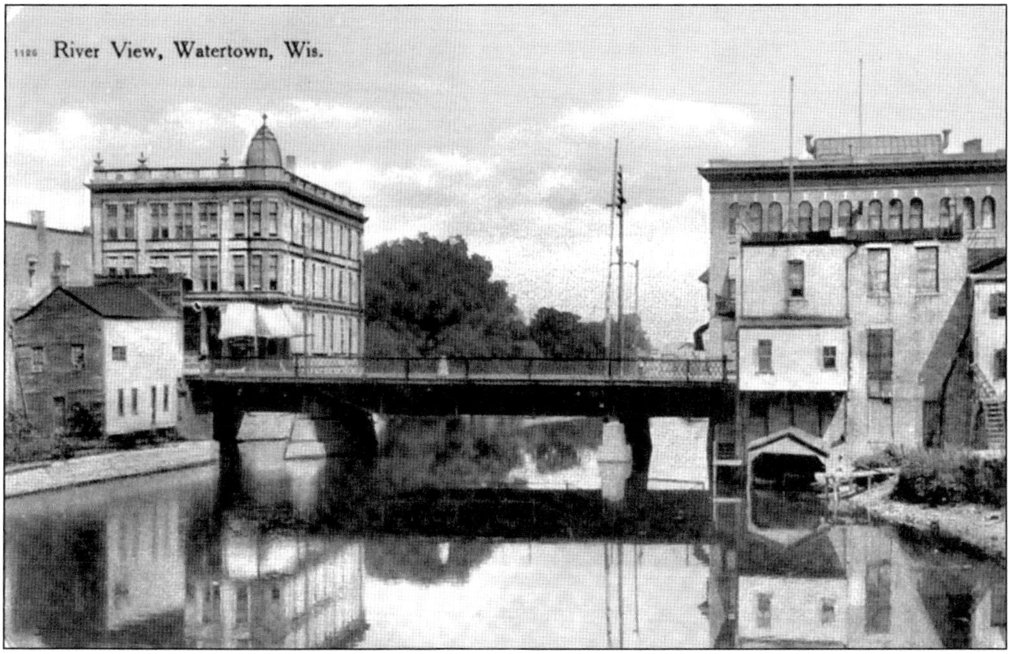

The Main Street bridge is again seen here in 1909, only this time from the south looking northward. The first bridge across the river was erected in 1844 and was replaced several times before the current bridge was erected in 1931.

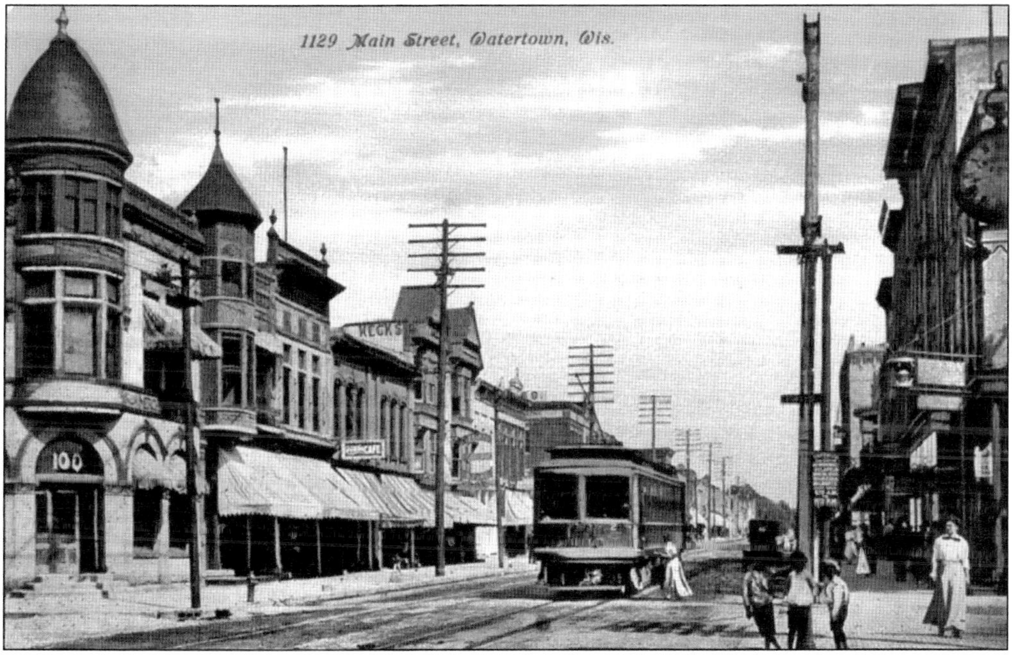

The intersection of Main and First Streets is seen here in an image from 1910. The Merchants Bank can be seen on the far left, and next to it is Clara Weiss's millinery shop. Today these buildings are all consolidated into one and comprise Fox Music, a retail music store.

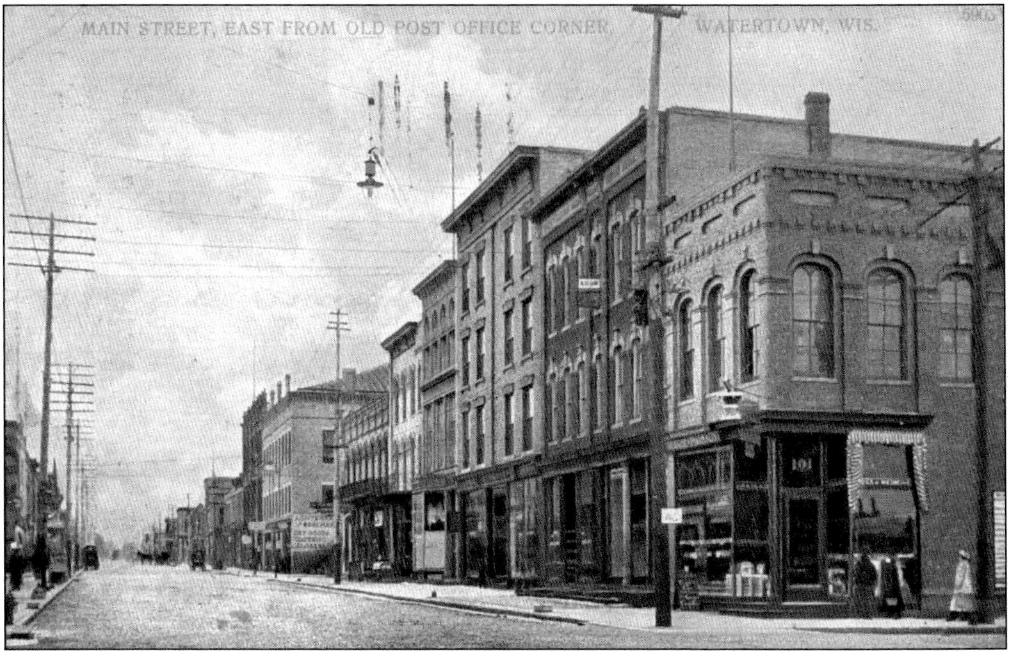

The intersection of Main and First Streets is shown in a view looking at the southern side of the street in 1909. The building on the far right is Gamm's Drug Store, which exploded due to mishandling of chemicals in 1910. This building, built by F. P. Brook, was erected about 1873 and replaced the former hotel, the Planters, that was on this site from 1843 until it burned to the ground in 1868. At one time, city hall, the post office, the offices of the *Watertown Daily Times* and the telephone company were here. Today this is a real estate office.

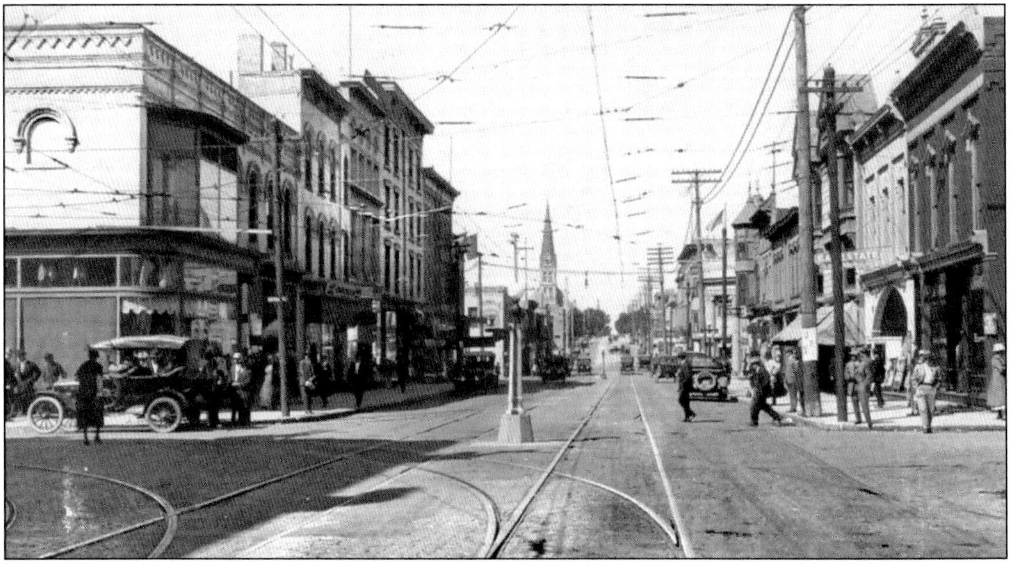

Main and Second Streets are seen here farther down the street in an image from about 1915. This view looks to the west. Note the trolley lines running above the street, a common sight from the arrival of the trolley in 1908 until it ceased operations in 1940. The building with the bowed opening, second to the right, is an early-day movie theater, the Pantorium. Next to it is the Joseph Harvey Saloon, later the Tetzlaff Pharmacy. Today this is a family restaurant.

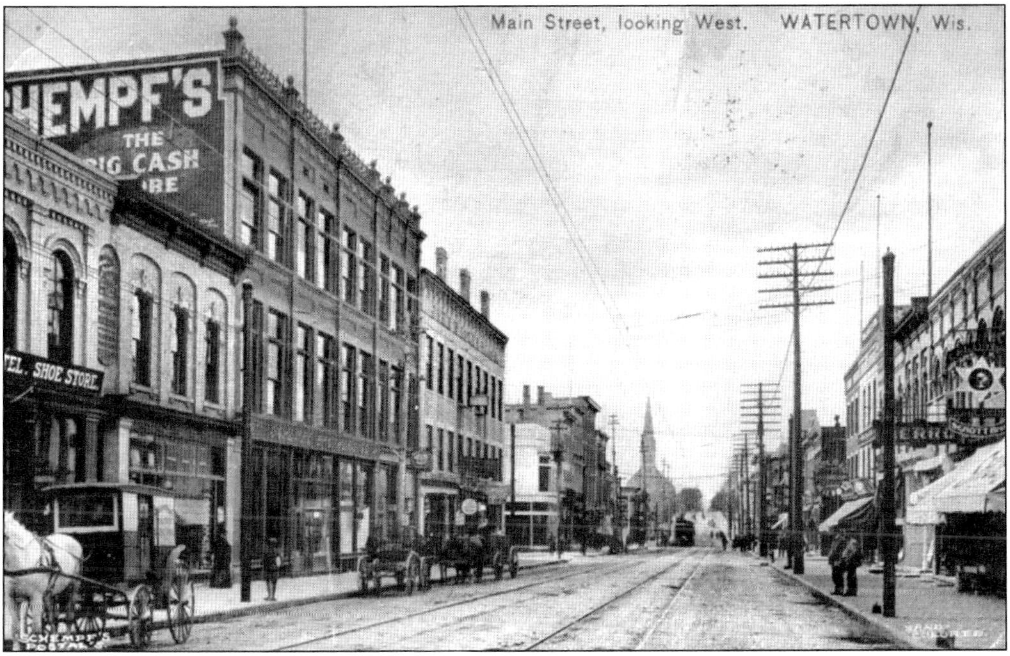

Farther down the street is the heart of the business district and the locations of some of the oldest buildings on Main Street. On the left, Schempf's can be seen. This was the leading department store in Watertown from the late 1840s to 1936, when it went out of business. To the right of the Schempf store is John W. Cole's block, which was built in 1854 and at one time housed a beautiful ballroom on its third floor. Today there is a microbrewery in the Cole building and a winery and gift shop in the Schempf store building. This image dates to about 1909.

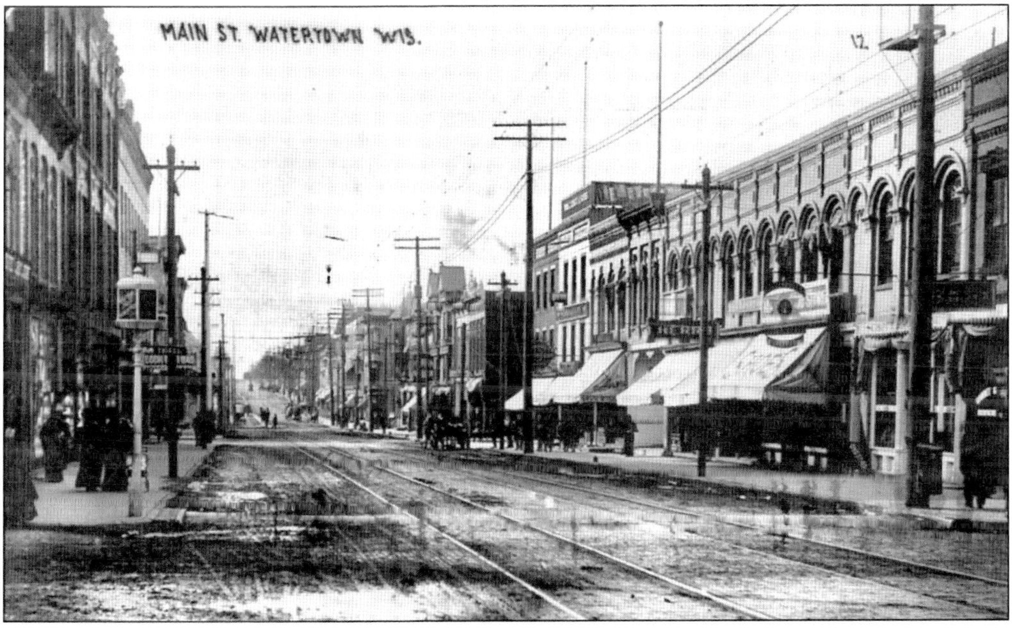

Here is a photograph of the north side of the street, taken from the intersection of Main and Third Streets about 1910. Most of the buildings on the far right still exist, but today they are consolidated into one massive shoe store.

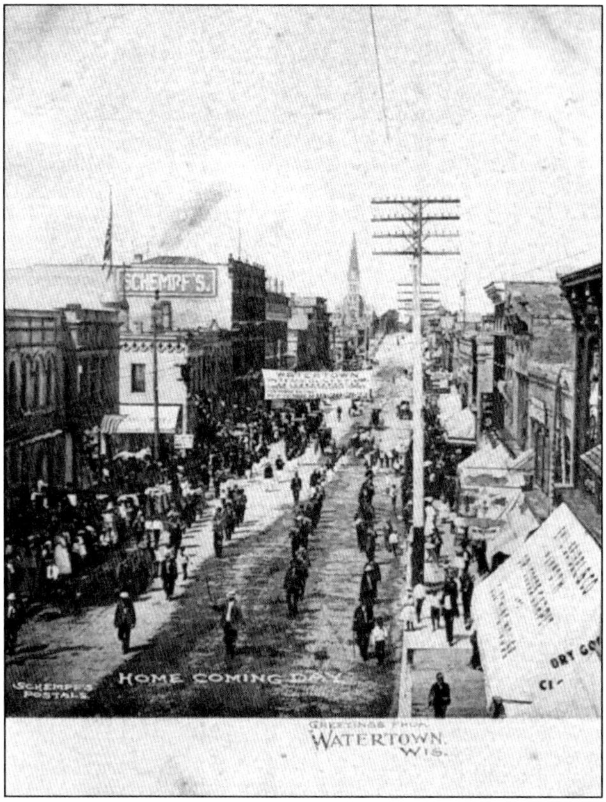

In this rare bird's-eye view taken from the intersection of Main and Fourth Streets looking to the west, one can get a good idea of Watertown's Main Street. This picture was taken during one of the city's annual "Home Coming" festivals about 1909.

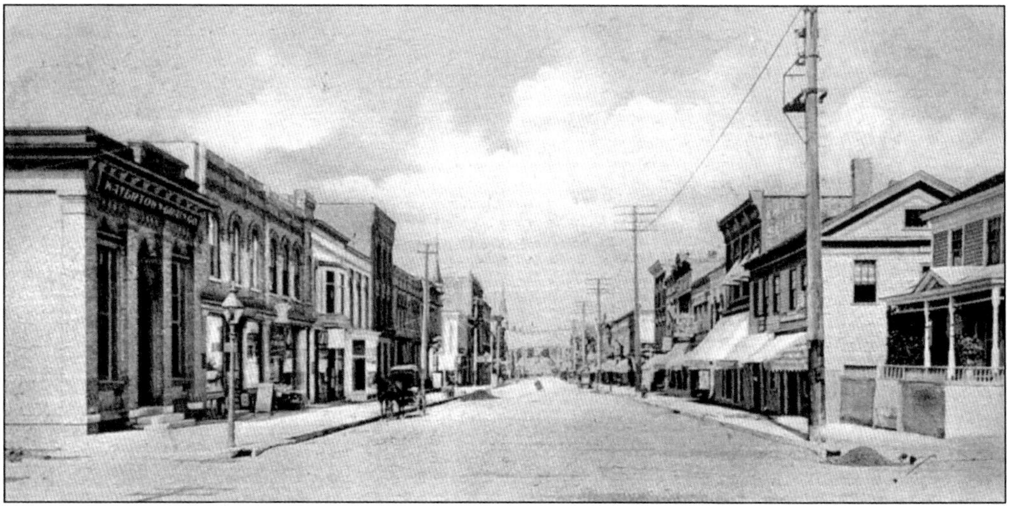

This is Main and Fourth Street around 1908, showing a rather quiet day in an otherwise high-traffic area. The frame buildings on the right were replaced in 1910 by a large brick block that housed the Miller Cigar Factory and later the F. W. Woolworth Company five-and-dime store. The building on the far left—at the time of this image housing the offices of the *Watertown Weltburger*, the city's German-language newspaper—still looks the same today as it does in this image.

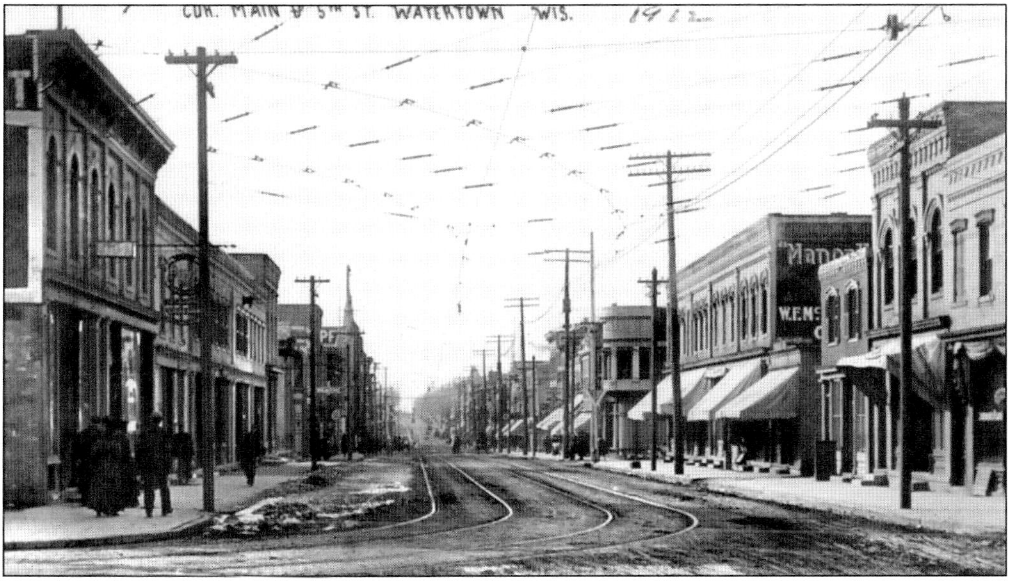

Leaving the heart of the business district, this image features the intersection of Main and Fifth Streets, about 1912. On the right, in the distance, one can just see the round bay window of the Miller Cigar Factory, erected in 1910. Though heavily "remuddled," most of these buildings still stand on Main Street today. (Kreitzman Collection.)

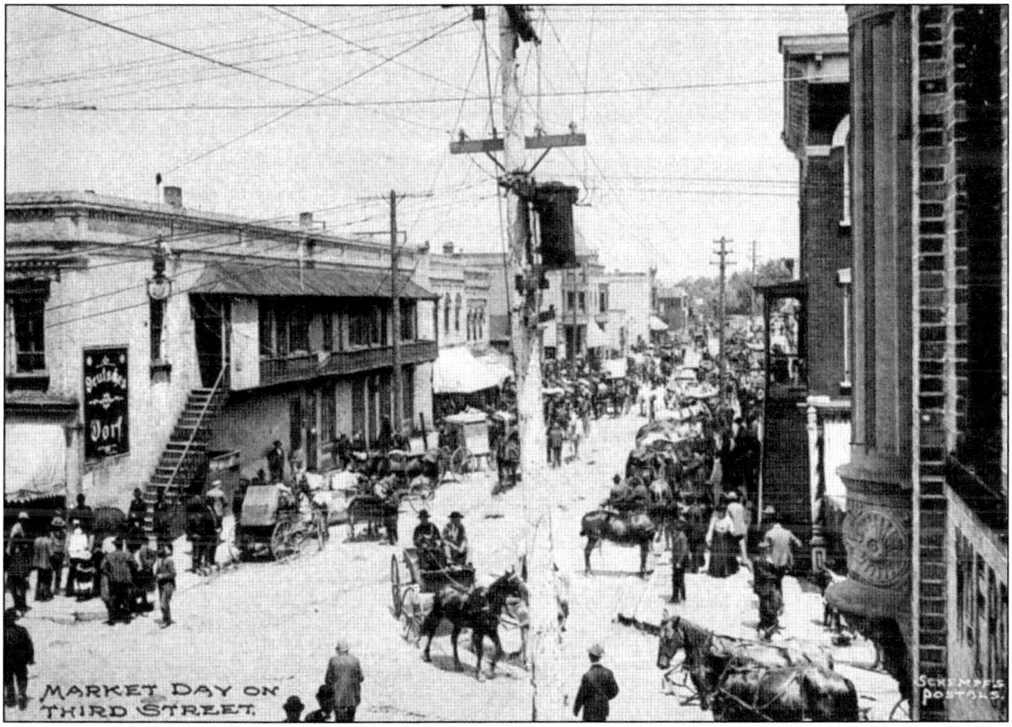

Heading back toward Church Street, we see the intersection of Third and Main in a dramatic image of "Fair Day," taken from the fire escape of the W. F. Brandt store, today a sports bar. These monthly fairs were once held downtown along the side streets. The fair later moved to North First Street, and today it is held at Riverside Park.

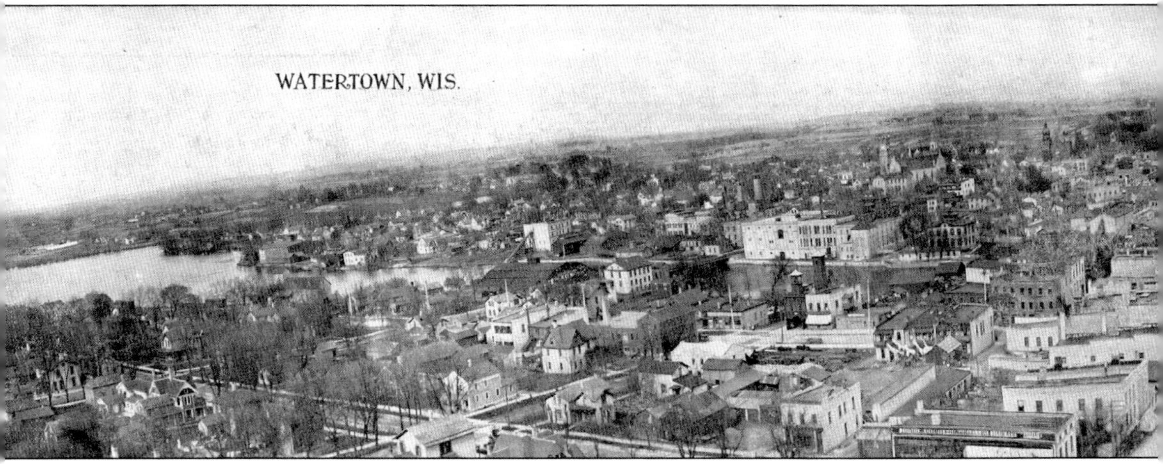

This breathtaking panoramic view of the city was taken from the steeple of St. Bernard's Catholic Church looking eastward about 1912. Here one can see all the glories of a bustling and

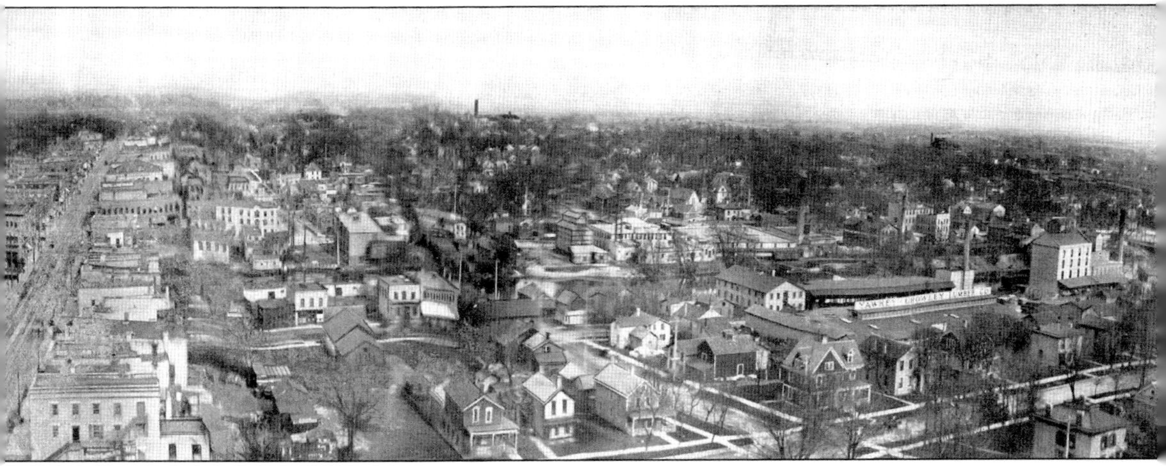

thriving Midwestern city in the early days of the 20th century. This was Watertown.

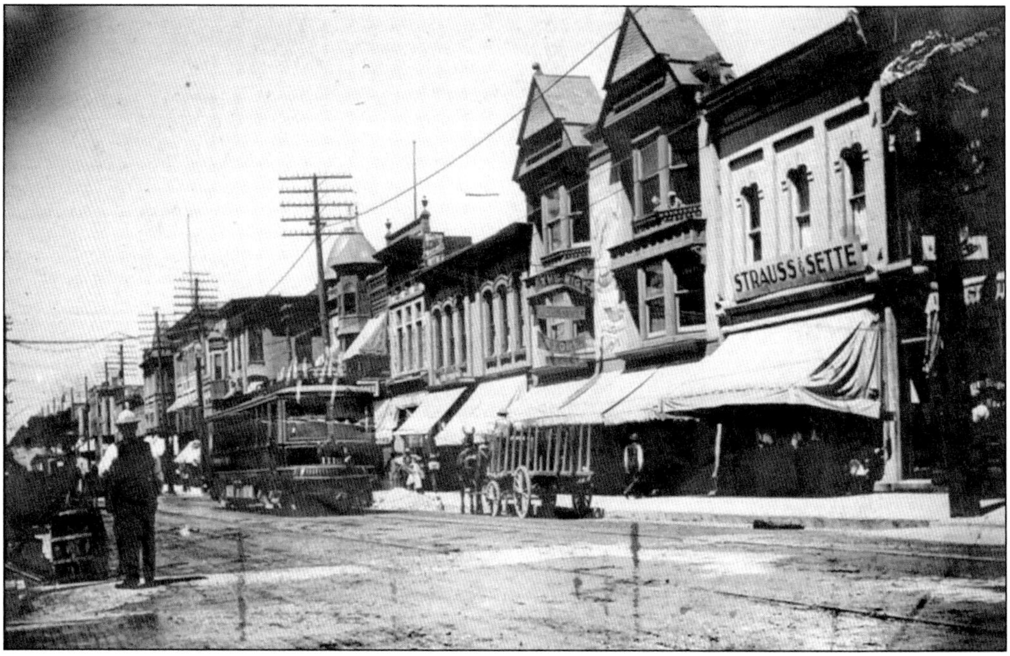

Farther west, a trolley car is encountered in the block between First and Second Streets, looking at the north side of the street in 1910. Note the distinctive gables on the Keck Furniture building, the oldest furniture store in Wisconsin, founded in 1853. These were replaced when the building was remodeled in the 1920s.

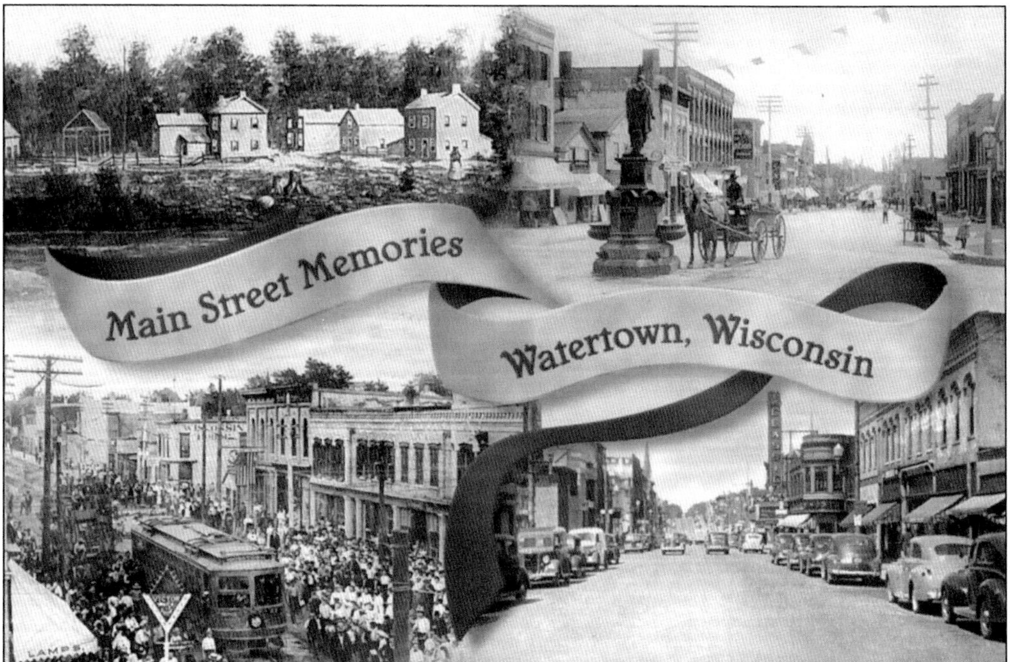

Thus ends the trip down Main Street. Here the many changing faces the street has taken over the years can be seen: 1842, top left; 1900, top right; 1908, bottom left; and 1944, bottom right. This card was issued recently by the Watertown Tourism Board.

Four

Schools and Churches

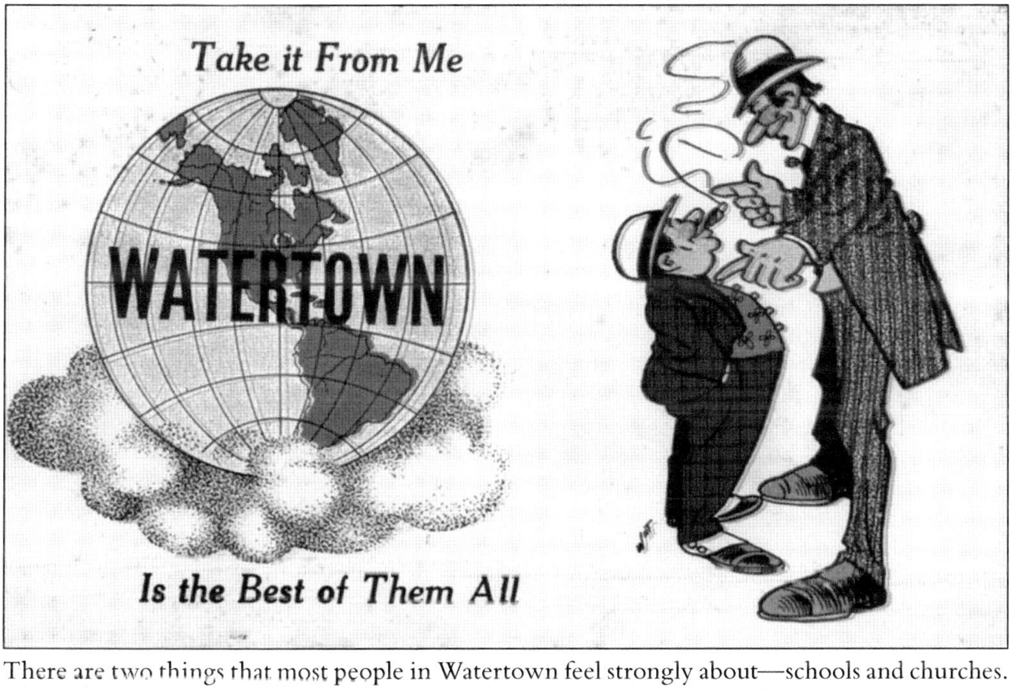

There are two things that most people in Watertown feel strongly about—schools and churches. The earliest settlers found no church awaiting them in the wilderness, so they held private services in various homes until a traveling circuit-riding minister came through and the first services were held in a common building. Thus religion came to Watertown. Likewise, education was not the first thing the pioneers thought of, but after clearing the land and establishing themselves, the idea of school began to appeal to their Yankee sensibilities, and a school was established in 1839. Through the years, there have been many churches that established themselves in Watertown, and currently there are over 25 religious bodies active in the city. There are more than 12 different schools, both public and private, primary and secondary, currently active in Watertown. Some of these schools and churches will be found on the following pages. This postcard from 1916 says it all for the author and for most people.

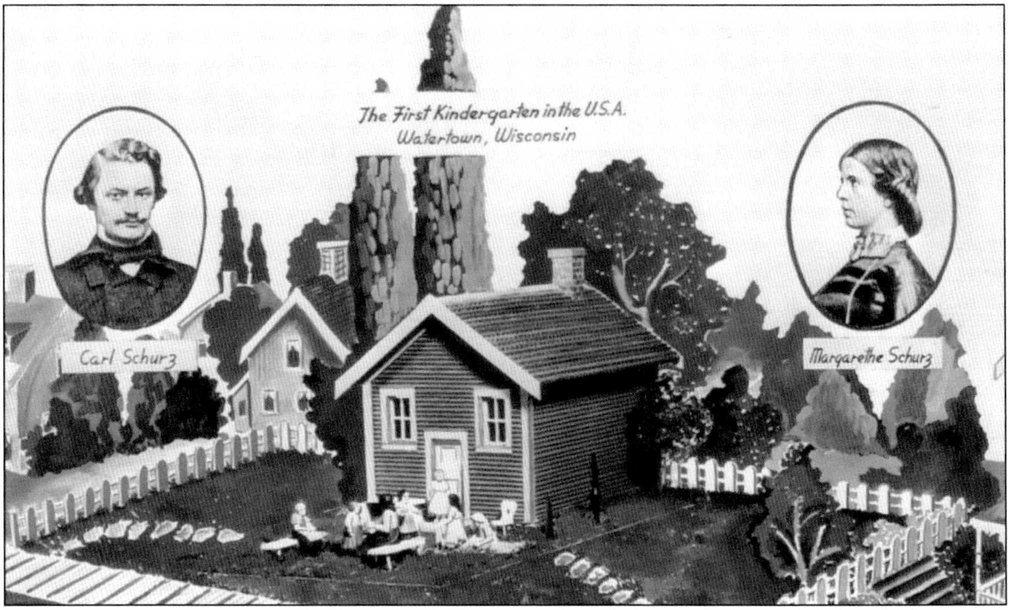

Watertown's chief claim to fame is that it is home to the very first kindergarten in America. The school was founded in 1856 by Margarethe Meyer Schurz, wife of the famous German American statesman Carl Schurz. Students first met in the Schurz home on North Church Street and then quickly moved to a building located at one time on the corner of North Second and Jones Streets. This idealized picture of the first kindergarten was done in the 1920s.

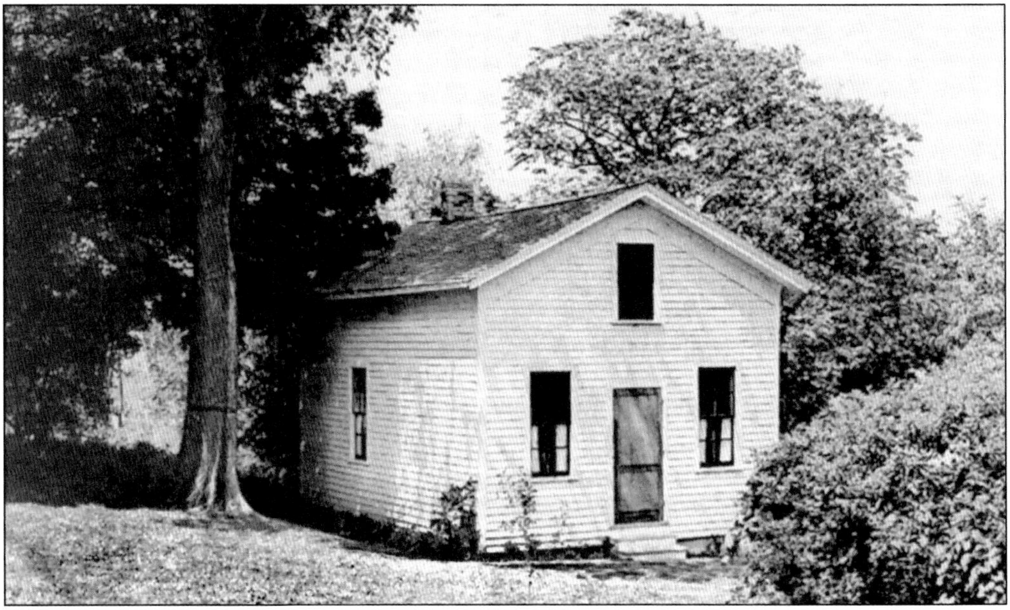

The original kindergarten building was only used by Mrs. Schurz for a year, and then the family moved on to Milwaukee. Through the years, this building was used for various enterprises, including a cigar factory, a religious bookstore, and a fish shop. In 1956, it was in danger of being demolished, and Gladys Mollart, a director of the Watertown Historical Society, saw to it that the building was moved. Today the kindergarten building is a public museum, and it is located on the grounds of the Octagon House Museum at 919 Charles Street in Watertown.

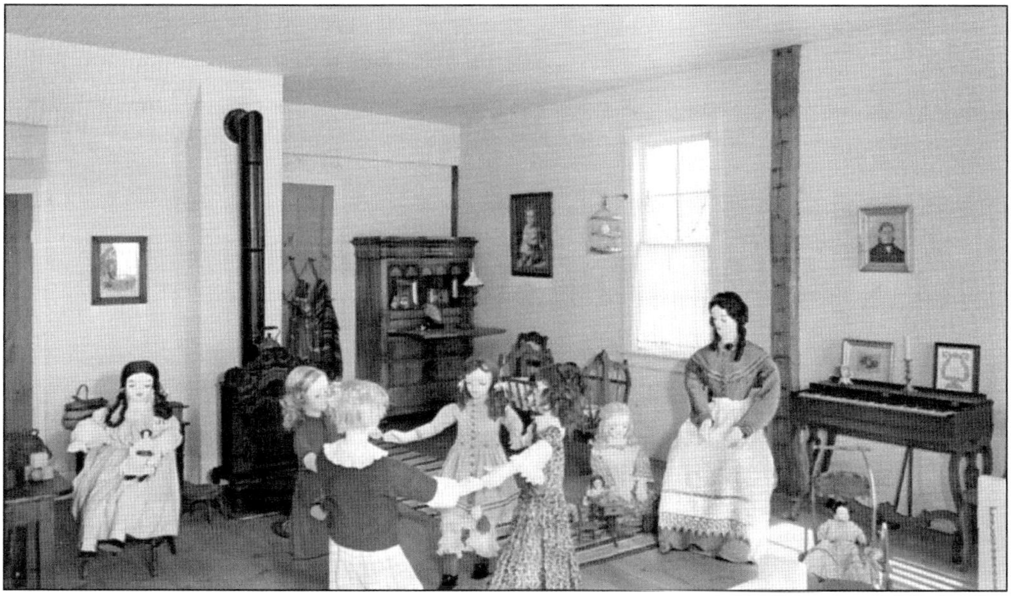

The kindergarten as run by Mrs. Schurz was originally a small, private school with only six pupils: her daughters Agatha and Marianne Schurz, three Juessen girls (their cousins), and one boy, Franklin Blumenfeld. This is the interior of the Kindergarten Museum today, showing manikins that replicate the original children who attended the school.

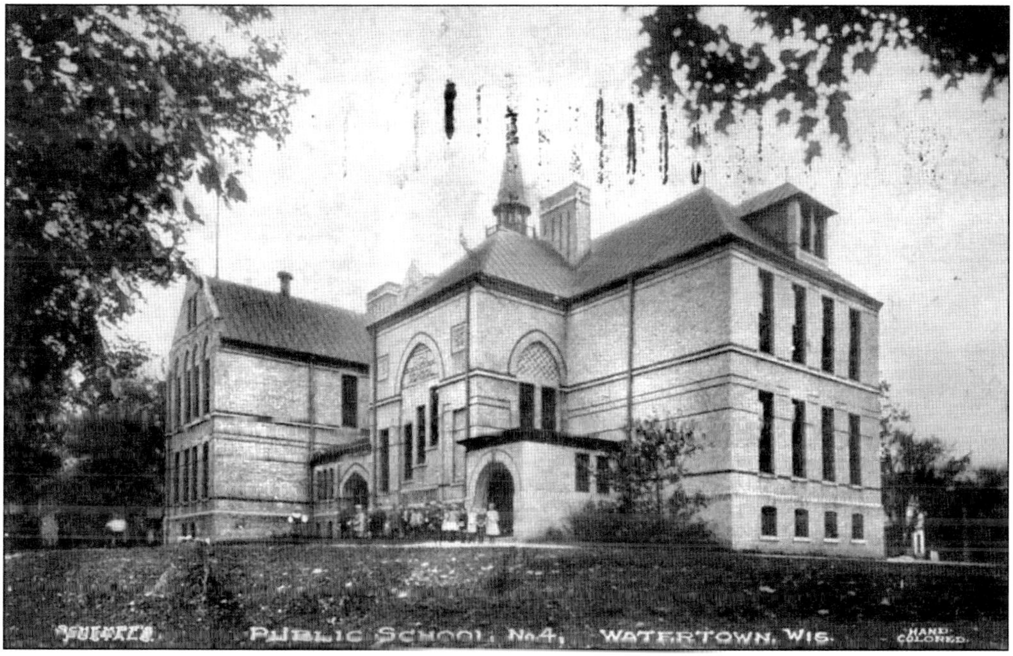

The first high school in Watertown opened in 1863 in a small frame house located on the corner of North Fifth and Jones Streets. In 1883, it moved to this splendid brick edifice located along Western Avenue, and here it would stay until 1897, when the high school moved to the former Union School No. 1, located on East Main Street. At that time, this school became an elementary school that was later known as Webster School. It was demolished in the late 1950s. This image dates to 1909.

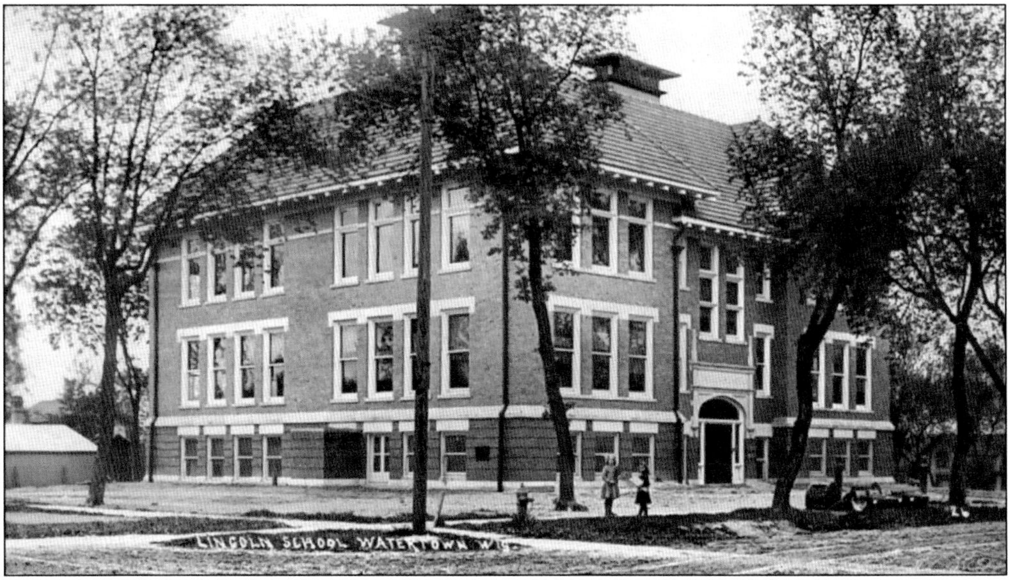

In 1909, the schools in Watertown began to take on names. Prior to this time, they were identified by their number, such as the school pictured here, which was originally built in 1864 and rebuilt in 1910, known as Union School No. 2. In 1909, the year before the school was rebuilt and dedicated, the students and faculty petitioned the school board to have the new school named after Abraham Lincoln, the nation's 16th president. This request was granted, and that opened the floodgates. Today there are, in addition to Lincoln School, schools named after Stephen A. Douglas, Daniel Webster, and even Margarethe Schurz. Lincoln School burned to the ground on February 23, 1946, and was rebuilt in 1949.

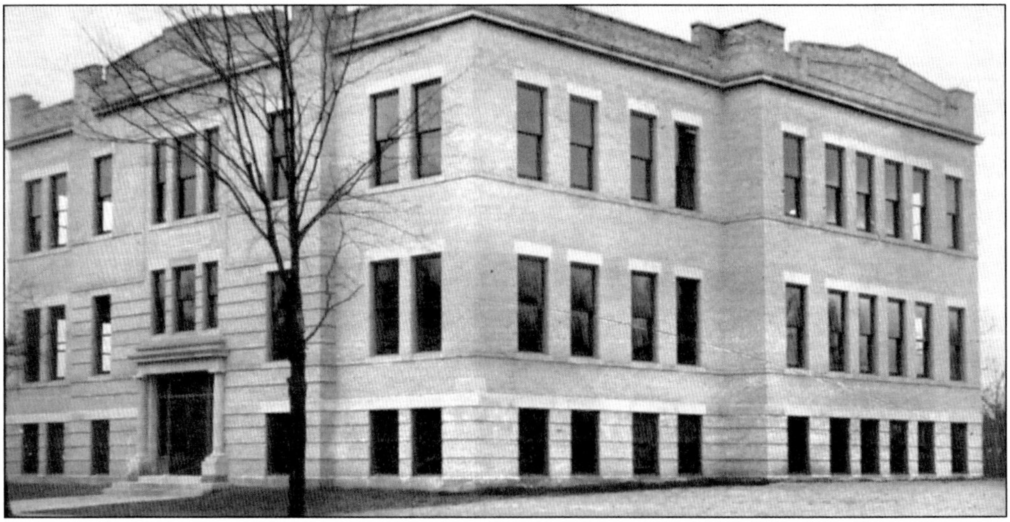

The first schools in Watertown were private schools and academies. Then, in the 1850s, the city decided to unify its schools and created the "Union School System," thus assuring that all pupils were taught a common curriculum. Not long afterward, churches began to open their own schools to not only educate the children of their congregations but also to give them a thorough grounding in religious education. This is St. Mark's Lutheran School, built in 1914. It was used for many years before being demolished in 1974 to make way for a more modern school building.

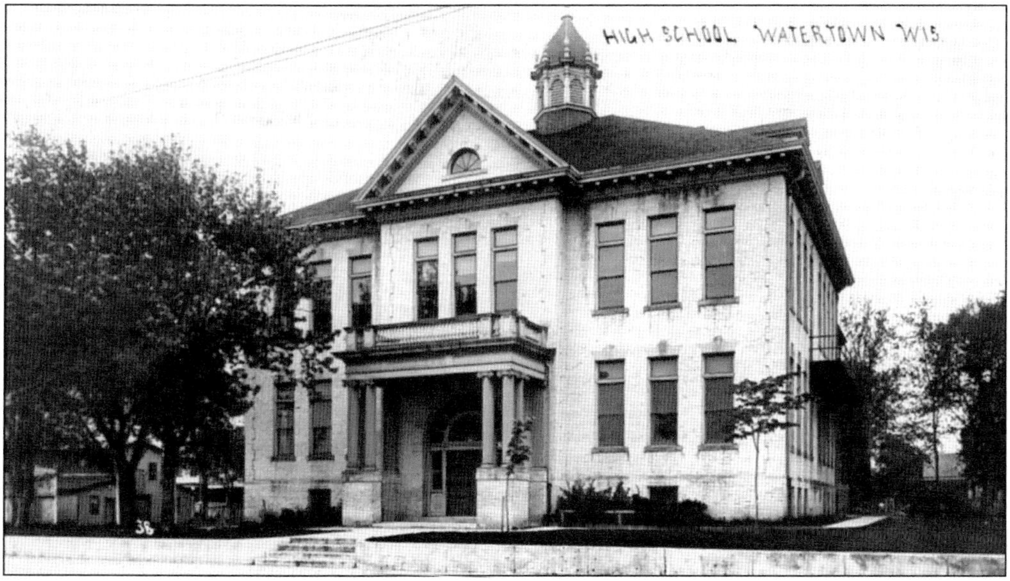

As stated before, the first high school opened in 1863 and later moved to Union School No. 1, shown here, in 1897. This building was erected in 1863 and served as the high school from 1897 to 1917. After the school left it, this structure became the city armory, and still later it housed the Youth Activity Center (YAC) before being demolished in the late 1960s. A hotel is on this site today.

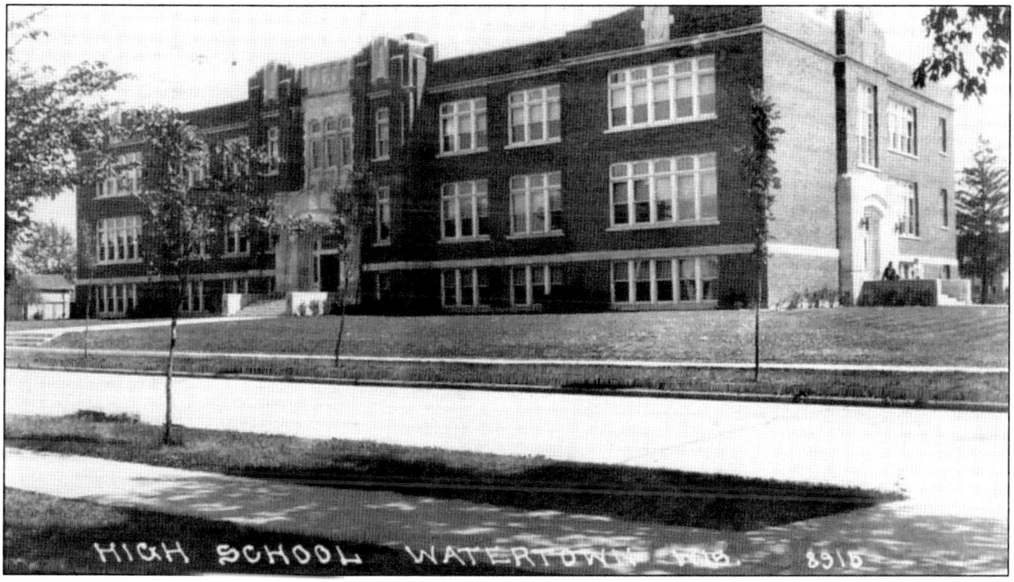

This is the author's alma mater and the alma mater of many hundreds of young people from 1917 to 1994. This is Watertown Senior High School, located on South Eighth Street, taken in 1922. This view shows the school as it appeared before an addition was added in the late 1920s to allow for a junior high school department. A later addition, built about 1957, was constructed to the north of the building. In 1994, this high school ceased to operate, as the high school moved into a brand-new state-of-the art building in the northern part of the city. For a time, it sat empty, before finally being demolished in 2000. A parking lot marks this site today.

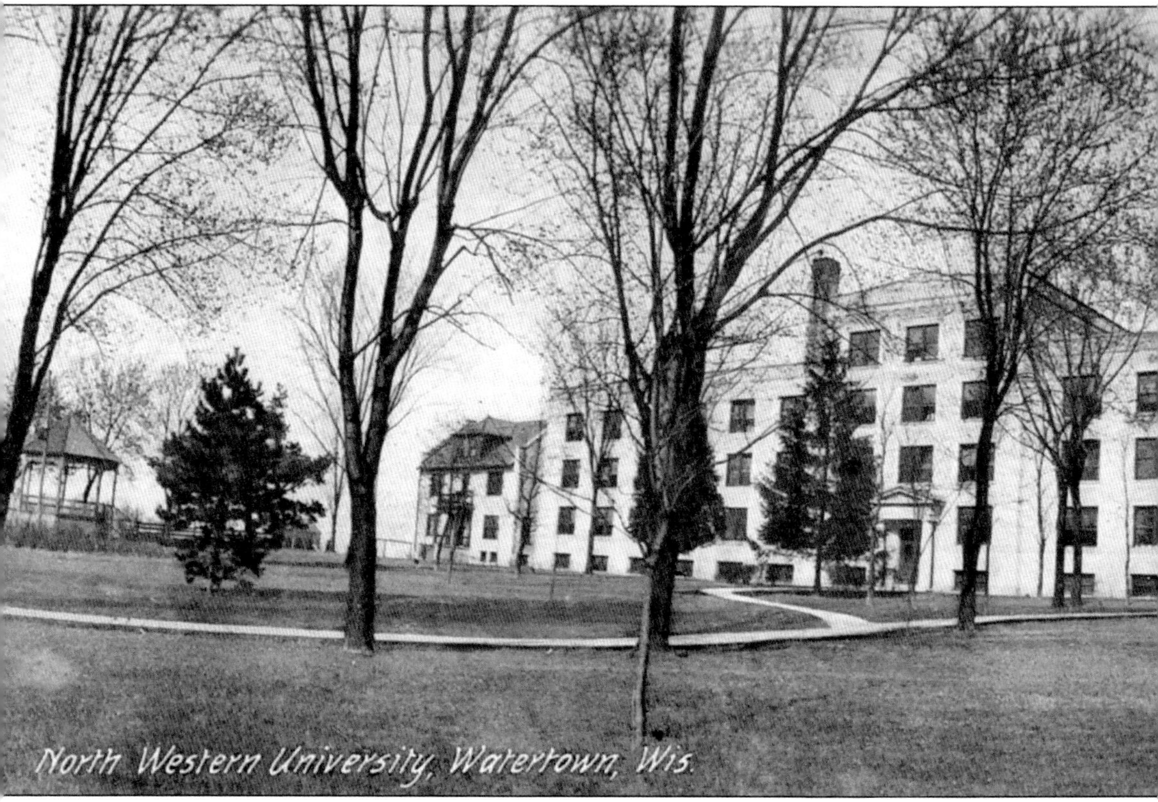

Watertown has always been home to two colleges. At one time, those colleges were Sacred Heart,

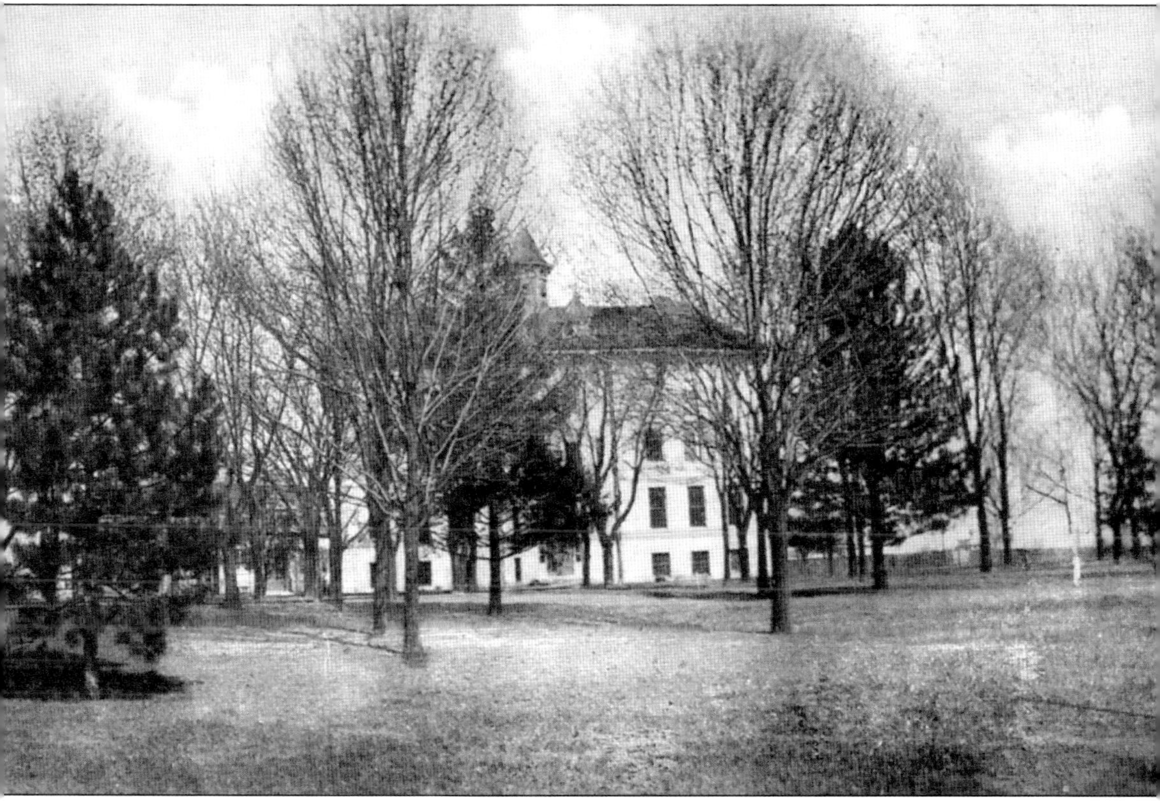

a Catholic school, and Northwestern College, pictured here in 1908, a Lutheran college.

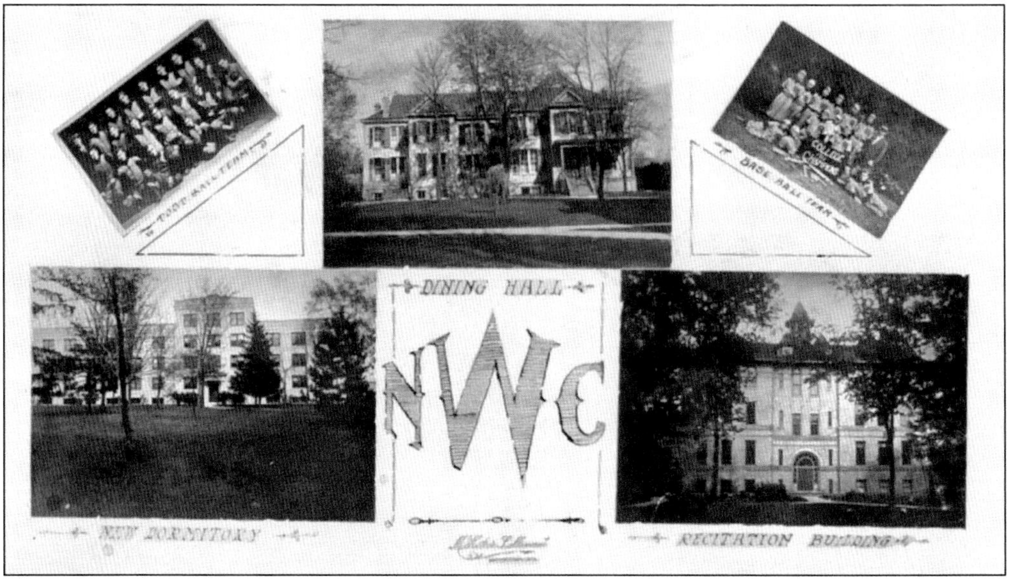

Northwestern College, shown here in a multiview postcard from about 1910, was founded in a small house on North Fourth Street in 1863. By the latter half of the 1860s, it moved to larger quarters on the corner of College and Western Avenues, where it remained and flourished. In 1994, the Wisconsin Synod decided to close the campus in Watertown and move the college to New Ulm, Minnesota. In its place, the synod opened a preparatory school, known as Luther Prep, which operates there today.

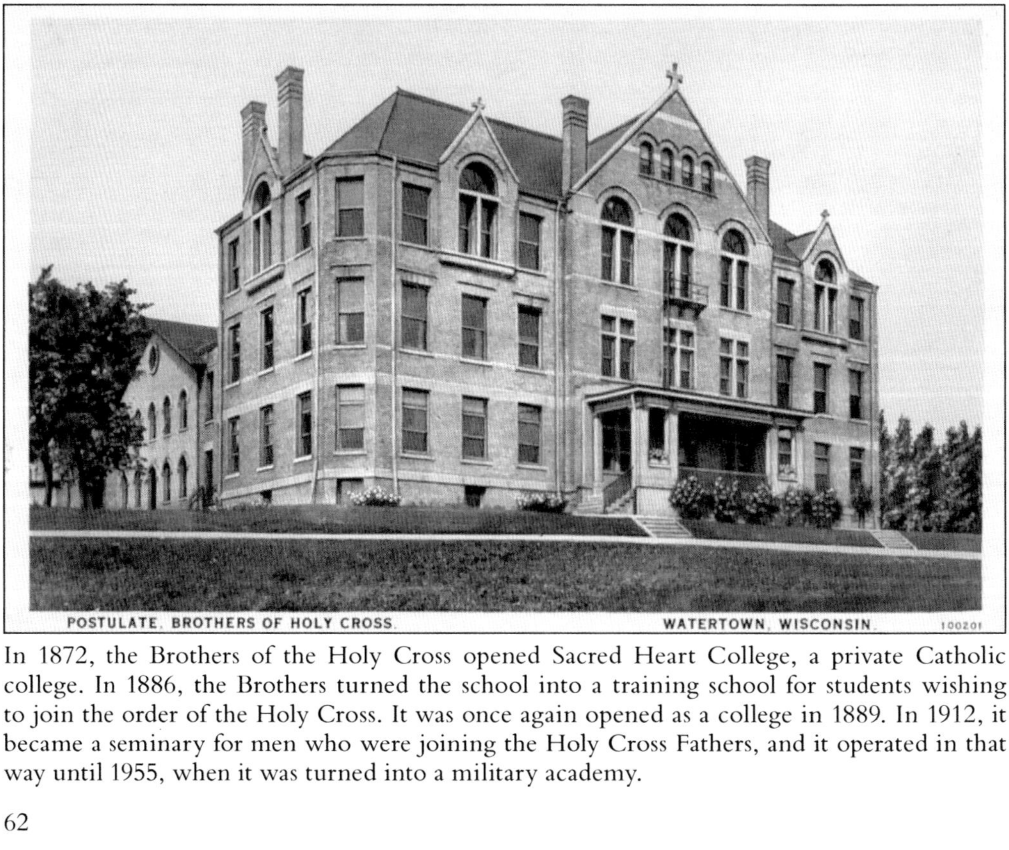

In 1872, the Brothers of the Holy Cross opened Sacred Heart College, a private Catholic college. In 1886, the Brothers turned the school into a training school for students wishing to join the order of the Holy Cross. It was once again opened as a college in 1889. In 1912, it became a seminary for men who were joining the Holy Cross Fathers, and it operated in that way until 1955, when it was turned into a military academy.

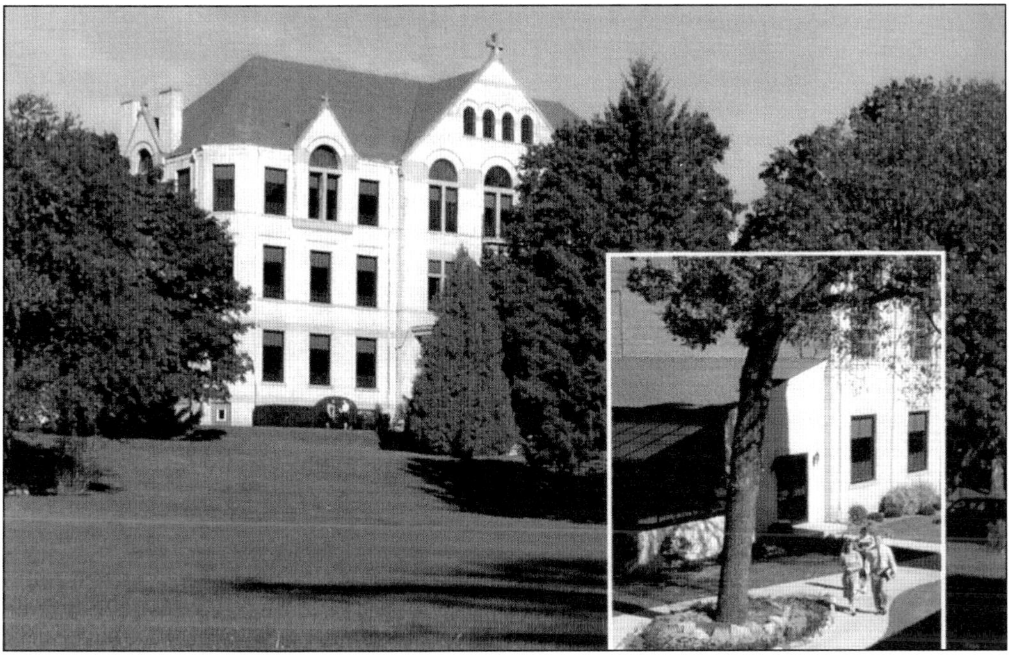

In 1968, Sacred Heart Military Academy was sold to the Baptist Church, and it is now known as Maranatha Baptist Bible College. Today, besides Maranatha, Watertown is also home to Madison Area Technical College. Thus the tradition of Watertown being a two-college town still holds true.

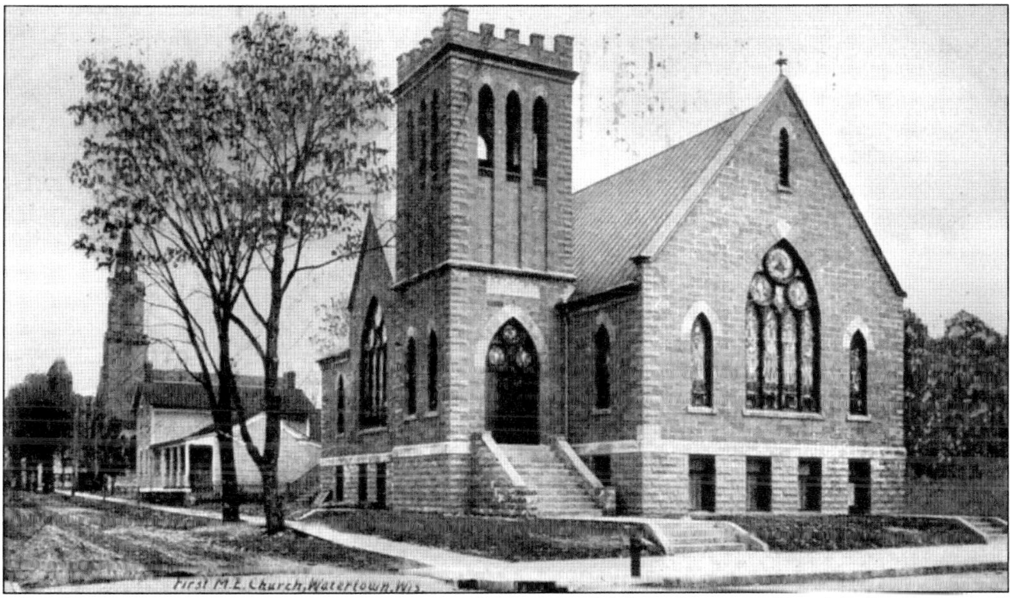

The first minister to reach Watertown was Rev. Jesse Halstead, a traveling Methodist circuit rider who arrived here in 1837. Until 1843, Methodism was the dominant religion here. This image shows the Methodist church on the corner of Fifth and Main Streets about 1909, a year after the church was erected, replacing a frame building. This church remained on Main Street until the mid-1970s, when it moved to a modern building on Hall Street on the eastern side of the city. Today a bank is on this site.

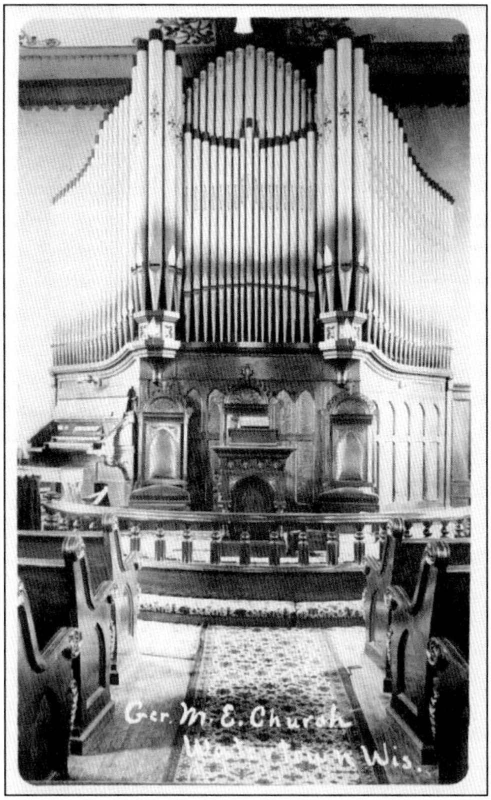

This is the interior of the German Methodist Episcopal Church, also known as the Wesley Methodist Church, shown about 1912. The German Methodist Episcopal Church was founded in 1849, and its first building was erected in 1851 at 201 North Fifth Street (it can be seen to the far left of the postcard on page 63). In 1957, the church merged with the Watertown Methodist Church and became Christ United Methodist. The building was demolished in the mid-1970s and is today a parking lot.

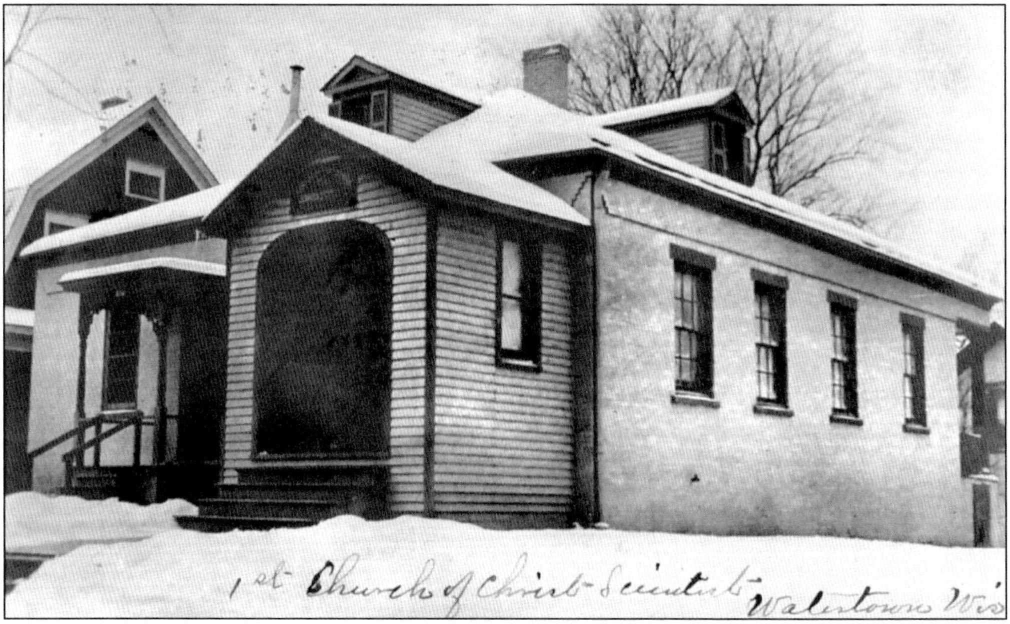

In 1906, a Christian Science church opened in this building on South Fifth Street. This building was replaced by a substantial brick edifice in the 1920s, and the church continued until the 1960s, when it went out of existence. The Seventh-Day Adventist congregation uses the old Christian Science church building for their place of worship today. This view dates to 1908.

In 1841, a Catholic missionary, Rev. Patrick O'Kelly, arrived in Watertown and said the first Catholic mass in the home of Bernard Crangle, an early Irish settler. This act led to the foundation of St. Bernard's Catholic Church, the oldest Catholic church in Watertown. Originally a small frame structure, the building was replaced by this brick edifice, which was opened for worship in 1876. The cornerstone of this church was cut from the famous Rock of Cashel in Ireland.

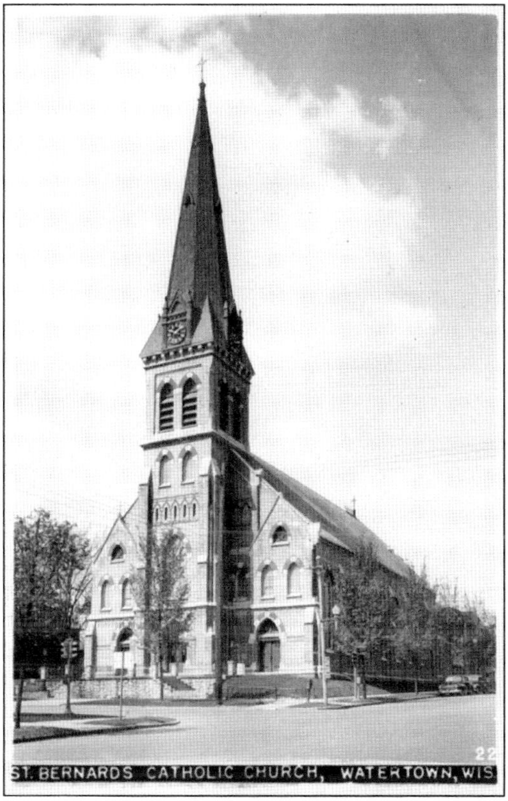

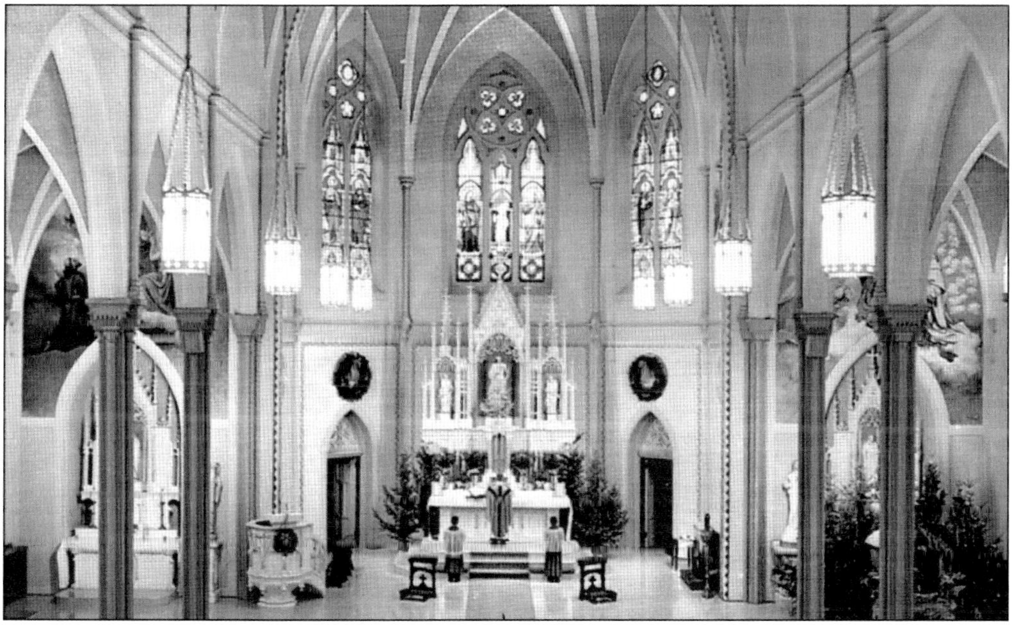

This postcard from the 1950s shows the interior of St. Bernard's Catholic Church. This is how the interior looked until 1974, when a massive remodeling took place, obliterating most of the former glory of the church. In the last few years, there has been a concerted effort to try to restore some of the former features of the church's interior.

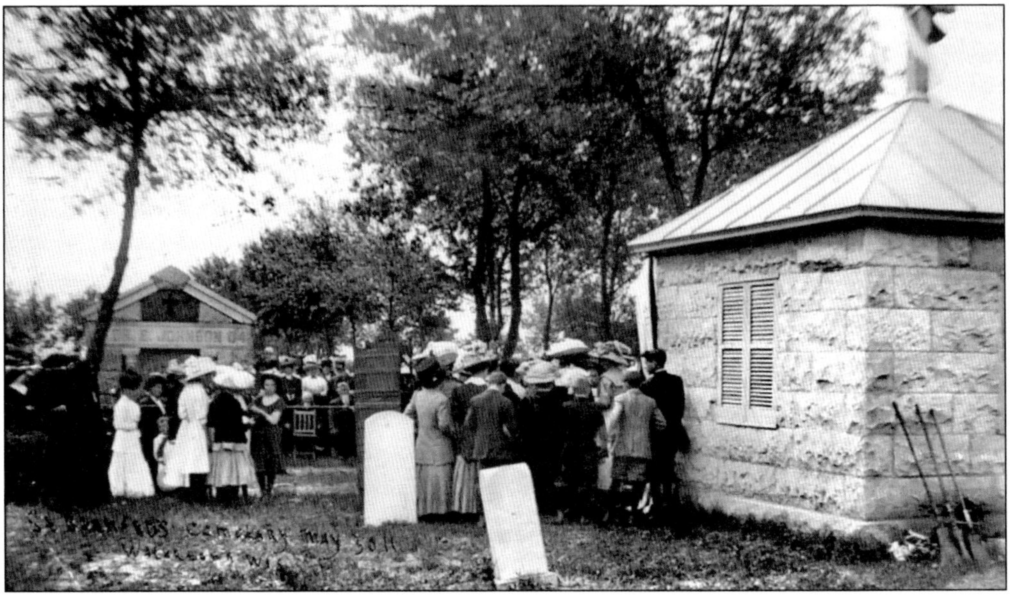

For many years, St. Bernard's held special church services at its cemetery located along Milford Street in the southwestern part of the city. This view shows one of those services held on Decoration Day, May 30, 1911. The mausoleum on the left belonged to Dr. Edward Johnson, the city's first druggist and a prominent member of and benefactor to St. Bernard's.

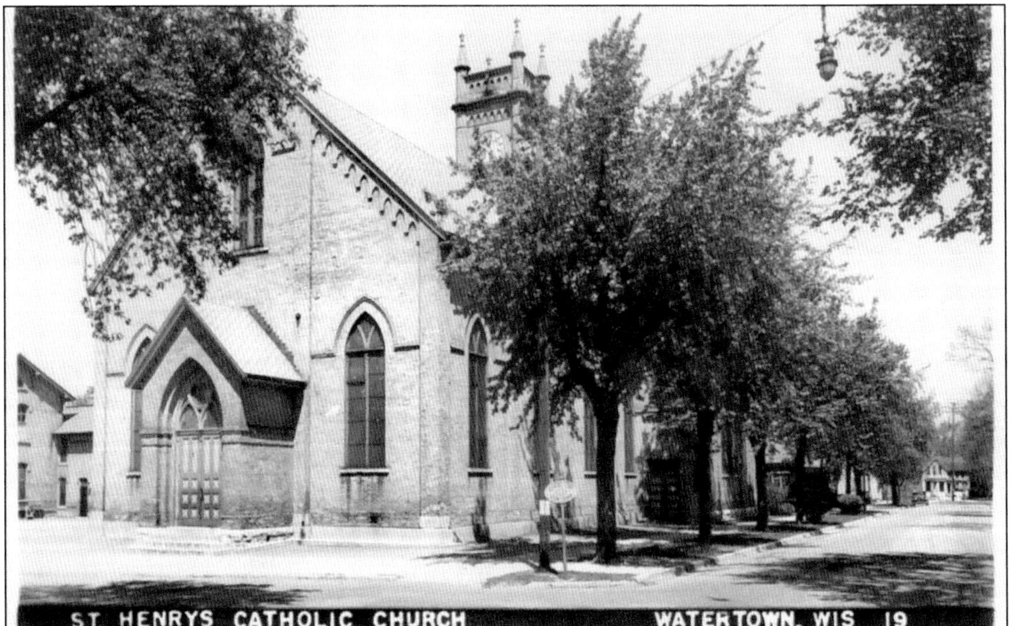

In Watertown, as in other places no doubt, a certain amount of tension existed between Irish and German settlers. In Watertown, the various ethnic groups kept to themselves for the most part, preferring to live in little enclaves or settlements within the city. A number of German Catholics tried to worship at St. Bernard's, but since that church was predominantly Irish, things did not always bode well. So, in 1853, a German Catholic church, St. Henry's, was established. This postcard shows the church in 1944.

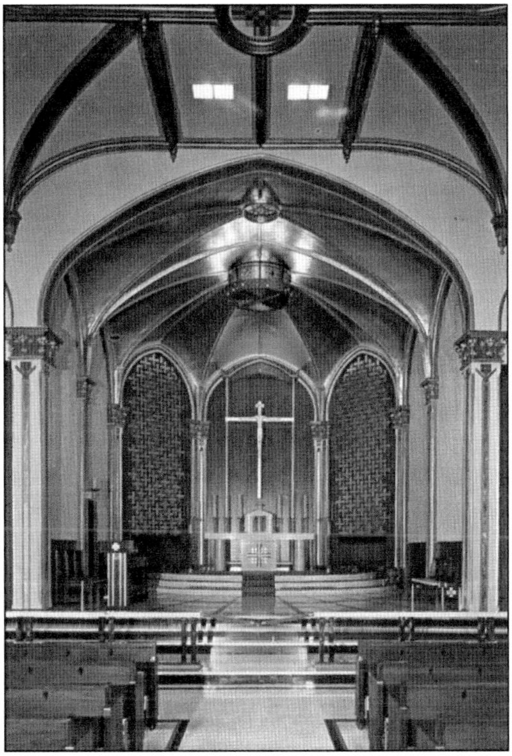

St. Henry's Catholic Church is located on the corner of East Cady and North Fourth Streets. This view shows the interior of St. Henry's just after it was remodeled in 1962. The interior of the church was remodeled once again in 2002, and much of its former brilliance and glory has since been restored.

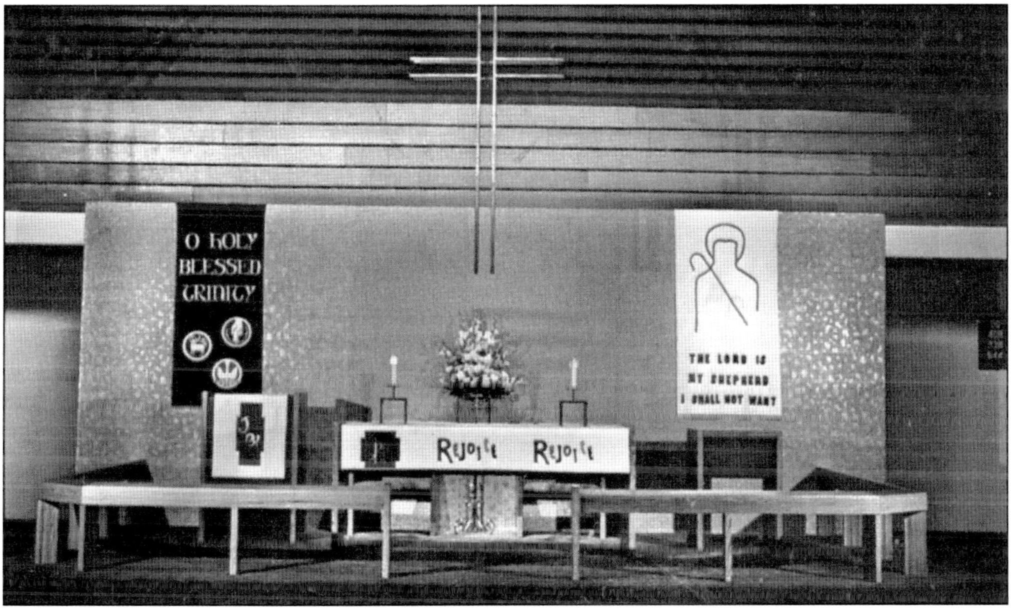

There is an old joke that goes something like this: no one can get along with Lutherans, especially other Lutherans. That certainly seems to be the case in Watertown, for there are seven Lutheran churches here, most of which broke from the two oldest Lutheran churches. This is one of the churches that broke away, Good Shepherd Lutheran Church, which left St. John's Lutheran Church in 1971, when the church left the Missouri Synod for the Wisconsin Synod. Good Shepherd is located along the Highway 16 bypass on the east side of the city.

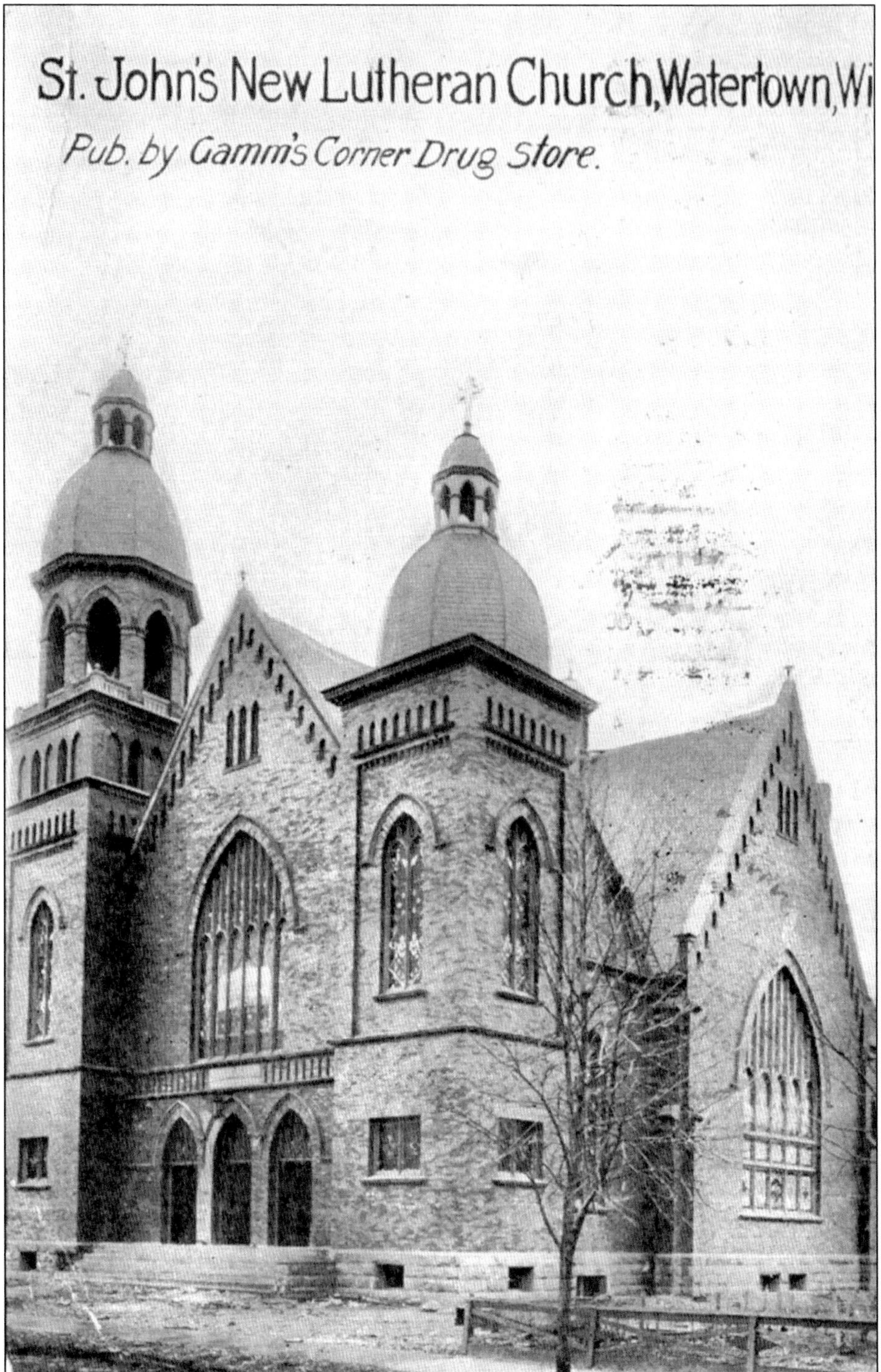

Perhaps the oldest Lutheran church in Watertown is this one, St. John's, which was established by German Lutherans in 1852. The original church was a traditional Gothic church, but in 1908, this unusual Greek Orthodox–inspired house of worship, pictured here, was constructed.

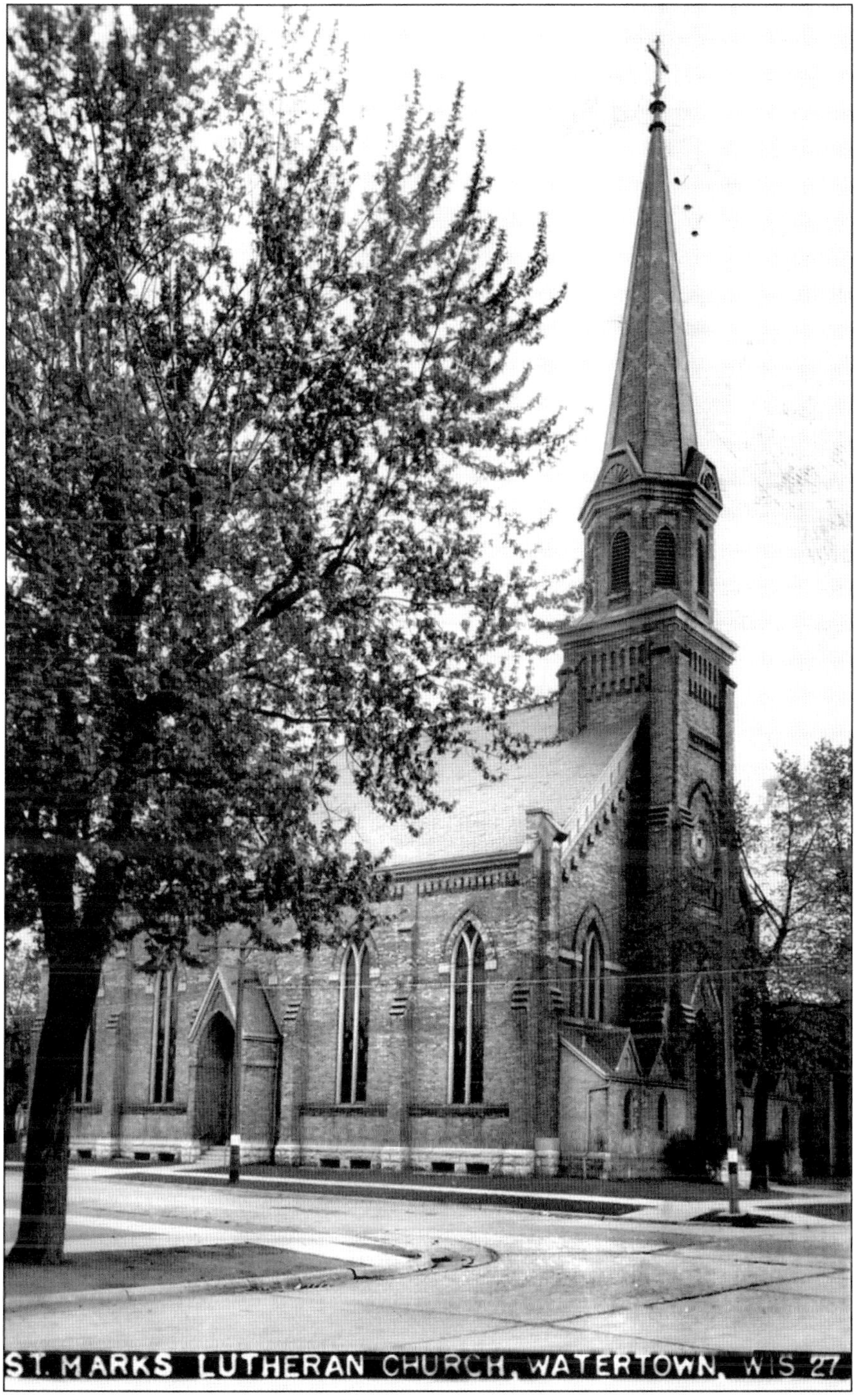

The second oldest Lutheran church in Watertown is St. Mark's Evangelical Lutheran Church, organized in 1854 by a very liberal and charismatic leader, Rev. Christian Sans. The original church was the first brick church building in the city. The present church building, pictured here in the 1940s, was erected in 1888. Apart from some additions, this is the same church in use today.

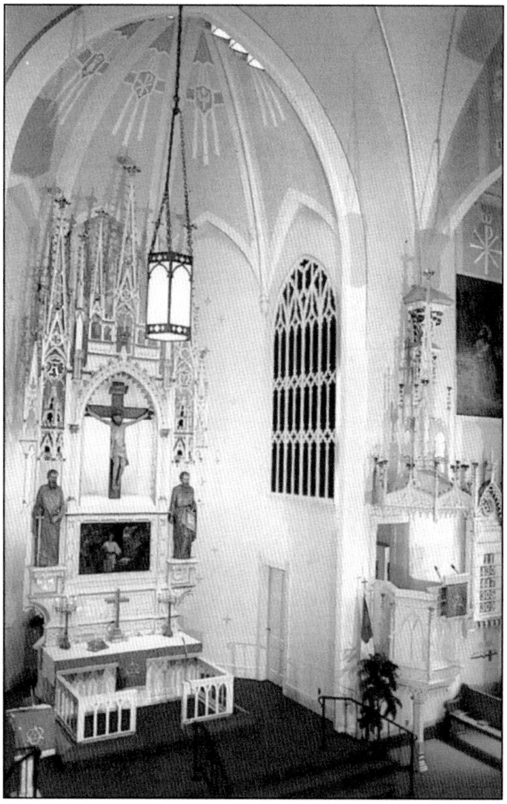

This interior view of St. Mark's shows the pulpit and altar. The church was first decorated in 1908, again in 1949, and in 1971, the date of this postcard. In 1997, the church was again remodeled on a massive scale, and the decorations first applied in 1908 were once again restored, making it one of the most striking churches in the city.

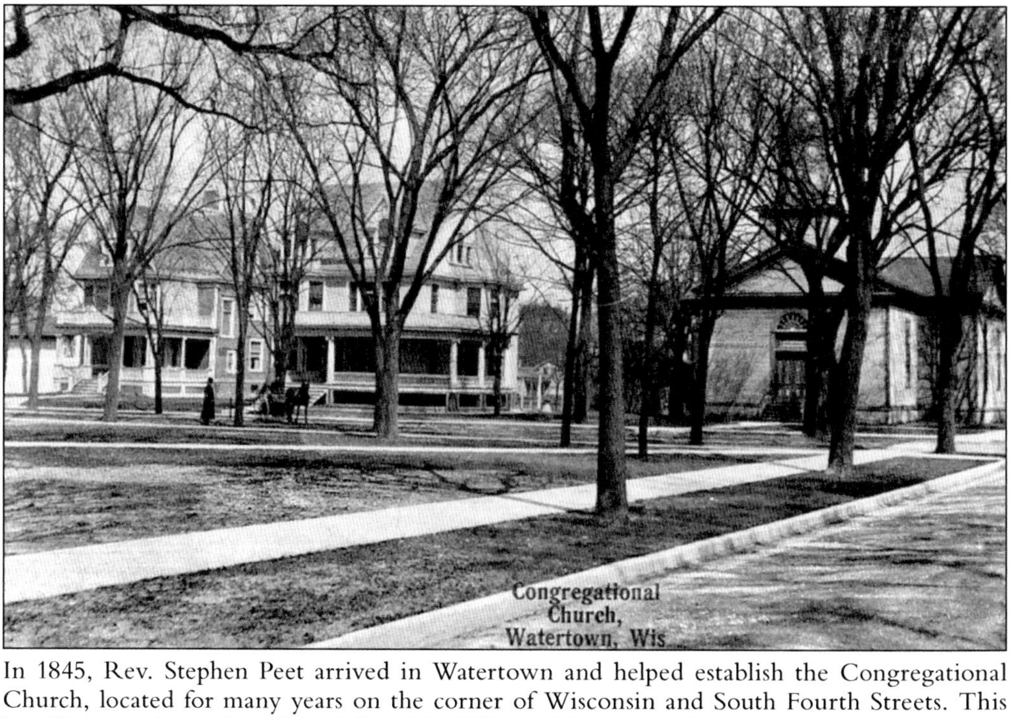

In 1845, Rev. Stephen Peet arrived in Watertown and helped establish the Congregational Church, located for many years on the corner of Wisconsin and South Fourth Streets. This bucolic scene shows the original church building, which was replaced in 1909.

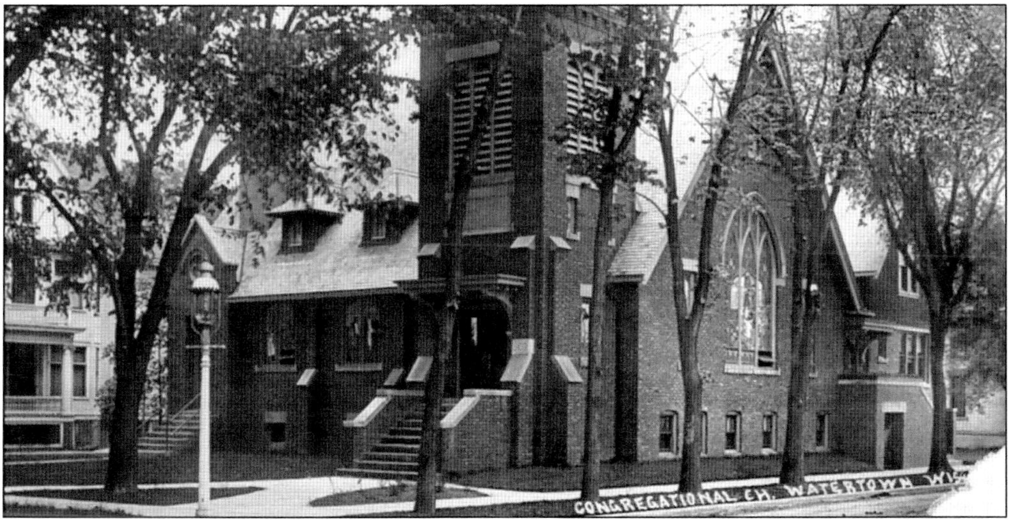

In 1909, the Congregationalists replaced their old church with a large, red-brick structure, shown here. Their old church was moved to the corner of South Second and Milwaukee Streets, where today it is an apartment building. The new church served as home to the congregation until 1993, when the church moved to the far eastern side of the city. Shortly thereafter, the 1st Brigade Band, a nationally known musical organization that re-creates the music of the Civil War, bought the building. Today this building is known as Heritage Hall, and besides the 1st Brigade Band, it is also home to the Dodge-Jefferson Counties Genealogical Society.

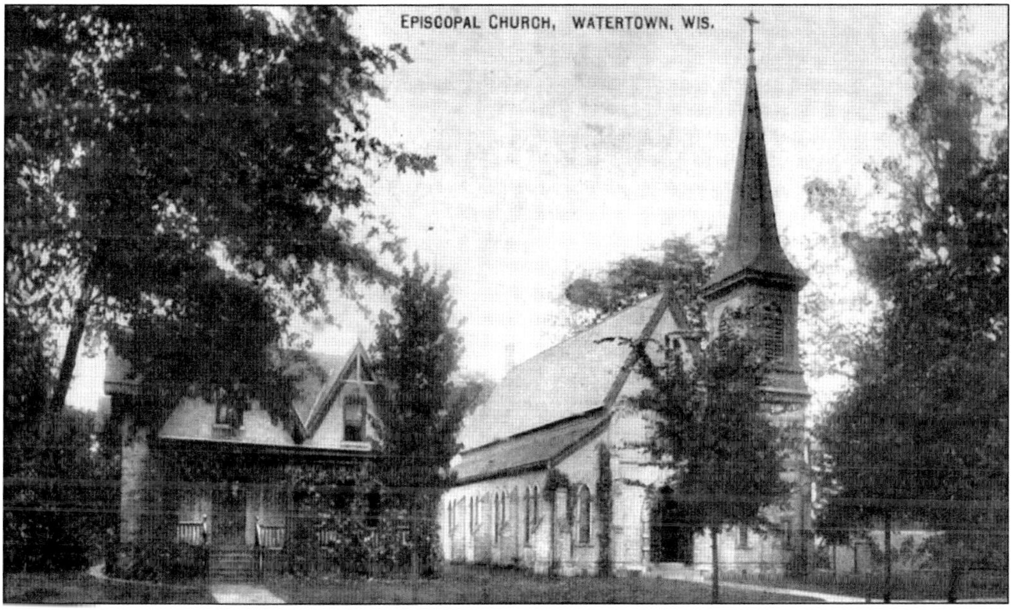

The oldest church building in the city is St. Paul's Episcopal Church, located on South Second Street. This church was established by Rev. Melancthon Hoyt in 1845. The original church was located on South Third Street, and in 1859, it moved to its present location. Over the years, several additions have been added to the church, including a chapel, a bell tower in 1890, and a fellowship hall in 1931. This 1910 view shows the front of the church and the parsonage, on the left. On July 23, 2005, the church was struck by lightning, and the roof and church steeple caught fire, doing serious damage.

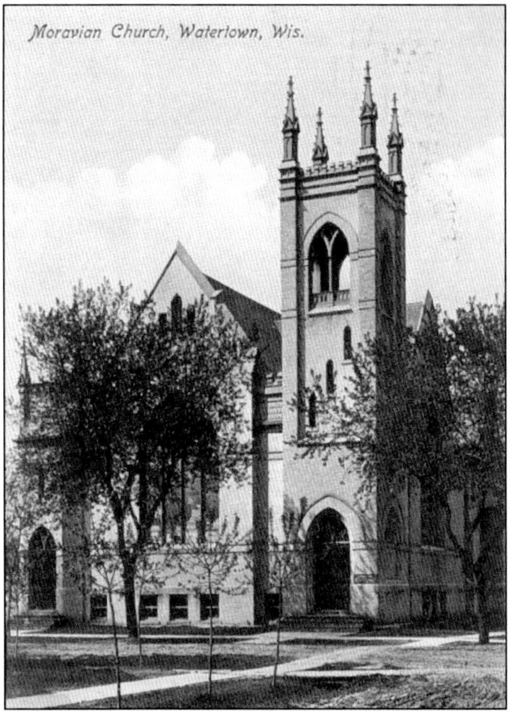

In 1853, the Ebenezer Moravian Church was established in the town of Watertown, south of the city. A sister church was established in the city proper at 609 Cole Street in 1855 by Rev. John Kaltenbrun. Over the years, this church has undergone several changes, including a completely new building in 1904, which is shown here about 1910.

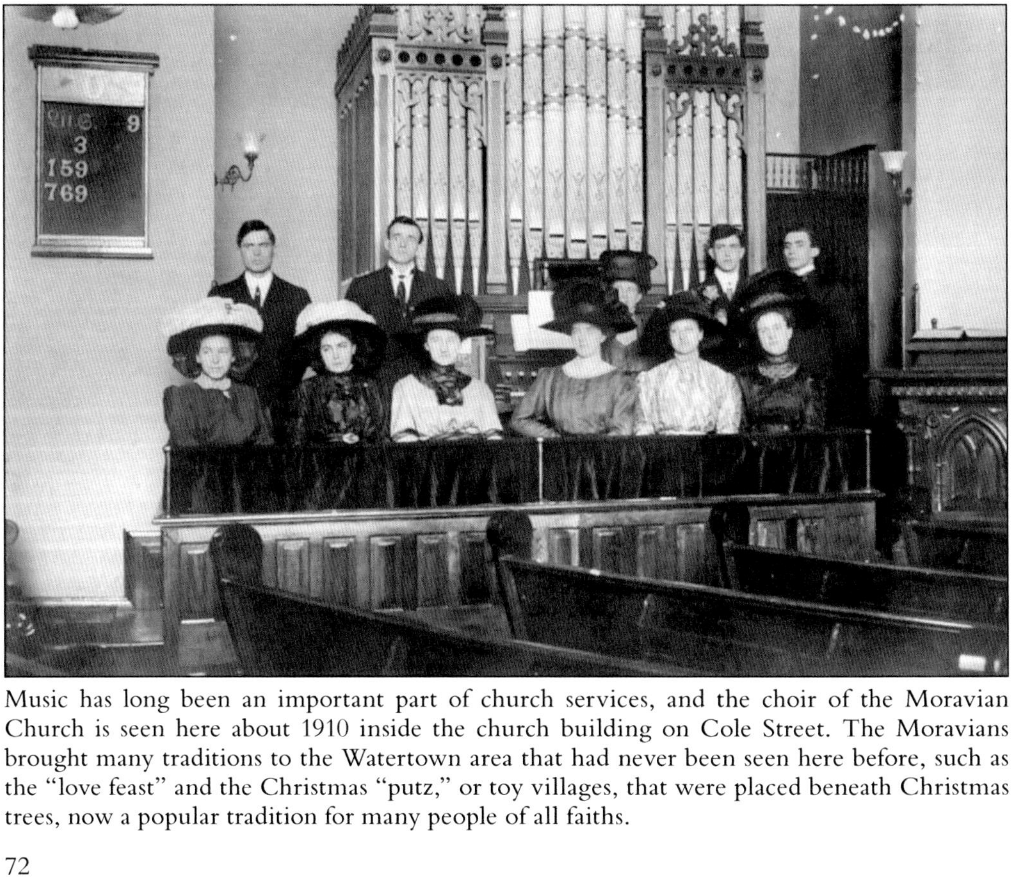

Music has long been an important part of church services, and the choir of the Moravian Church is seen here about 1910 inside the church building on Cole Street. The Moravians brought many traditions to the Watertown area that had never been seen here before, such as the "love feast" and the Christmas "putz," or toy villages, that were placed beneath Christmas trees, now a popular tradition for many people of all faiths.

Five

Recreation and Entertainment

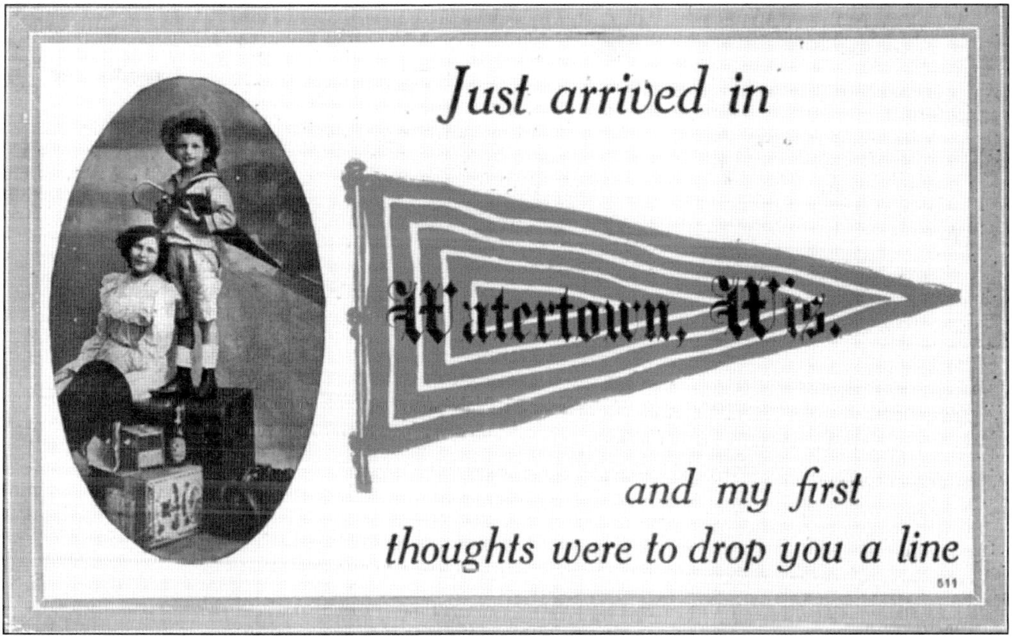

In Watertown, residents work hard and play hard. From the earliest days of the settlement, when the pioneers took time out from their labors in carving a home out of the wilderness to attend a barn raising, quilting bee, or a dance to the band concerts, dances, and sporting events of today, Watertown citizens have always used their leisure time to the fullest. Here is a glimpse of some of the forms of recreation once found (and in some cases still to be found) in Watertown. Above is a 1912 greeting from Watertown.

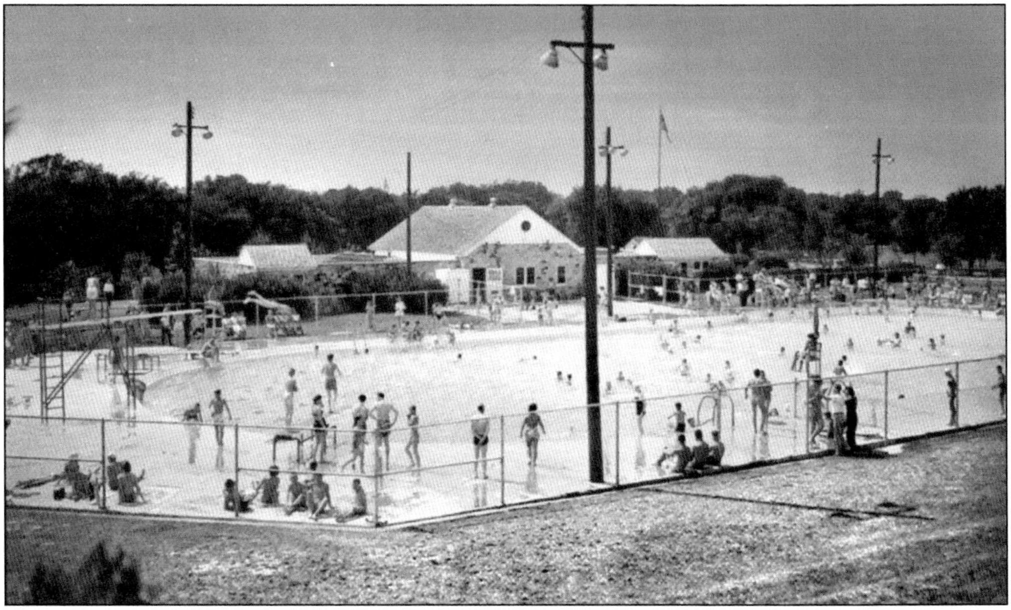

What is more rare than a day in June—especially a day spent at the swimming pool. On hot summer days, hundreds of people of all ages can be found taking a refreshing dip in the cooling waters of the pool. Built in 1942, the Watertown Municipal Pool, seen here in 1951, provided hours of cool relaxation to those who frequented it. The pool was remodeled in the early 1990s, and such amenities as a waterslide and a new bathhouse were added, and in 1993, the newly christened Watertown Aquatic Center opened for business.

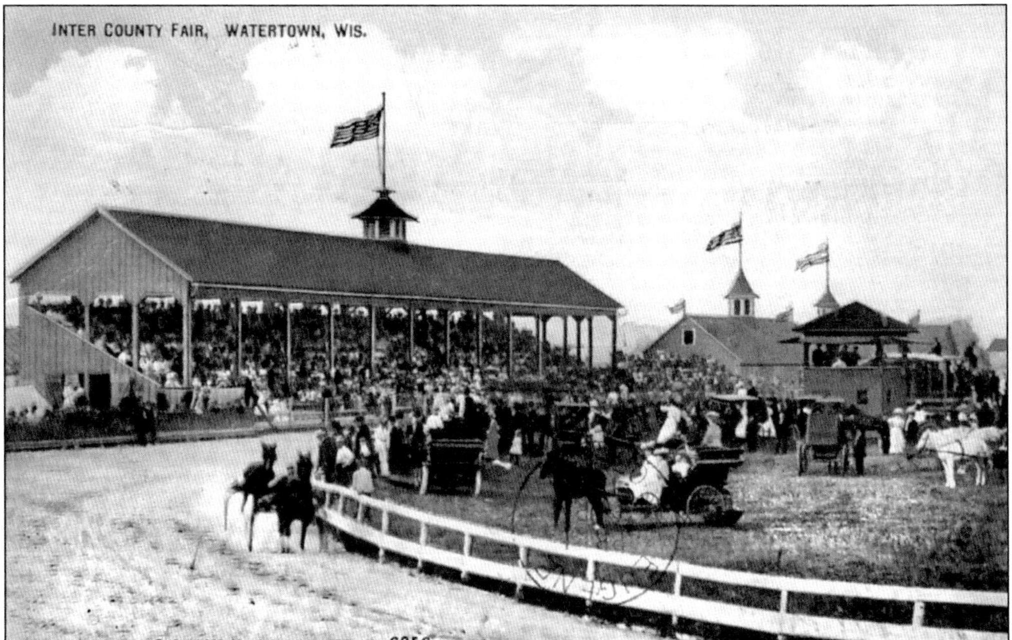

From 1904 to 1926, Watertown was host to the Inter-County Fair, held each September on grounds in the south of the city along Utah Street. This photograph shows the racing track and grandstands as they appeared in 1911.

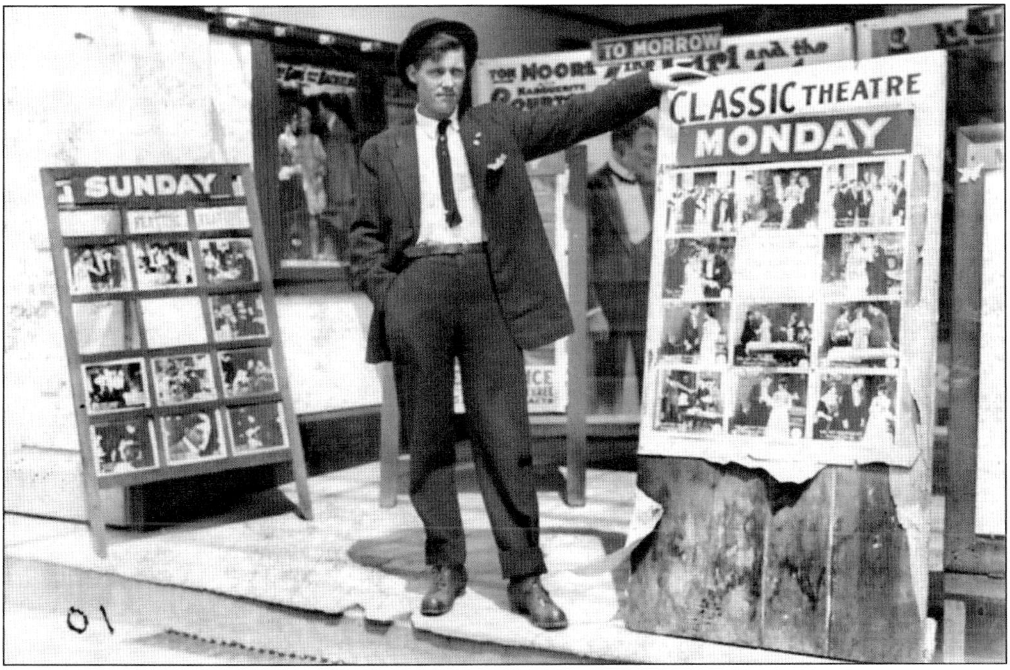

Movies are a popular form of entertainment, and they first appeared in Watertown in the late 1890s as part of traveling exhibits and lectures. At one time, there were over five or six theaters operating here. The oldest theater still operating was the former Classic Theater, opened in 1913 by Willis Norton and located at 308 Main Street. This image is from about 1915.

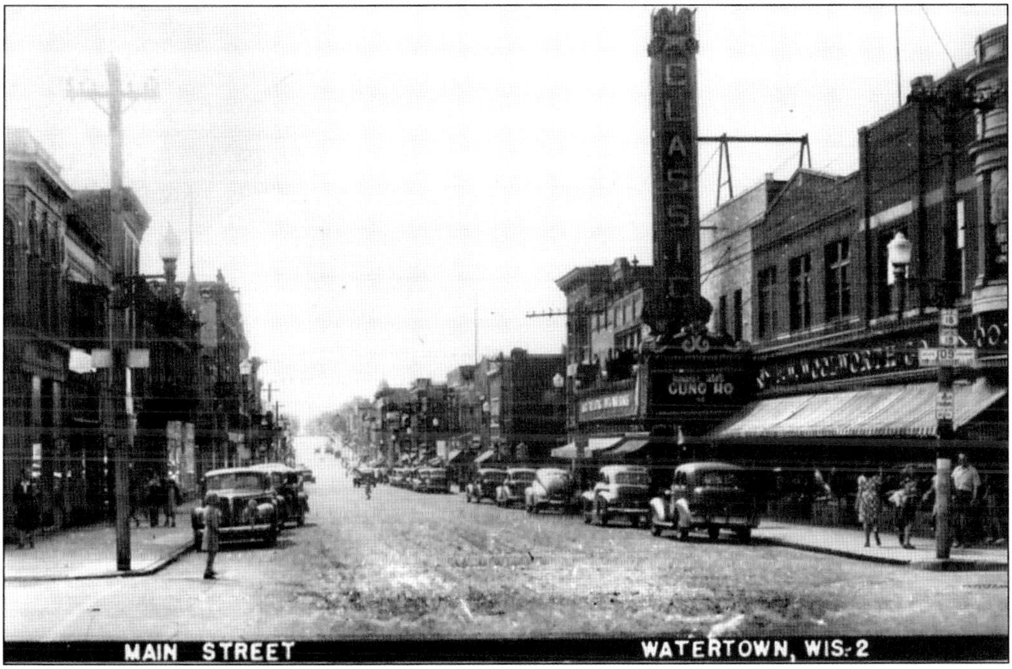

The Classic Theater is shown here in a 1944 view of Main Street, to the left of the Woolworth store. Since 1972, it has been known as the Towne Cinema, and in the 1990s it became a multiplex theater, with three different studios or theaters inside.

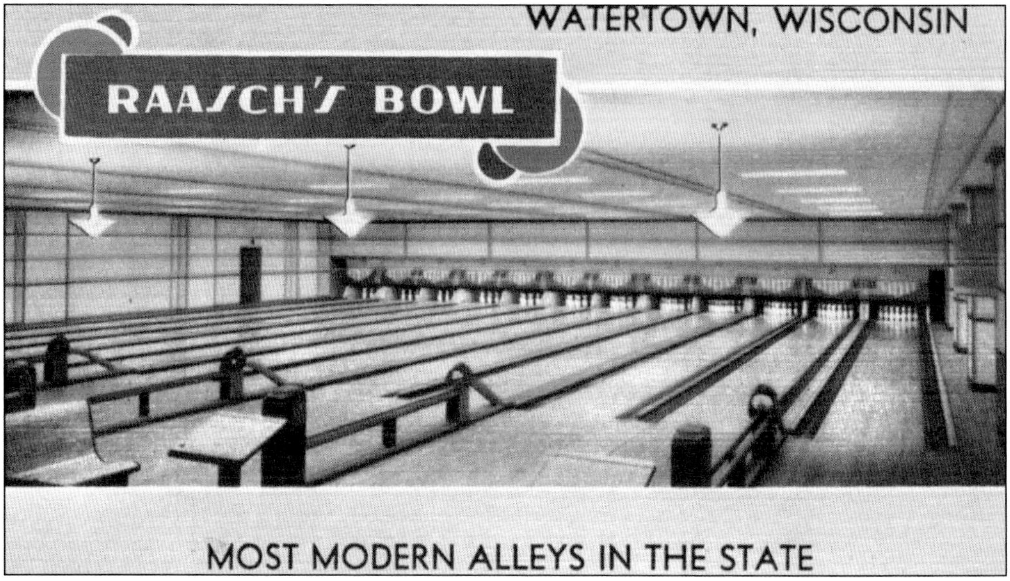

Each ethnic group that came to Watertown brought with them their own traditions and special types of entertainments. The Germans, for example, brought with them "kegelbahn," or the game of bowling. Many outdoor alleys could be found in sommergartens. Indoor bowling alleys began to appear in the late 1890s, with one of the first being in the basement of the Concordia Opera House. Today there are several bowling alleys, and many teams compete to win trophies. One of the oldest still in operation is Raasch's Bowl, today known as Watertown Bowl 18 on West Cady Street. Opened by Earl Raasch, this bowling alley, seen here in the 1940s, was opened in the former Eaton Ice House.

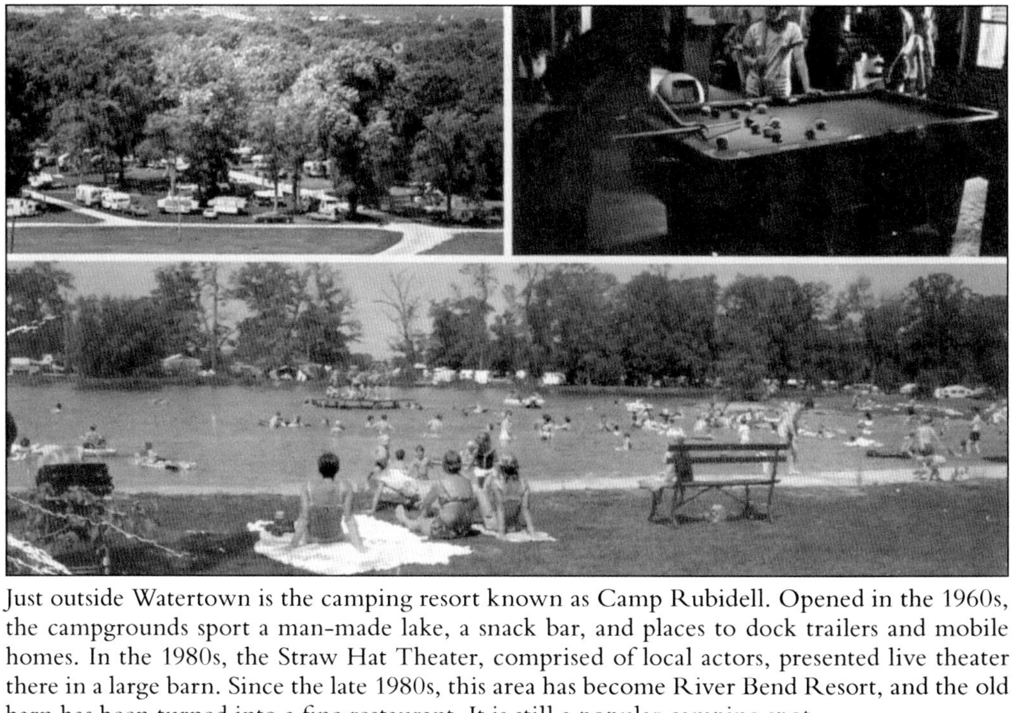

Just outside Watertown is the camping resort known as Camp Rubidell. Opened in the 1960s, the campgrounds sport a man-made lake, a snack bar, and places to dock trailers and mobile homes. In the 1980s, the Straw Hat Theater, comprised of local actors, presented live theater there in a large barn. Since the late 1980s, this area has become River Bend Resort, and the old barn has been turned into a fine restaurant. It is still a popular camping spot.

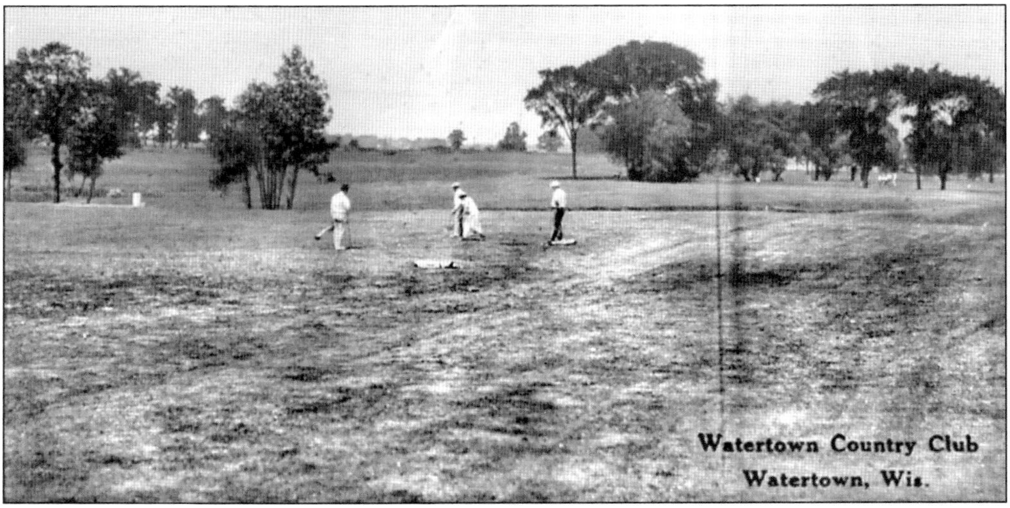

Golf, an ancient Scottish game, became a popular sport with common folks in the 1920s. In Watertown, this led to the founding of the Watertown Country Club in 1922, shortly after this image was taken. The Watertown Country Club maintains beautifully cared for greens and is a popular spot for members and guests. It maintains a lovely clubhouse, and many dances and receptions have been held there over the years.

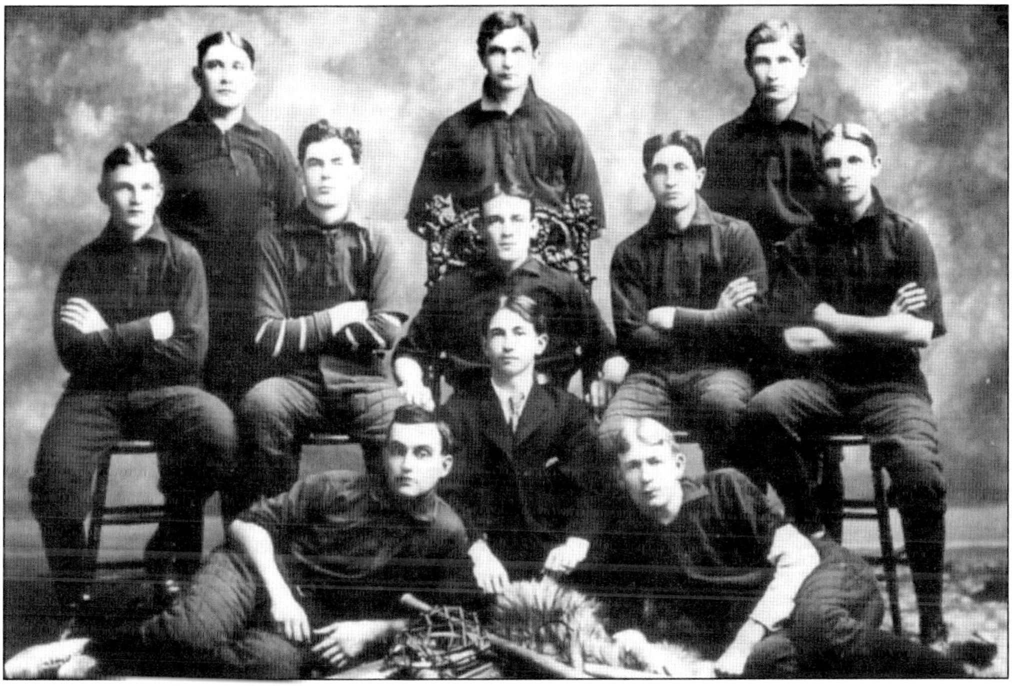

America's favorite pastime is baseball, which has its roots in the 1840s in the Northeast. The sport did not become popular in Watertown until the latter half of the 1860s, when the first ball team was organized, known as the Live Oaks. This team was followed by countless other teams. This image shows a baseball team from 1905 made up of Watertown men. From left to right are (first row) Ed Schultz, J. Miller, and ? Boettcher; (second row) George Richards, Frank McAdams (former mayor), William Richards, R. Hahn, and W. Krueger; (third row) Pete Kronitz, John Bergan, and F. Leschinger. (Kreitzman Collection.)

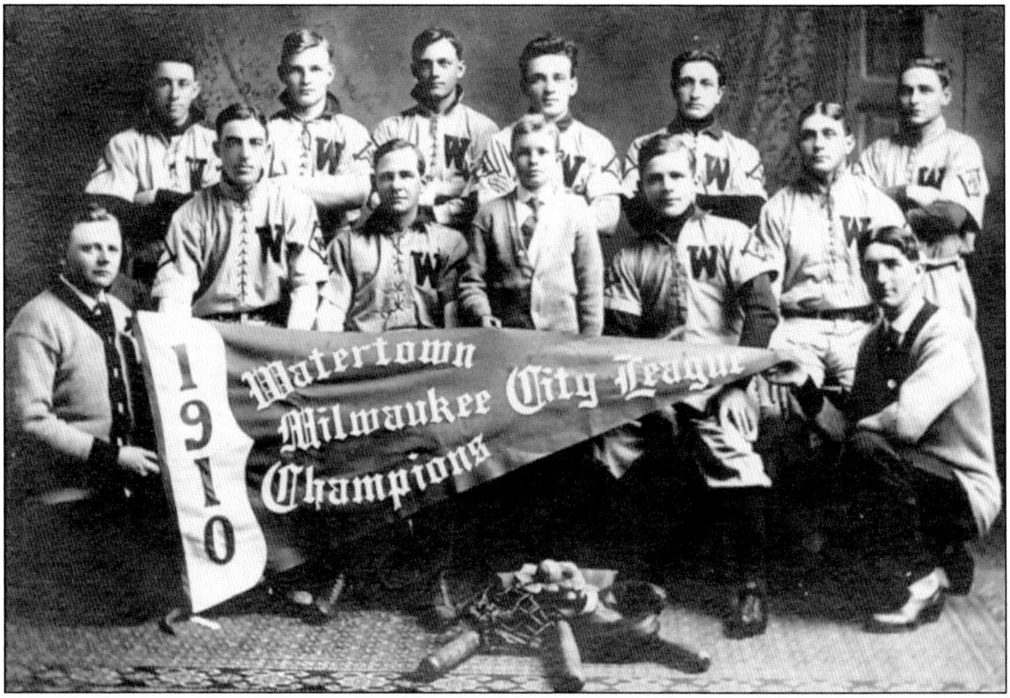

Over the years, many teams and individual players have risen to great prominence, among them Adrian "Addie" Joss, who became a celebrated pitcher in the National League, and Fred Merkel, whose mistake allowed the Giants to win the pennant in 1908 and earned him the epithet Bonehead. Pictured are the 1910 Watertown city league champions.

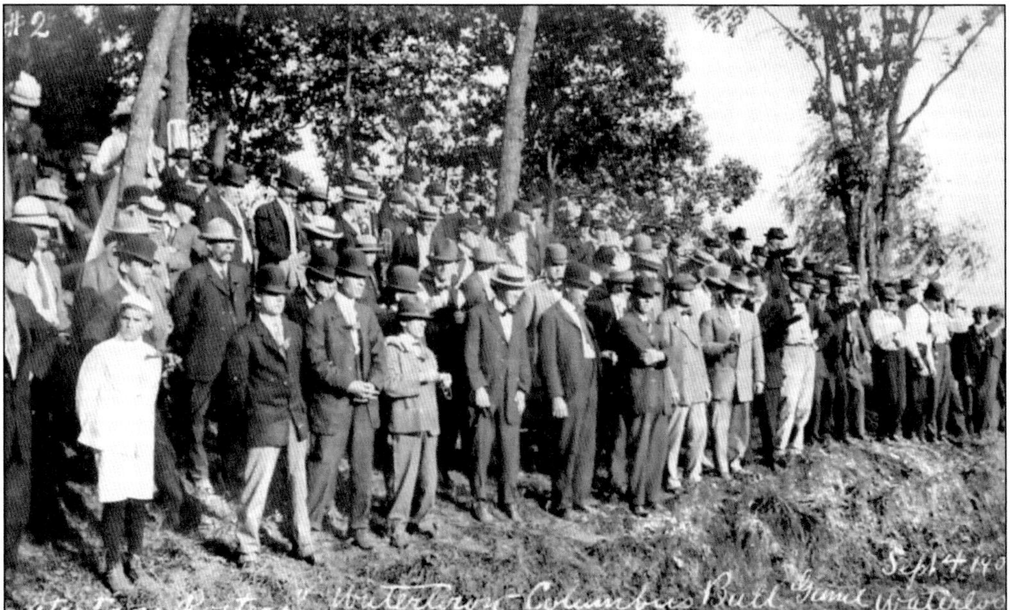

The Watertown fans were very loyal in their support of their favorite teams. Here we see "Watertown boosters" at a Watertown-Columbus game held in nearby Waterloo on September 4, 1908. (Kreitzman Collection.)

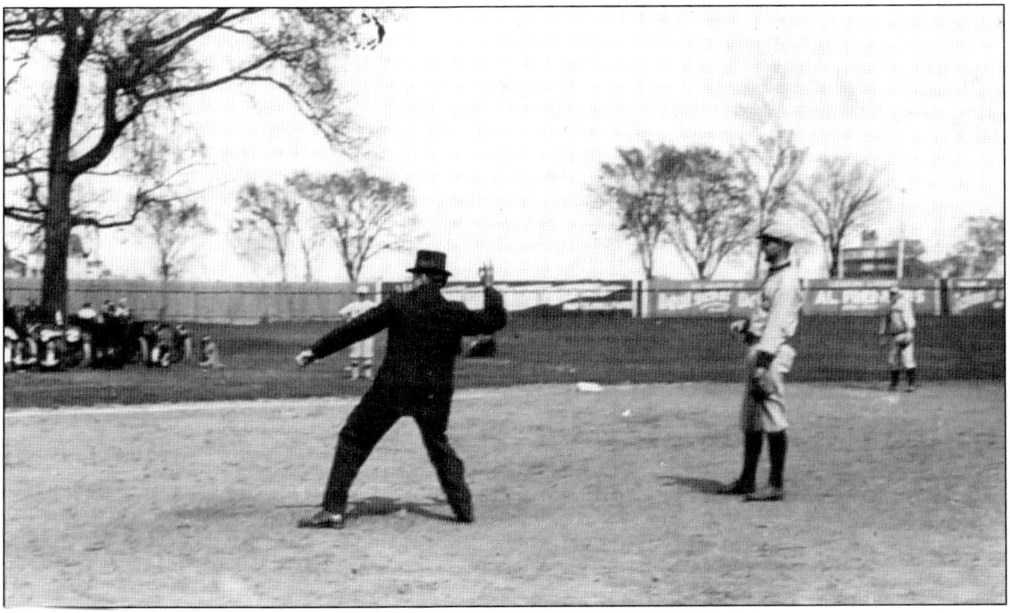

One of the milestones of Watertown's baseball history would have to be the day the Chicago Cubs came to play an exhibition game in the city on September 10, 1915. Here is the opening pitch of that historic game, which ended with the Cubs winning against Watertown 5-6. The game was held at Washington Park, just west of the Octagon House, which can just be seen in the distance.

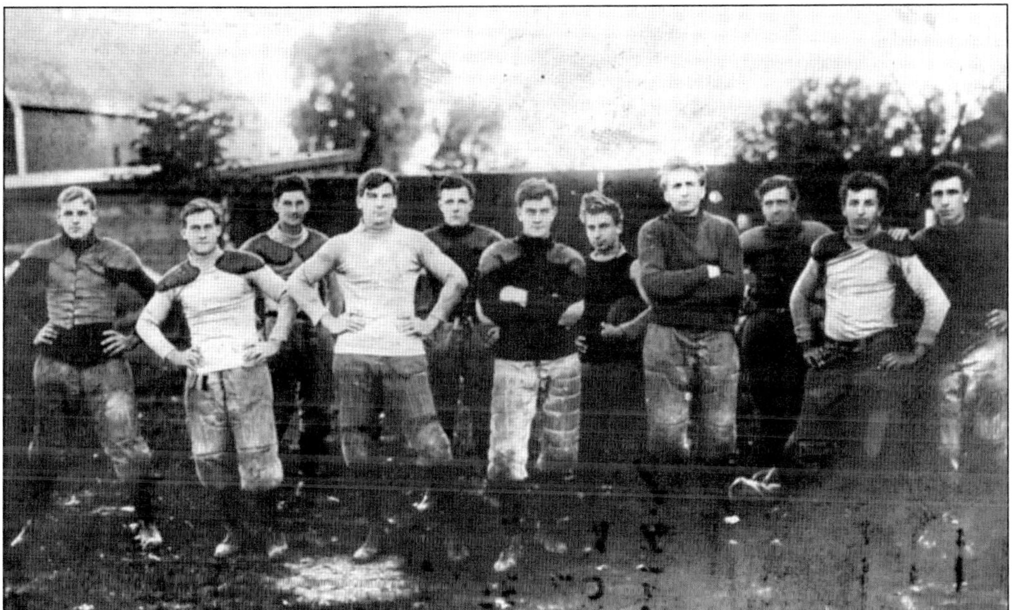

Football, a much more intense contact sport, was first played in Watertown in the 1890s, and then mainly by the two colleges here at the time, Sacred Heart and Northwestern. It proved a popular sport, but it was viewed by some as too rough and dangerous, so much so that in 1895 the game was outlawed for a time. Here is the Northwestern College "moleskin warriors" football team in 1905.

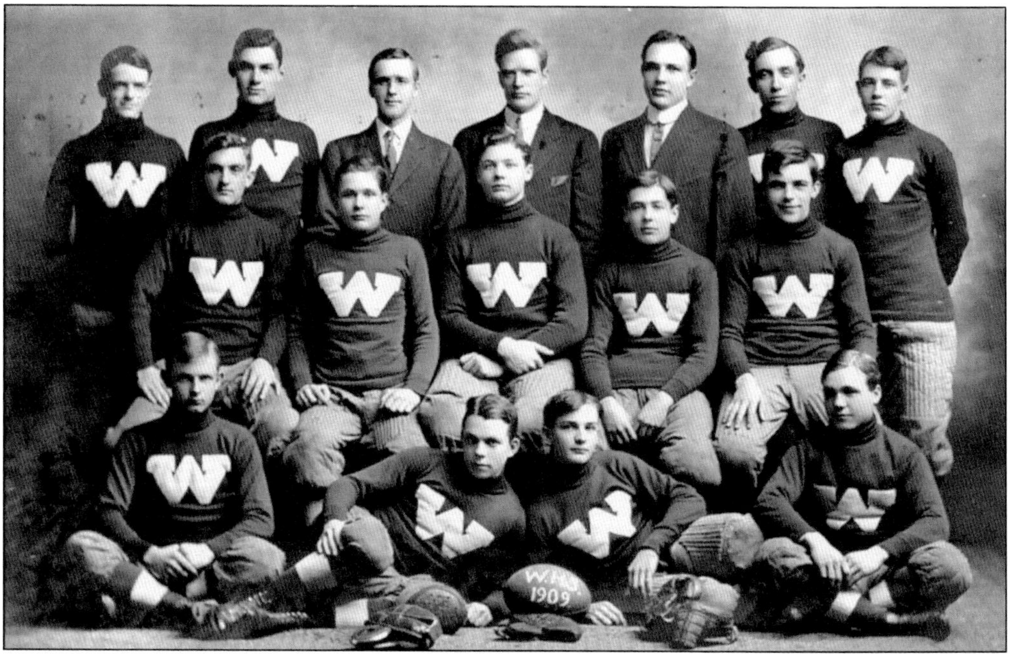

Not long after the turn of the century, football, baseball, and basketball were added to the curriculum of the school system. Here is the 1909 Watertown High School football team. Not long after that, the school adopted the name Goslings for all of its sporting teams in honor of the cottage industry of "noodling" or force-feeding geese to fatten their livers, which would be extracted to make pate. Many awards, trophies, and pennants have been won by Watertown teams, and many players have gone on to great fame in the field of sports.

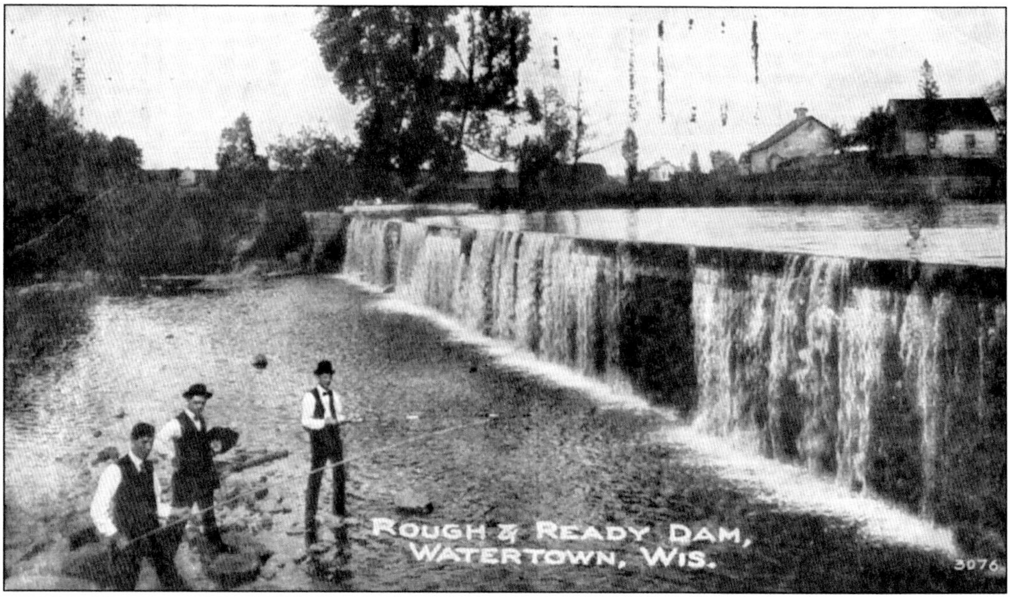

Another pastime indulged in by many is fishing. The Rock River at one time contained many species of fish, though today its predominant denizen is the carp. But some plucky devotees of Isaac Walton still manage to pull out the occasional northern or bluegill. This image dates to 1908 and was taken near South Concord Avenue on the city's east side.

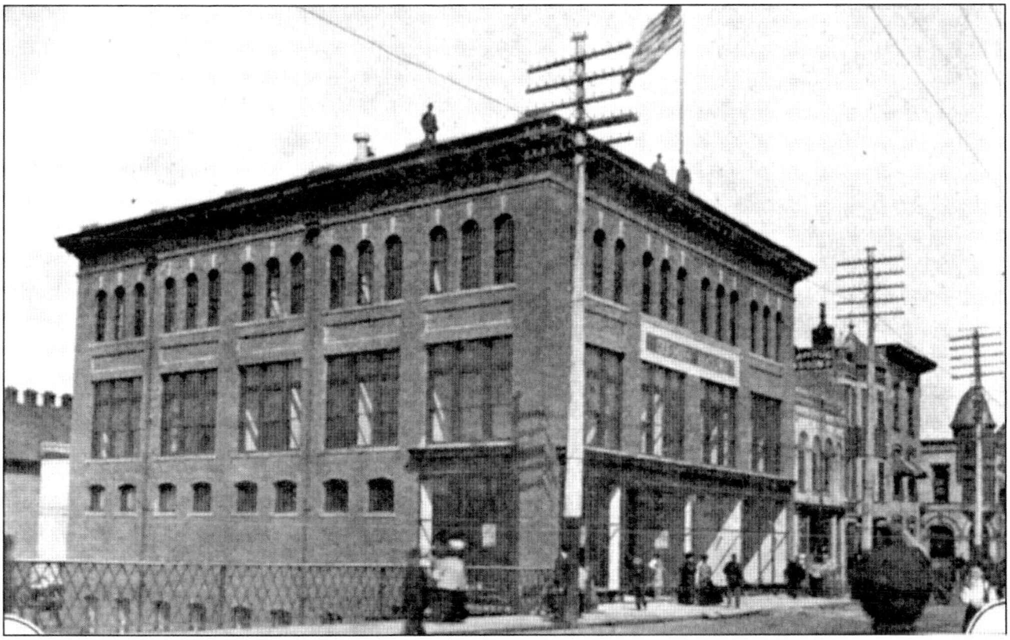

Clubs, fraternal organizations, and secret societies have long proliferated in Watertown. One of the oldest clubs was the Masonic order. The Masonic Lodge No. 49 was established in Watertown in 1854 and met in many different places before they built their magnificent temple at 2 Main Street in 1905, shown here about 1908. It was occupied by them and Fischer's department store (on the main and basement levels) for many years until the 1960s, when the Masons sold their building to the Fischer family and moved to small quarters along East Madison Street. The Masons ceased to exist as a lodge in Watertown in the late 1990s.

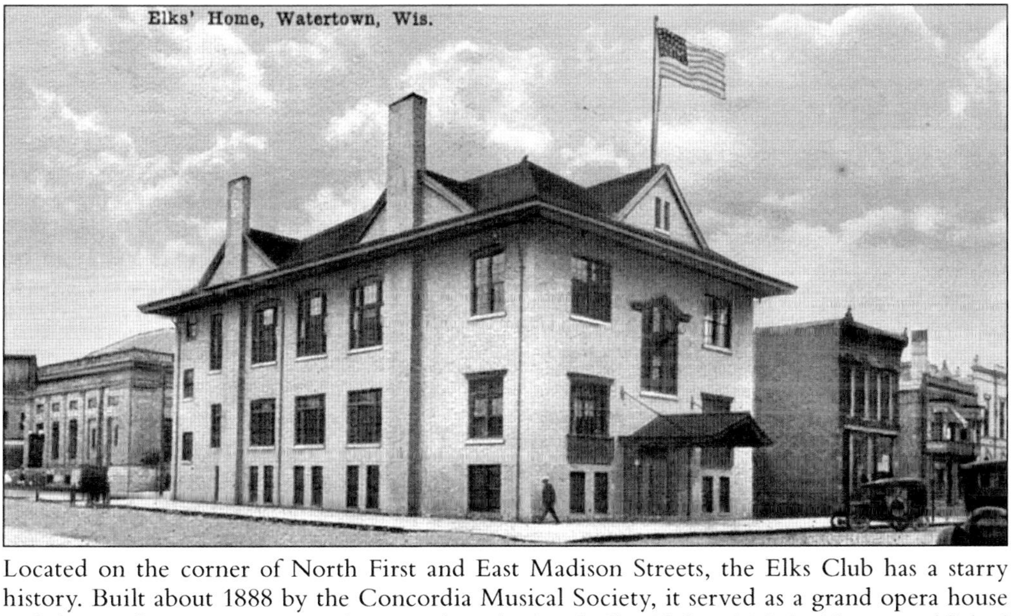

Located on the corner of North First and East Madison Streets, the Elks Club has a starry history. Built about 1888 by the Concordia Musical Society, it served as a grand opera house and theater for many years until 1917, when the local Elks Club, which had been established in Watertown in 1901, bought the building for their clubhouse. In the early part of the new century, the clubhouse was remodeled and restored to some of its former glory.

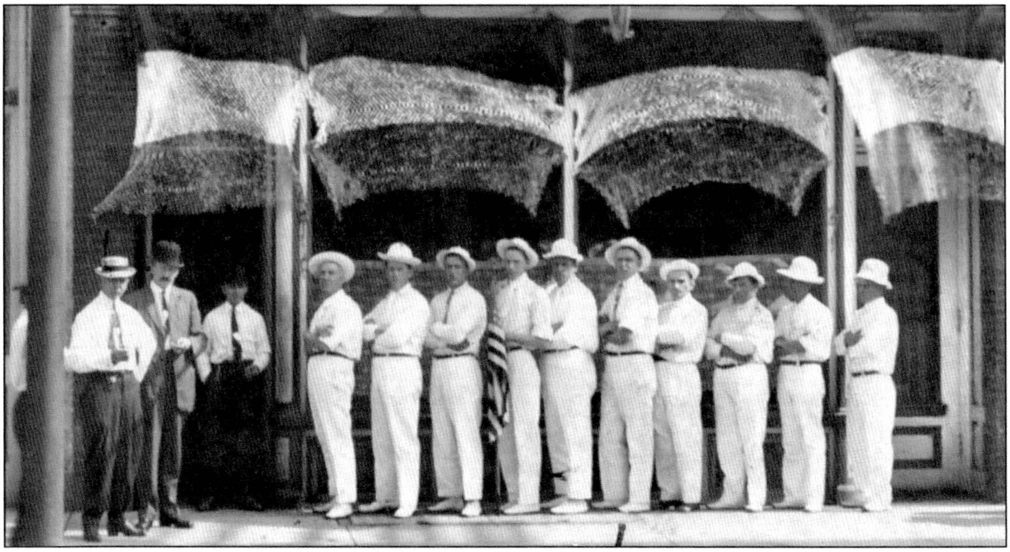

Among the many clubs that were popular here at one time but have since disbanded is the Eagles Club, established in Watertown in 1905. It was active in fraternal work, and the membership included many prominent citizens. Pictured here are some of the members, including the author's grandfather, William Jannke Sr., resplendent in white, fifth from the right. This image dates to about 1915. The Eagles ceased to operate in the city by the 1920s.

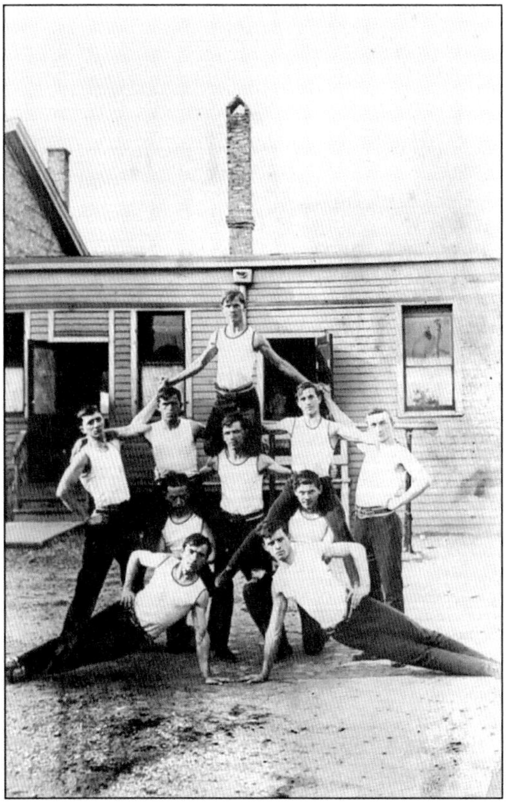

Perhaps the oldest club still in existence in Watertown is the Turner Society. Founded in 1860 by German freethinkers, it was originally a forum for political activism, athletics, and fine arts. In 1868, the Turners built a grand opera house on South Fourth Street, which burned to the ground in 1928. A new hall soon rose from the ashes, and the group still maintains the hall. The emphasis today is on civic works and hall rental for events. This image, taken about 1905, shows some of the athletic Turners in a human pyramid.

Six

Our Beautiful Park System

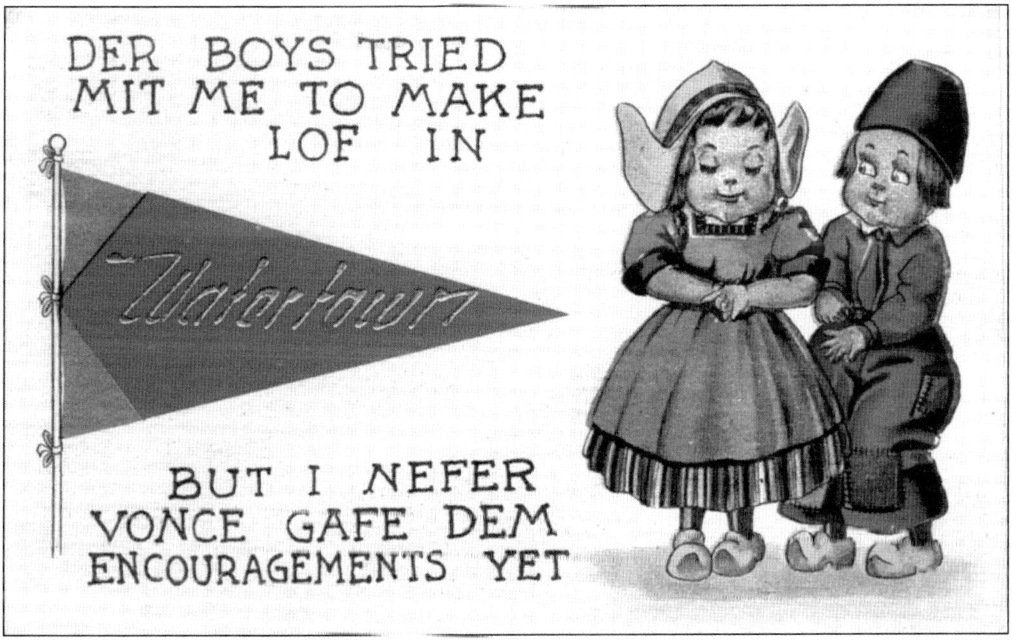

There are more than a dozen parks in Watertown, all maintained by the good folks at the Watertown Park and Recreation Department. The city's park system dates back to the early days of the 20th century and the establishment of the Watertown Outdoor Art Association. This group of dedicated citizens made the beautification of the city their top priority. One of the first things the group did was pressure the city fathers to purchase a former picnic ground from Samuel Kussel, located on the east side of the Rock River, and together they saw to it that this area was developed into a city park, one of the first in Watertown, today known as Riverside Park. People of all ages enjoy strolling in the city's parks, partaking in the many festivals, and enjoying the playground facilities. Summer in Watertown is a time to be outdoors, and the city parks are *the* place to be.

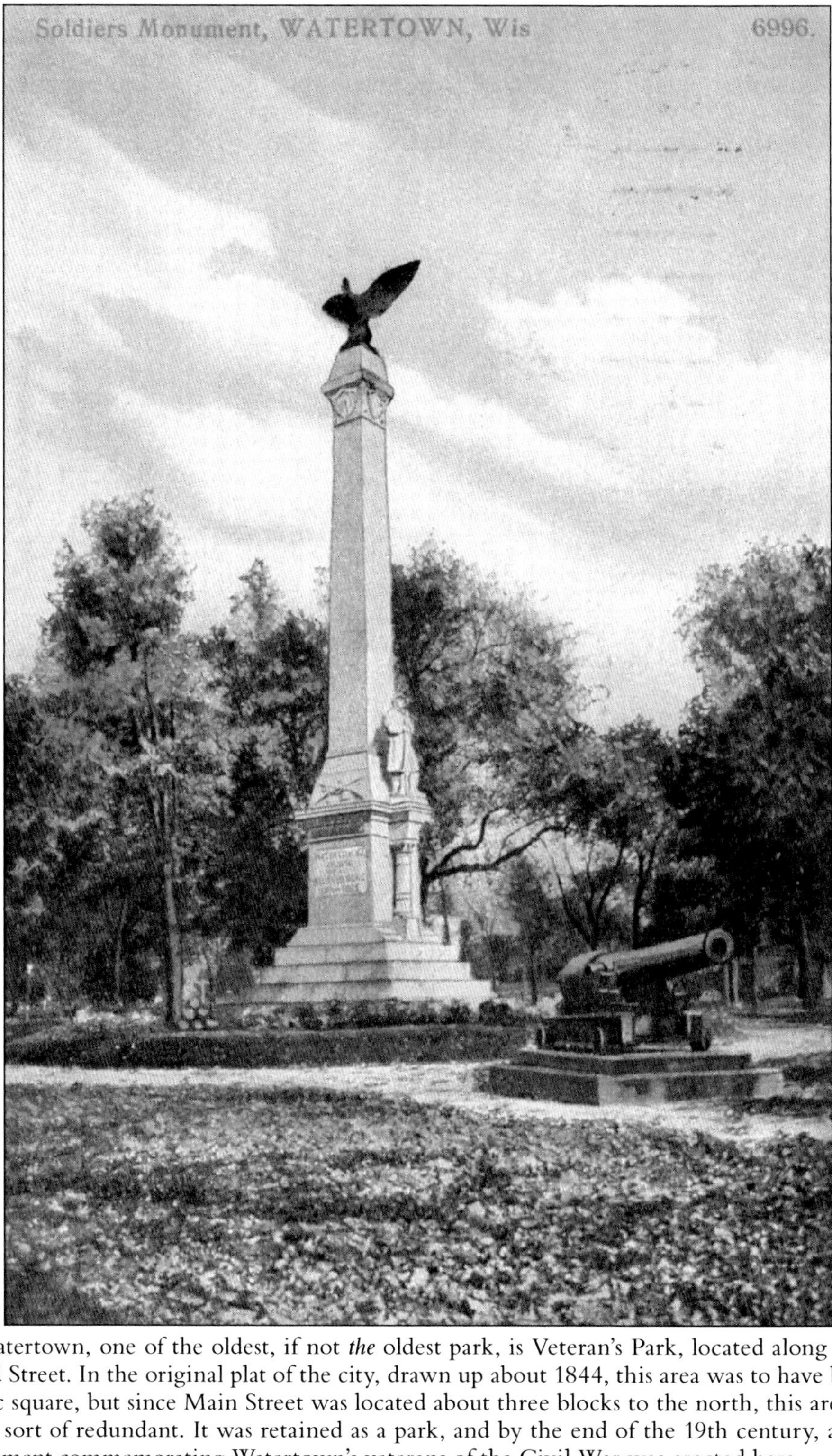

In Watertown, one of the oldest, if not *the* oldest park, is Veteran's Park, located along South Third Street. In the original plat of the city, drawn up about 1844, this area was to have been a public square, but since Main Street was located about three blocks to the north, this area was made sort of redundant. It was retained as a park, and by the end of the 19th century, a large monument commemorating Watertown's veterans of the Civil War was erected here.

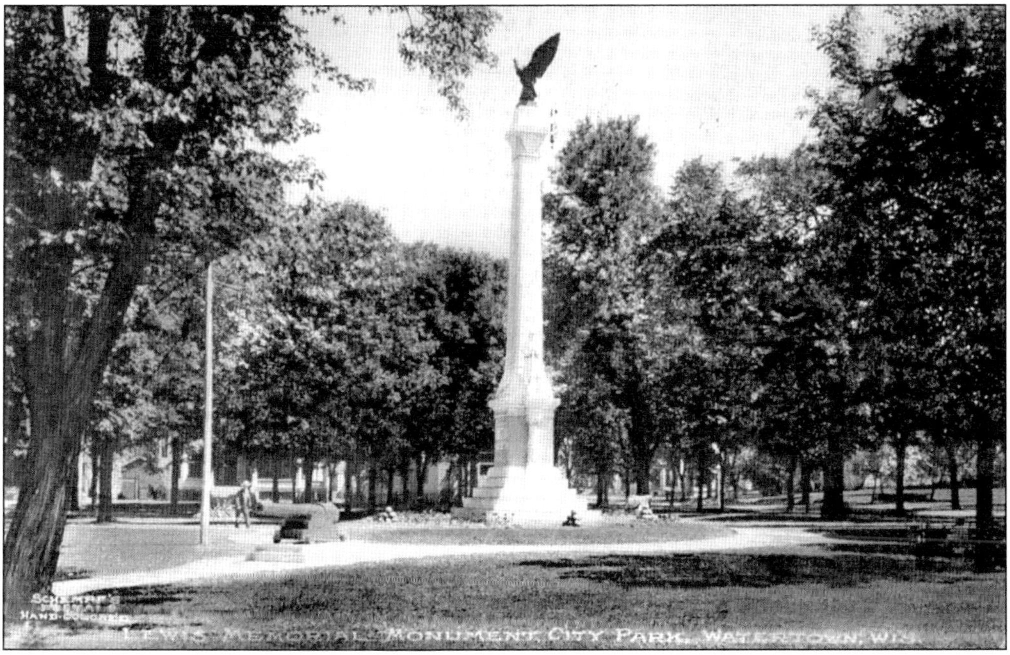

The soldiers' monument, seen here from the southwestern section of the park, was presented to the city of Watertown in 1899 by industrialist and benefactor G. B. Lewis and his wife, Fannie. Shown here in an image from 1909 are the two cannons that once flanked the monument. They have since been removed, and a World War II–era cannon now rests in the southwest corner of the park.

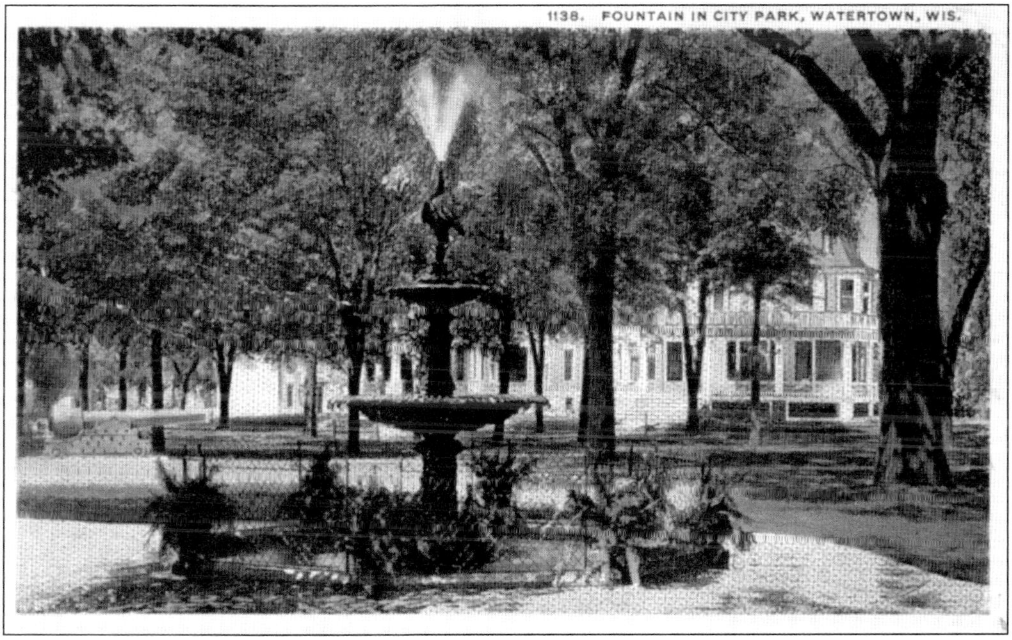

Also found in Veteran's Park at one time was this elegant fountain, also presented by the Lewis family. The fountain was located in the northern part of the park, along Wisconsin Street, and has since been removed.

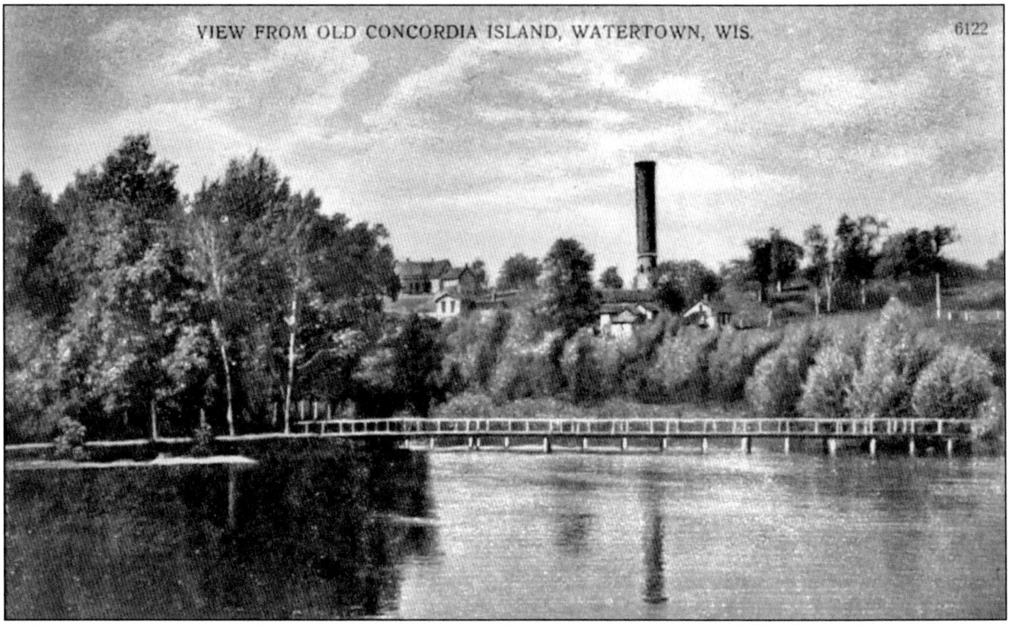

There are several islands in the Rock River, the largest being located on the eastern side of the city. Once known as Boughton's Island, in the 1870s it had passed into the hands of the Concordia Musical Society, who built a large pavilion and dance hall and erected a beautiful fountain. It was known as Concordia Island for many years and was the city's chief pleasure spot. This view shows the island in 1905 and the original bridge that linked the island to the mainland.

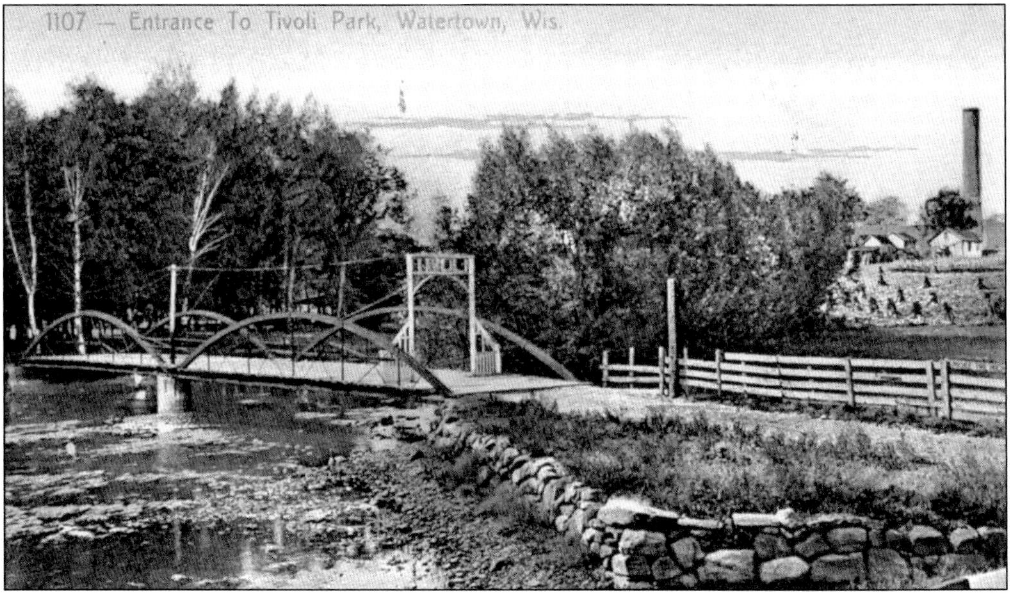

Sometime after the turn of the last century, the Concordia Musical Society ceased operations and sold their island to the Ohm brothers, who renamed it Tivoli Island after the hanging gardens of Tivoli and continued to let out the park for picnics and dances. This view shows the island in 1908 and the bow-span bridge that still leads into the island. This bridge is considered a very rare form of architecture now.

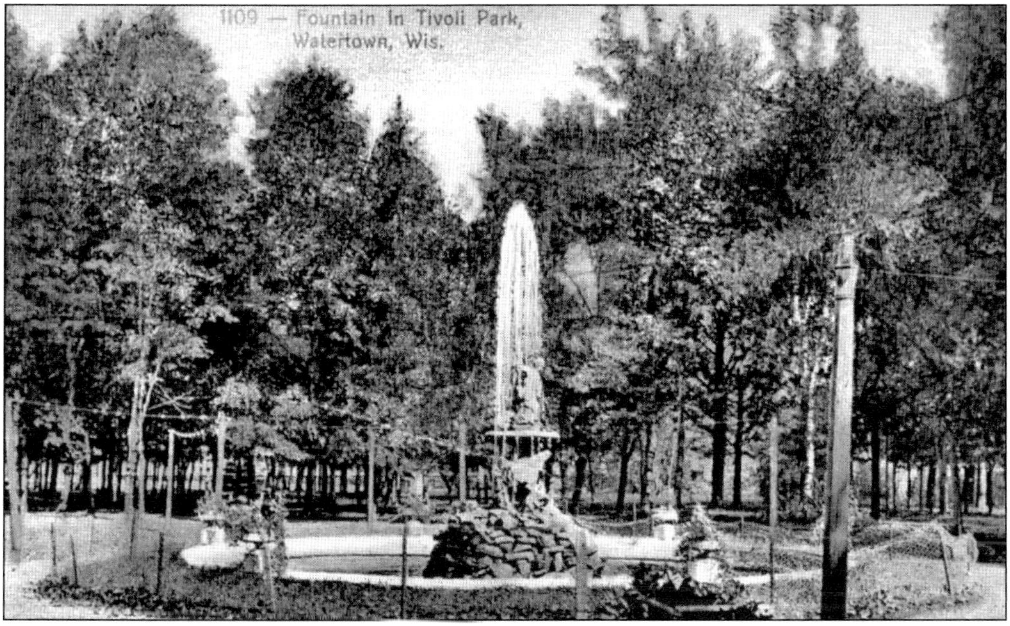

This view from 1909 shows the center of the island and the lovely fountain that once graced it. By the second decade of the 20th century, the island had fallen on hard times and was being used as a duck farm. It was later used by the local Boy Scouts for a campground. In 1957, the pavilion burned down, and shortly thereafter the entire island was acquired by the city. Tivoli Island, much smaller than it was due to erosion, is now a nature preserve.

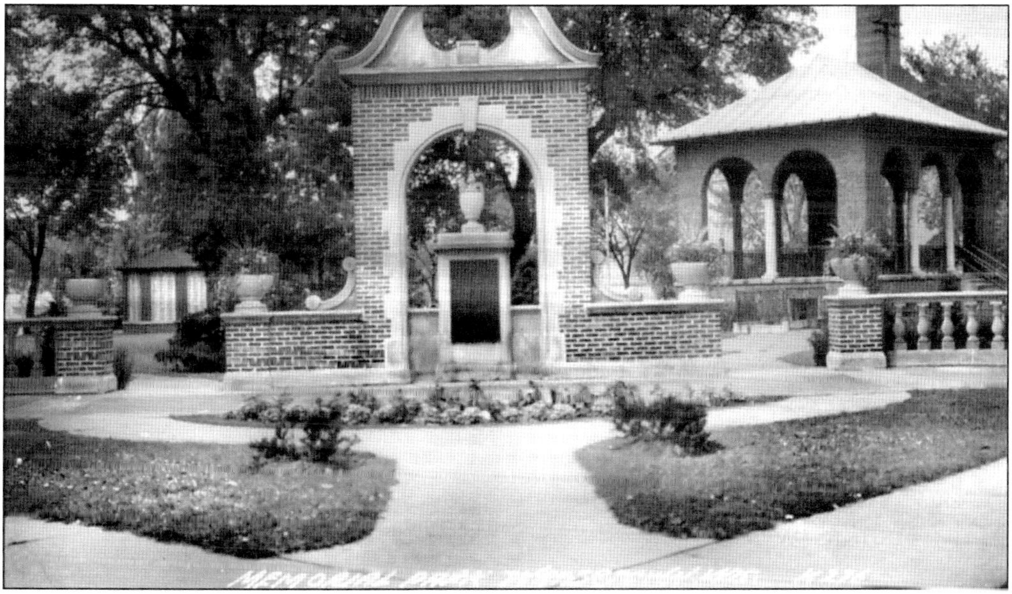

Memorial Park, shown here in the 1940s, was developed on land formerly housing the Fuermann Brewery. The buildings were removed around 1915. The park was finally created in the 1920s and proved a popular spot for children and adults to congregate during shopping expeditions and Fair Day events since it was located in the heart of the business district along North Second and Jones Streets. In the early 1960s, this park fell victim to the need for a new municipal building and ceased to exist.

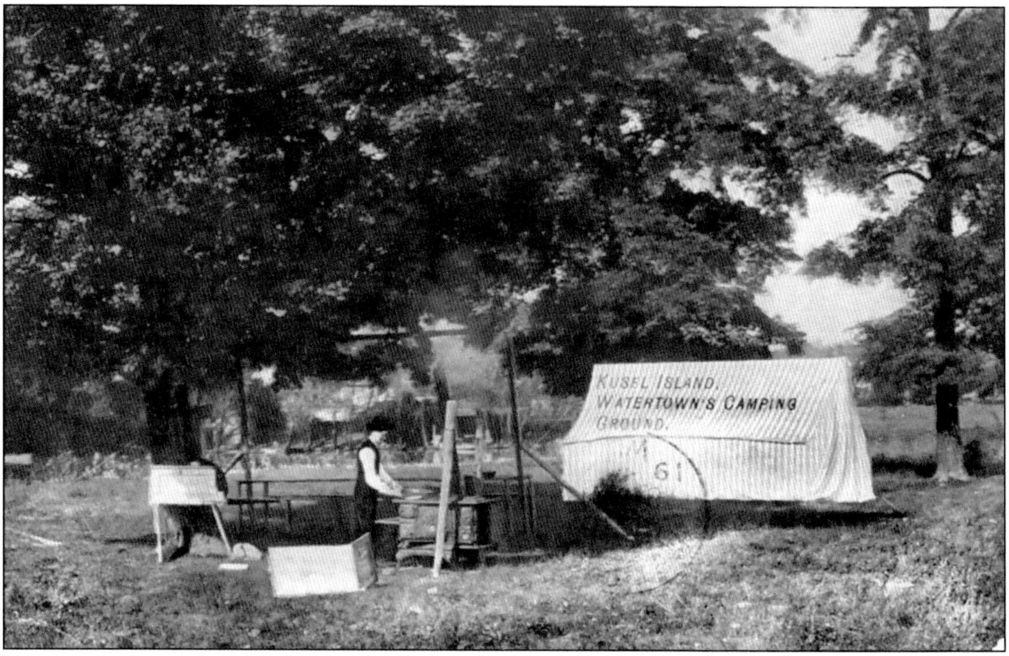

Shown are the Samuel Kussel picnic grounds, located where Riverside Park is today. This area was purchased by the city at the urging of the Outdoor Art Association, and by 1910, they had developed it into Riverside Park, one of the largest parks in the system today.

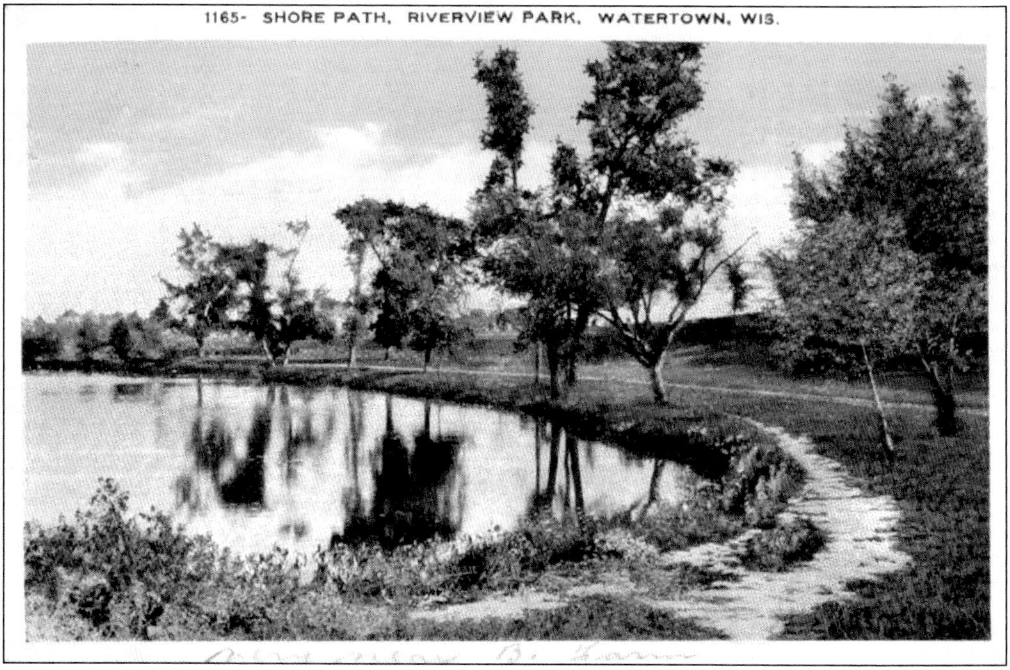

Some improvements to the park were made in the early 20th century, including the placement of footpaths such as the one seen above in 1925, which rings the river in the southern extreme of the park. The hill on the right is where the Aquatic Center is today.

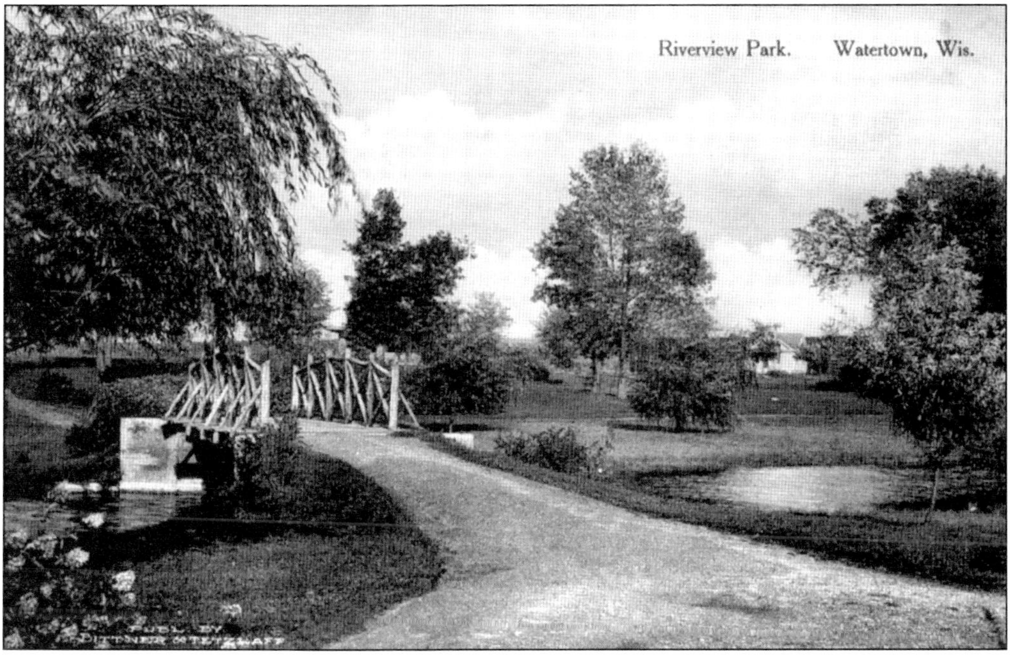

Another improvement was the placing of a rustic bridge from the mainland of the park to "the island." Many postcard images exist of this bridge. This view, from the early 1920s, shows the bridge from the island, looking into the park.

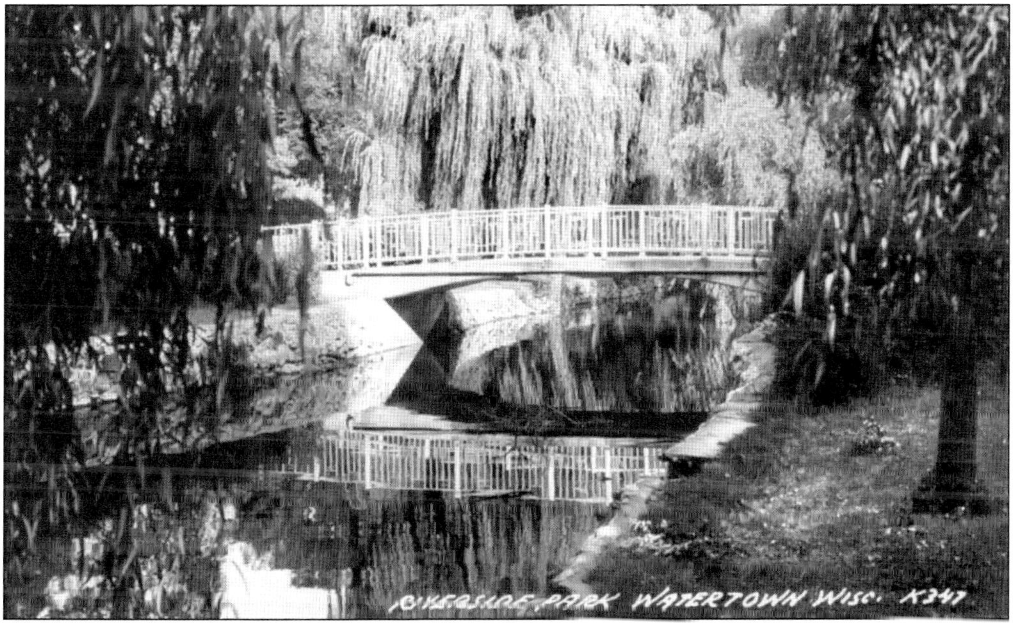

During the Great Depression, and for many year afterward, the Watertown Park and Recreation Department was headed by Ewald "Honey" Brumm, who oversaw much beautification of Riverside Park. Men hired through Works Progress Administration programs helped make improvements that included building several stone bridges, a small dam over a stream that runs through the park, and the replacement of the rustic bridge with this metal bridge to the island, shown here about 1944.

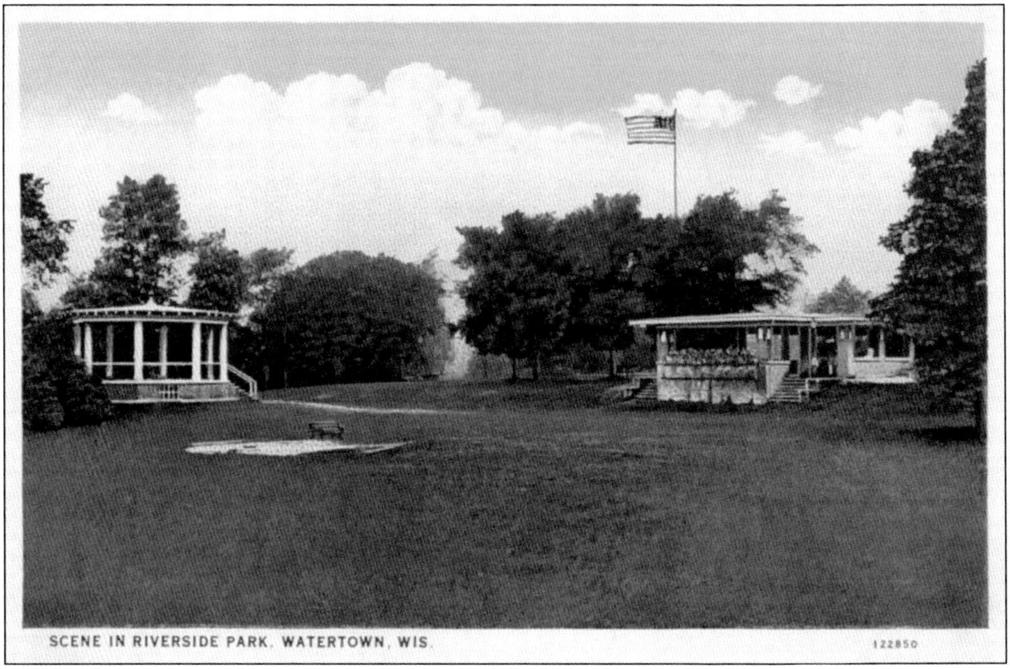

Pavilions went up sometime in the second decade of the 20th century. The bandstand shown here on the left was demolished long ago. The pavilion shown on the right still stands, with several additions added later.

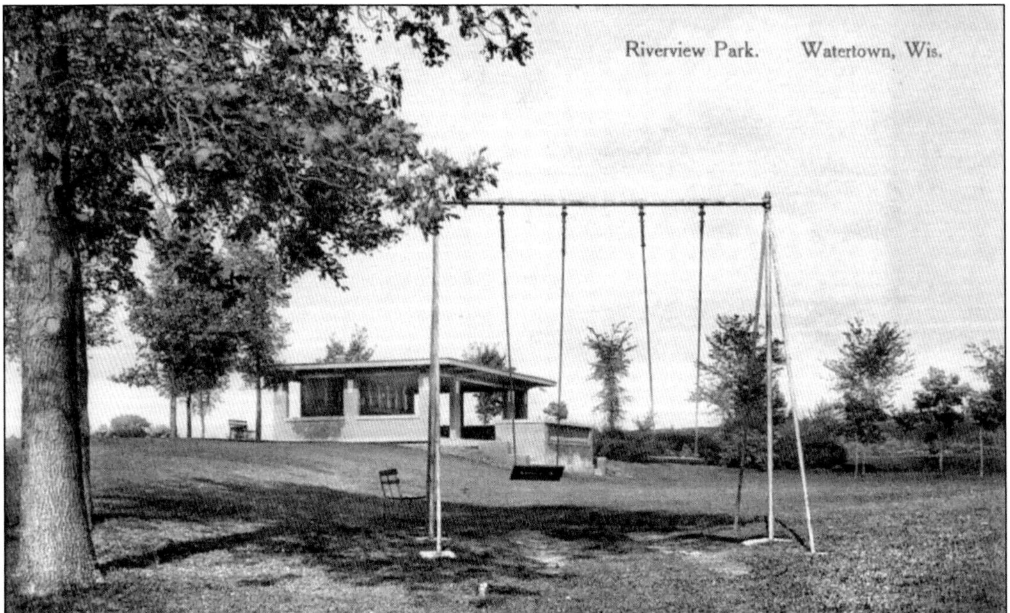

This 1916 view shows the first playground equipment put in for the pleasure of children. One must admit that two swings in a large park was poor planning, and by today's standards, this is positively "low-tech."

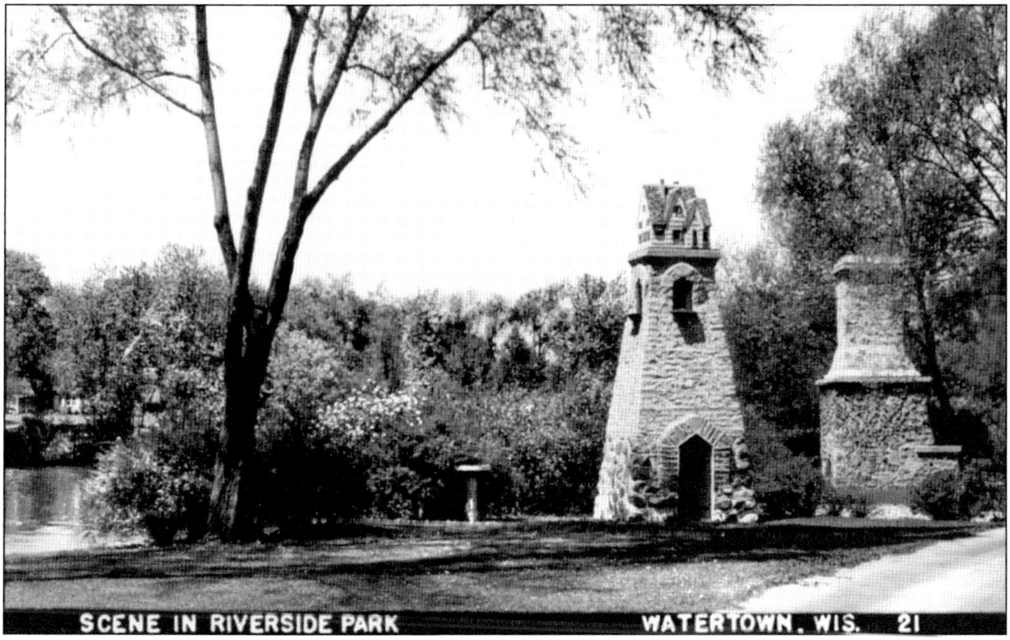

In the 1930s, a more substantial playground area was established in the northwestern part of the park along Laberee Street. At about the same time, these stone structures resembling castle turrets were erected, shown here in 1944. They still stand at the park today.

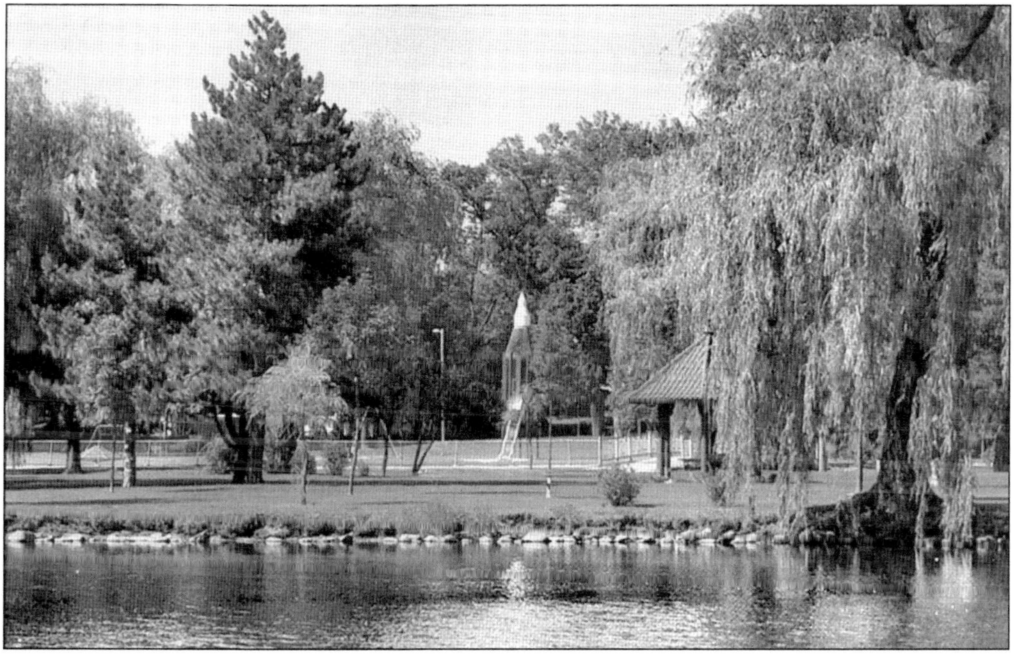

By the 1970s, the playground was updated to include this metal "spaceship" slide. By the 1990s, it was considered too dangerous for children, and, accordingly, it was replaced by a kid-friendly play area known as Chamberland, which was sponsored by the chamber of commerce and built by all-volunteer labor in early 1996.

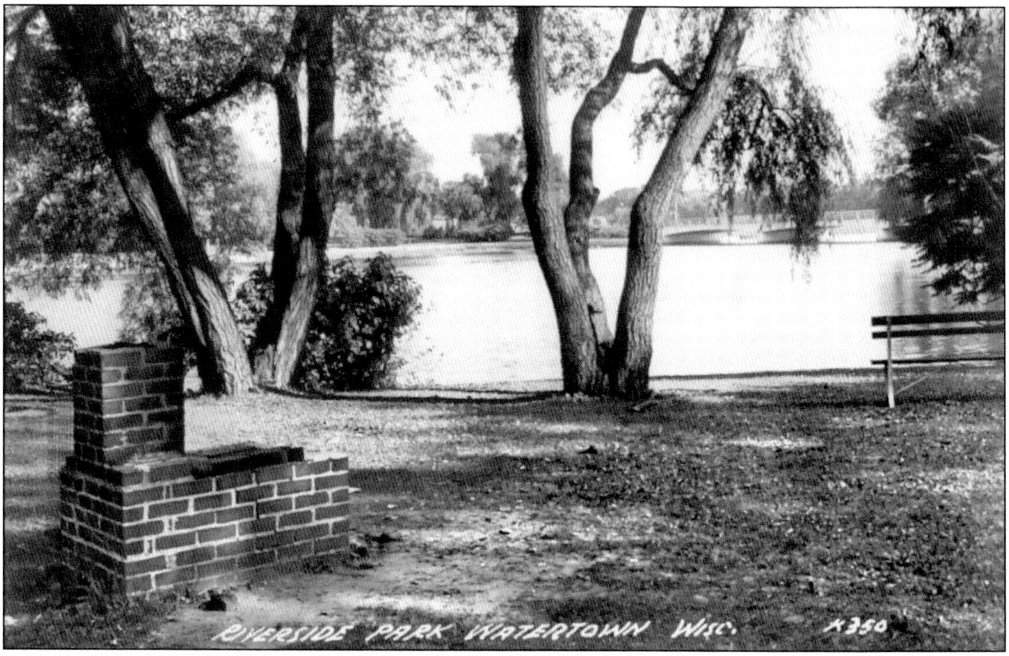

Riverside Park has been the scene of many church picnics, wedding receptions, family reunions, and company picnics. However, it has been more often used by the local citizens as a picnic spot, and to accommodate those visitors, metal grills were at one time found in the park, and even a brick grill was found on the island, as this 1940s view shows.

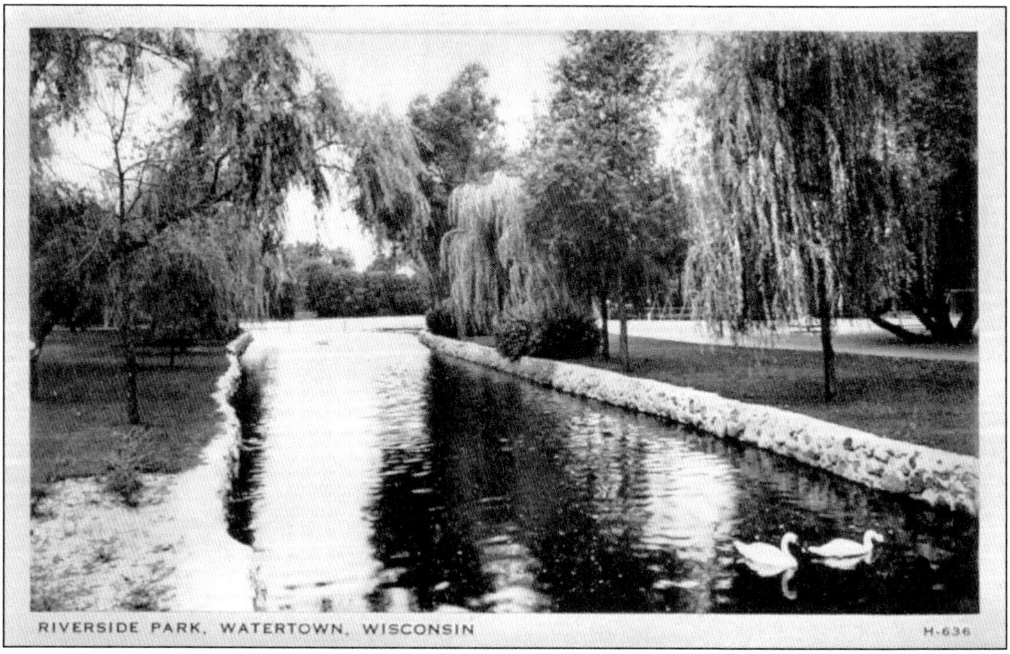

This late-1930s view shows the channel running between the main area of Riverside Park and the island. Note the swans, which once were common sights in the Rock River and added to the overall beauty of the area.

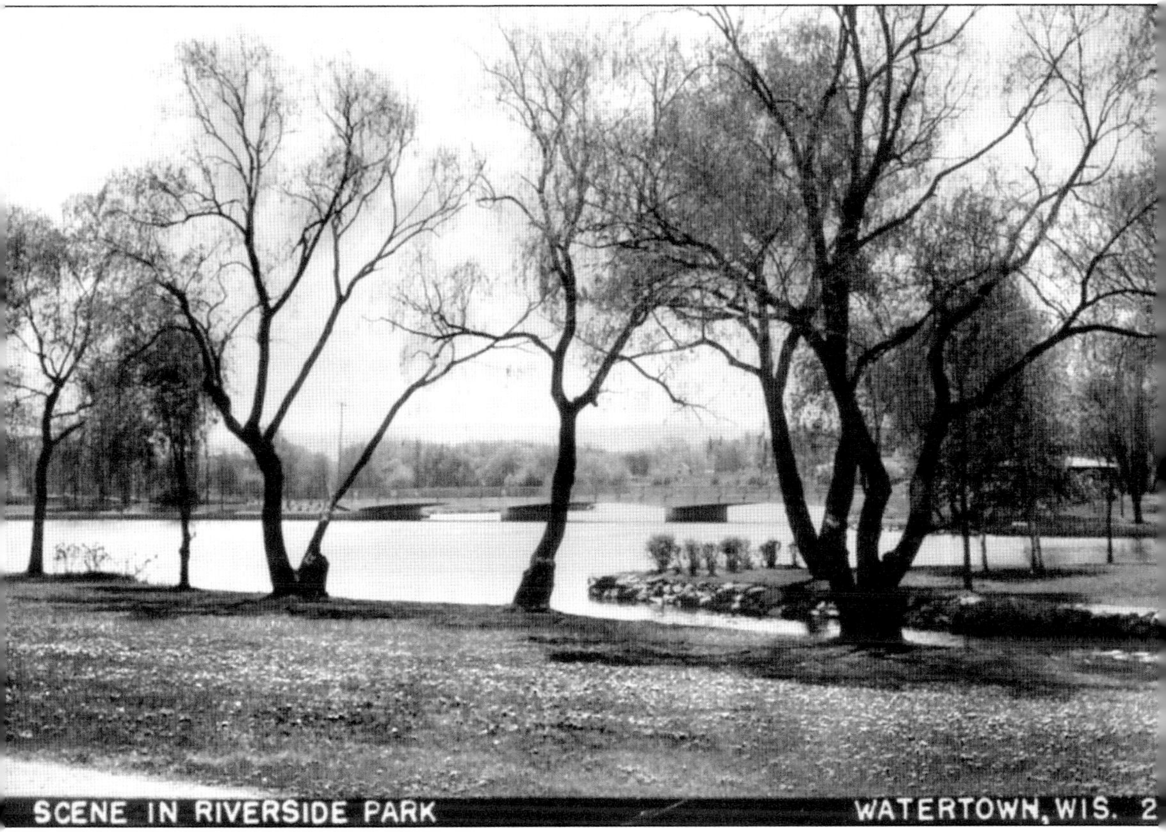

It is the beauty of the river and the serenity of the surroundings that make Riverside Park one of the most popular parks in the city. This 1940s view, which looks to the south from the island, shows the river and the East Division Street bridge in the distance.

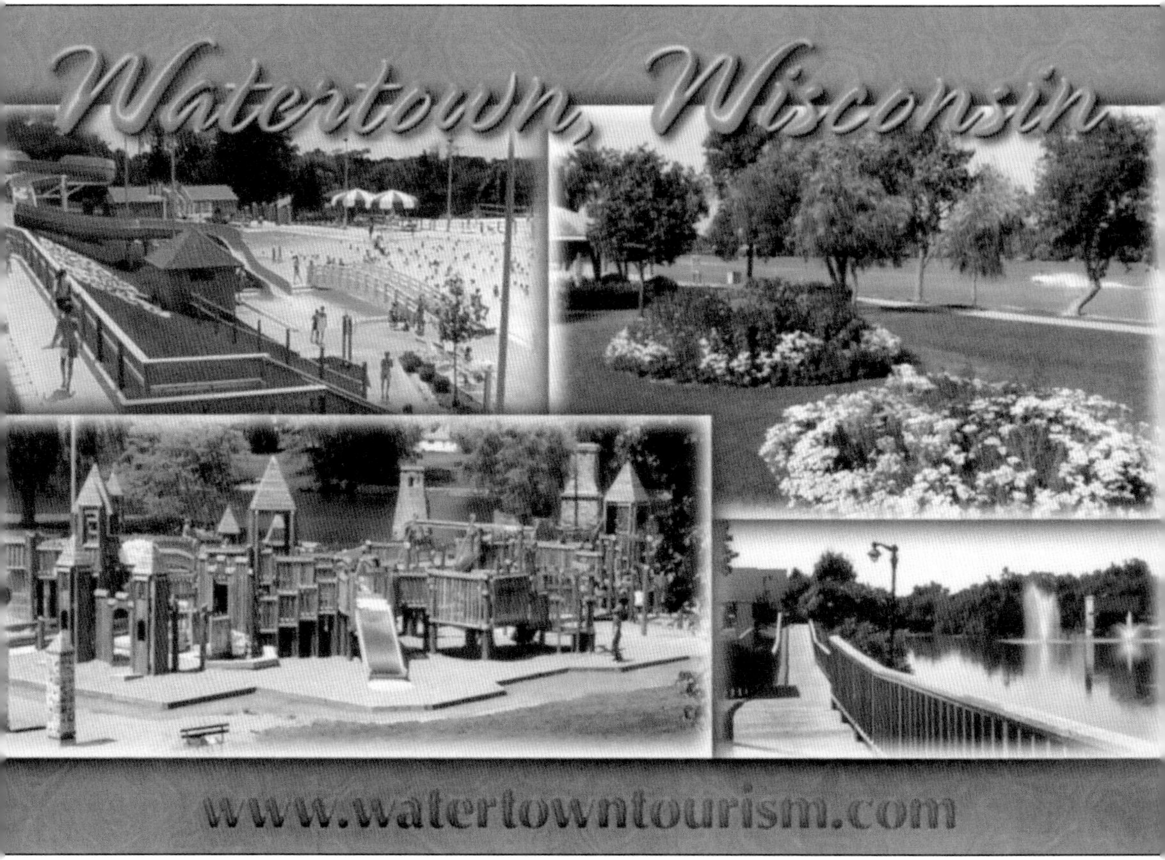

Some of the many parks that Watertown is proud of can be seen in this multi-image card issued recently by the Watertown Tourism Board. Shown here are, clockwise from the right, Fannie P. Lewis Park (located along North Water Street), the river walkway (located along the Rock River in downtown Watertown), Chamberland in Riverside Park, and the Watertown Aquatic Center. Watertown's parks have something to offer everyone.

Seven

Health Services

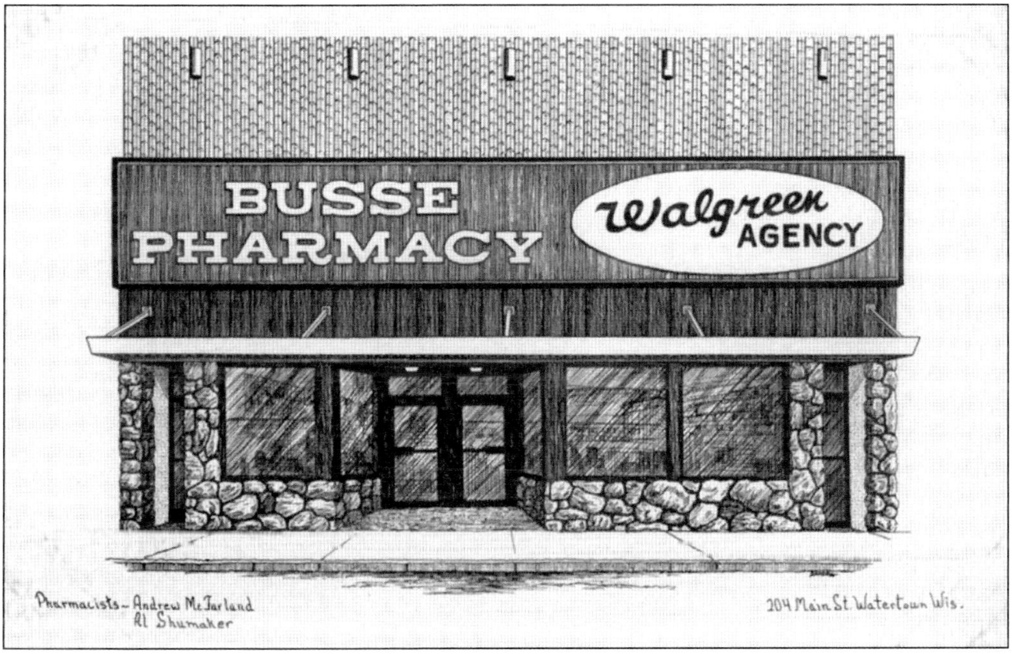

No matter how lovely a place Watertown may be, people *do* occasionally get sick. Fortunately, the city has had medical men and women among its residents since its founding. A hospital did not exist until the early days of the 20th century, but since then, Watertown has kept pace with medical progress, and today the city can offer the best medical care available. In addition to the hospital, there are also several care facilities for the elderly and infirm, and of course Watertown is the home of Bethesda Lutheran Home, a nationally recognized care facility for mentally and physically challenged individuals. So, while people may get sick here, there is never need to worry about not getting better, thanks to the health services readily available in Watertown. This is Busse Pharmacy, located on Main Street. It is one of five pharmacies still left in Watertown. Founded in 1930, it is known today as Aurora Pharmacy.

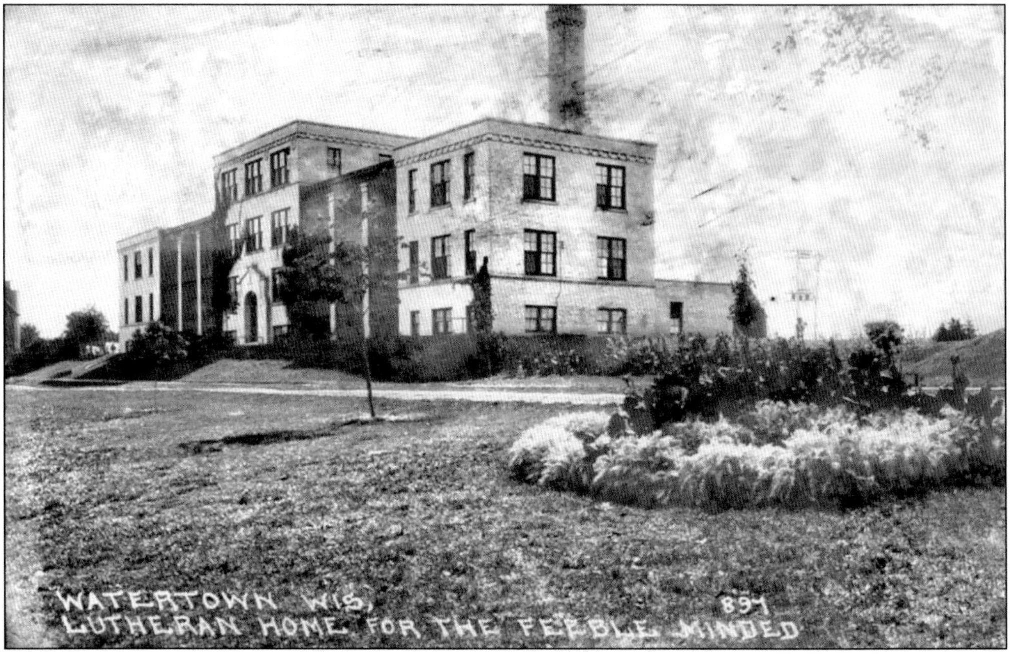

Bethesda Lutheran Home opened in Watertown in 1904 in the former "Faith Home" on Margaret Street, a sort of holistic spiritualist haven. It was part of the Kinderfreund, or Children's Friend Society of the Lutheran Church, and its mission was to care for the mentally challenged. It moved from the city for a short time, only to return in 1910 and locate in the southwest section of the city. Shown here is Bethesda's original main building about 1920.

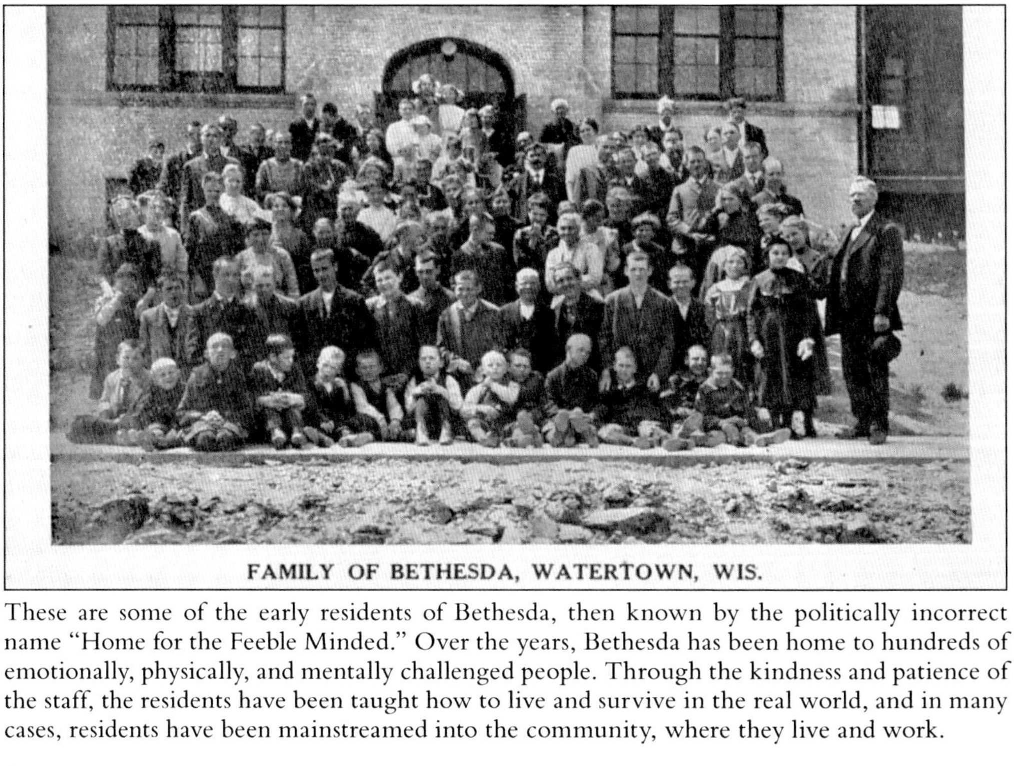

These are some of the early residents of Bethesda, then known by the politically incorrect name "Home for the Feeble Minded." Over the years, Bethesda has been home to hundreds of emotionally, physically, and mentally challenged people. Through the kindness and patience of the staff, the residents have been taught how to live and survive in the real world, and in many cases, residents have been mainstreamed into the community, where they live and work.

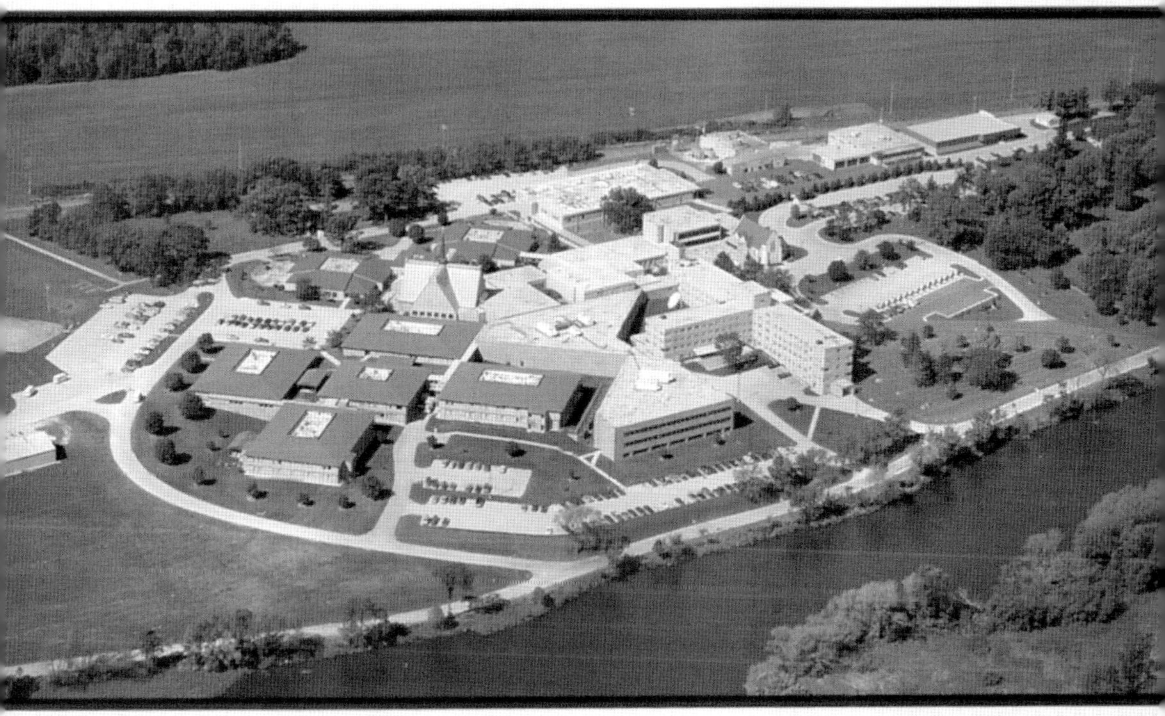

ETHESDA LUTHERAN HOMES AND SERVICES, INC
Watertown, Wisconsin

This is Bethesda today. The campus provides residential care and training for 700 children and adults with mental retardation at 38 sites in 10 states.

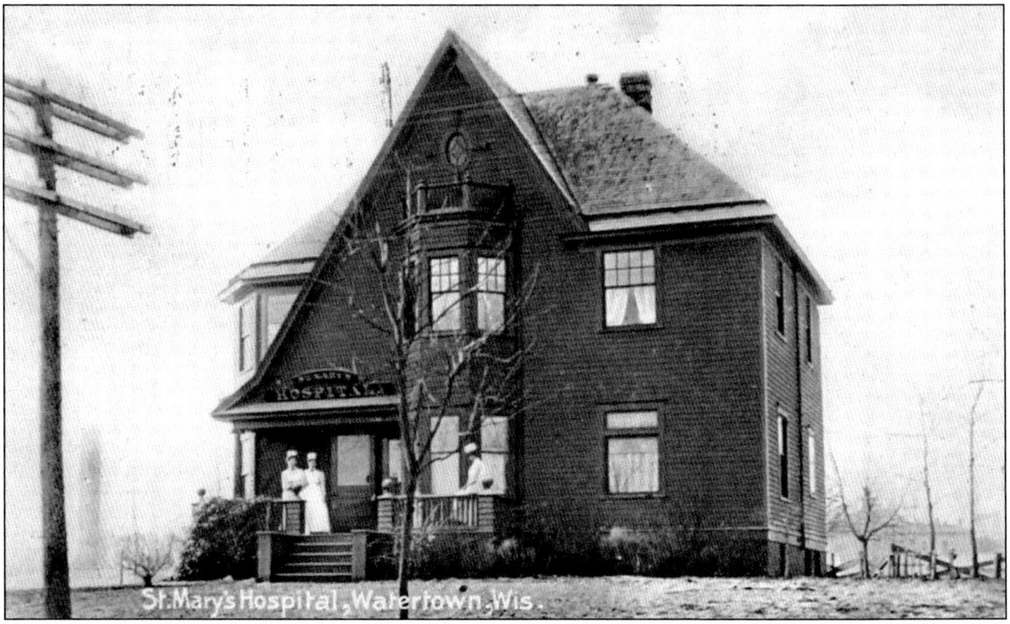

Seen here is St. Mary's Hospital about 1915, during the earliest years of its operations. The first hospital in Watertown was in a small room above a building along South First Street. In 1909, the hospital moved to this building, formerly the Charles Schiffler home on East Main Street. The running of the hospital was handled by the Sisters of the Holy Ghost, a Catholic order.

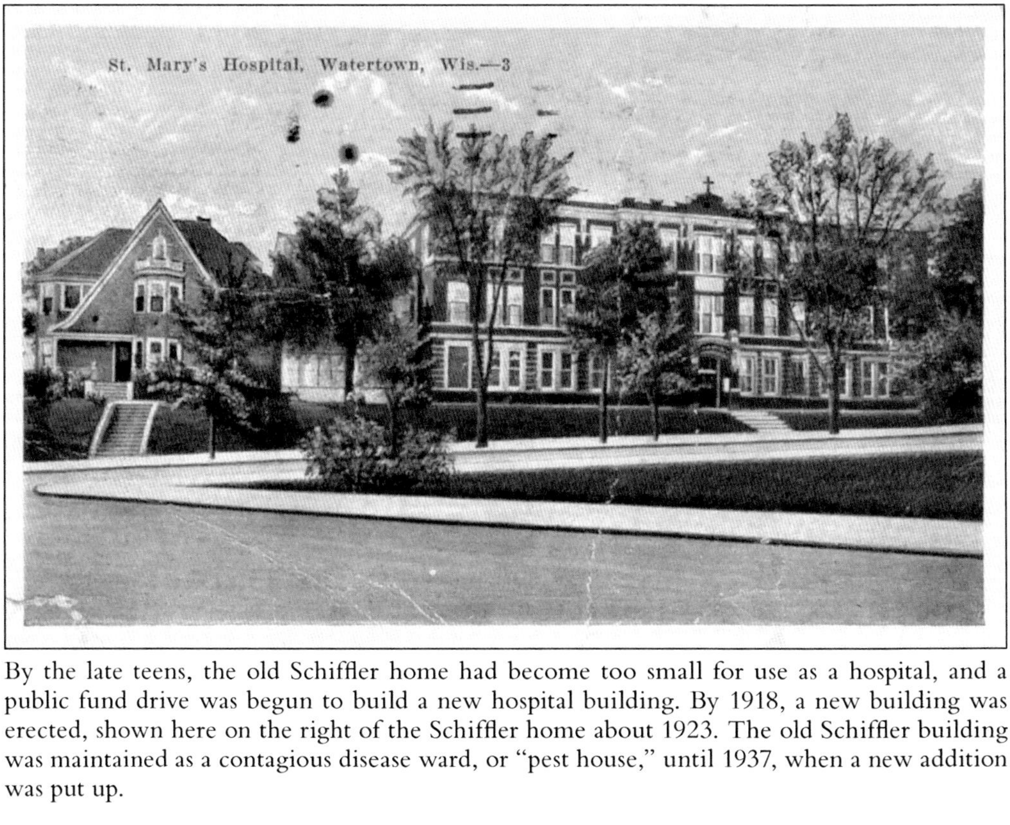

By the late teens, the old Schiffler home had become too small for use as a hospital, and a public fund drive was begun to build a new hospital building. By 1918, a new building was erected, shown here on the right of the Schiffler home about 1923. The old Schiffler building was maintained as a contagious disease ward, or "pest house," until 1937, when a new addition was put up.

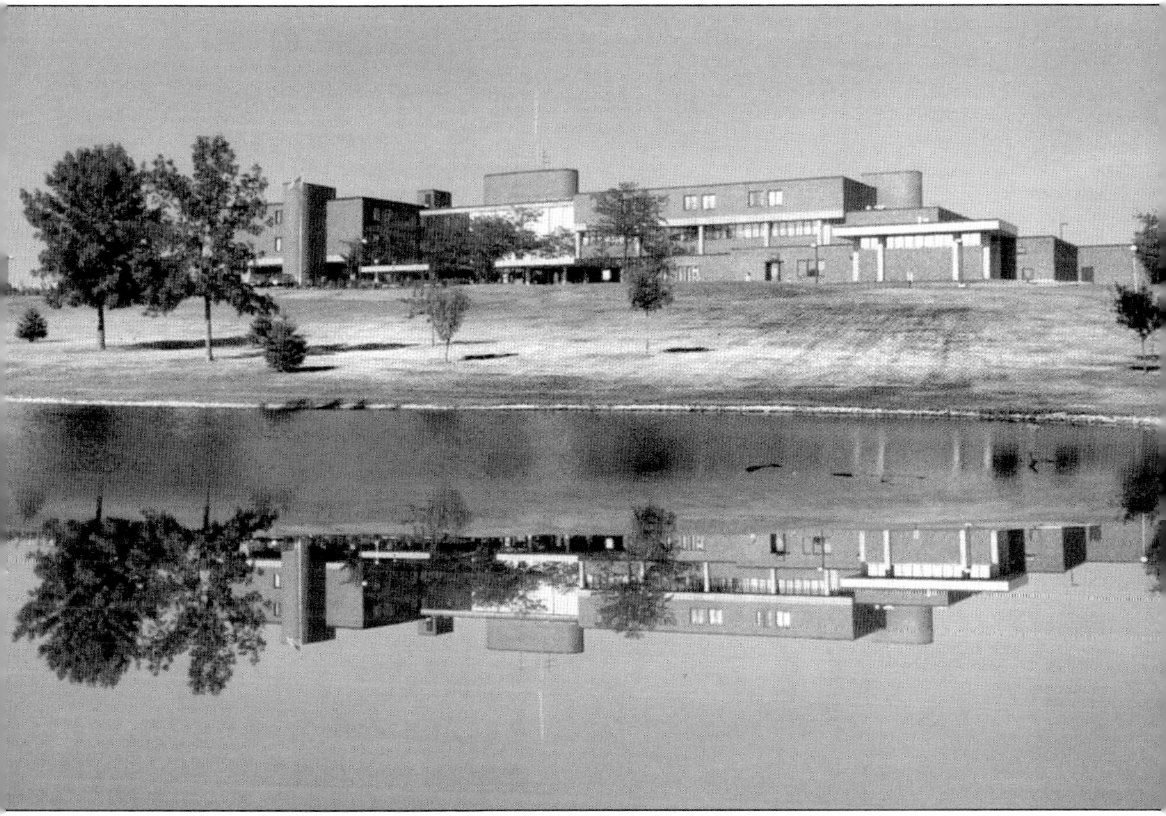

Despite the new addition, St. Mary's proved too far gone to remodel and update, and in 1971, a new hospital was constructed on the east side of the city and opened to the public. Watertown Memorial Hospital, shown here in a 1980s postcard, is very much a work in progress, with new construction taking place on a regular basis. All of this is to better serve those who need to use the hospital. Watertown Memorial Hospital continues to rise to meet the challenges and demands modern medicine brings.

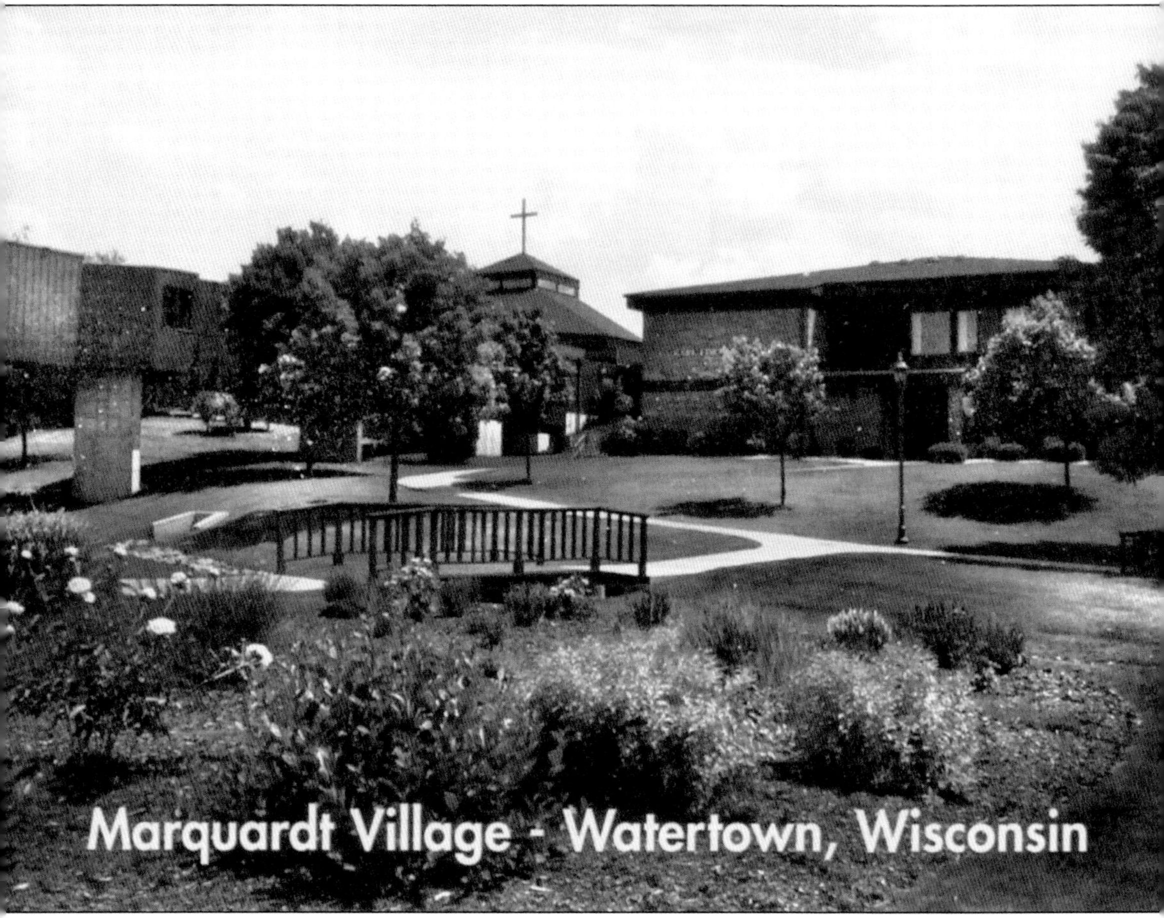

Care for the elderly and infirm has always been of great importance, and one of the many care facilities in Watertown is Marquardt Manor, which opened in 1969. Located in the northern part of the city, Marquardt Manor encompasses not only a care facility but also several apartment buildings and duplex homes. Today the complex is known as Marquardt Village, which is sponsored by the Western District of the Moravian Church.

Eight

Disasters, Natural and Otherwise

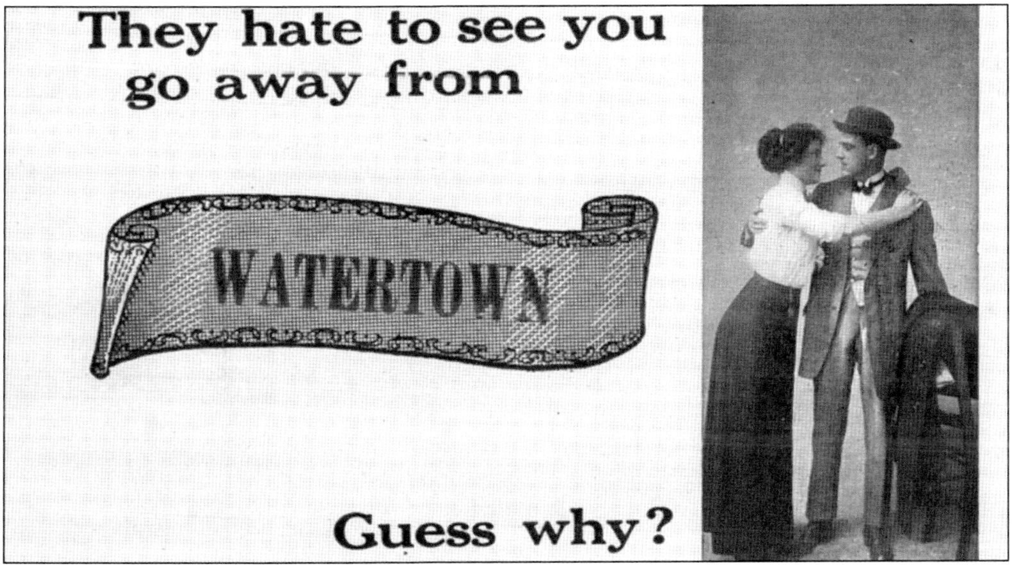

It is said that bad storms tend to miss Watertown because it is located in a valley, and when storms come overhead, they tend to break up. Whether or not this is true, it does seem as if the city has been spared the brunt of many harsh spells of weather. But not quite, because Watertown was the scene of tornado damage in the 1850s and again in 1873, 1914, and 1965. Fortunately, the damage has always been fairly minimal, with the exception of the so-called Cyclone of 1914, which caused considerable destruction. Likewise, Watertown has also been the recipient of heavy snowfalls, most notably in 1881 and again in 1978. As for other forms of disasters, there the city has not always been so lucky. Main Street was the scene of several very destructive fires in 1862, 1865, and again in the late 1940s, when the Tetzlaff Drug Store burned out just before Christmas. Besides Main Street, fires have struck the city's mills, schools, factories, and churches—in short, if it could burn, chances are a fire could break out. But Watertown is lucky to have a very efficient fire department that is skilled and dedicated to the suppression of fires, and thus the city has been spared major conflagrations. When all is said and done, it is worth remembering that the citizens of Watertown are a hearty lot and can handle just about anything Mother Nature can throw at them. The next few pages feature a few of the more extreme disasters that have taken place in Watertown.

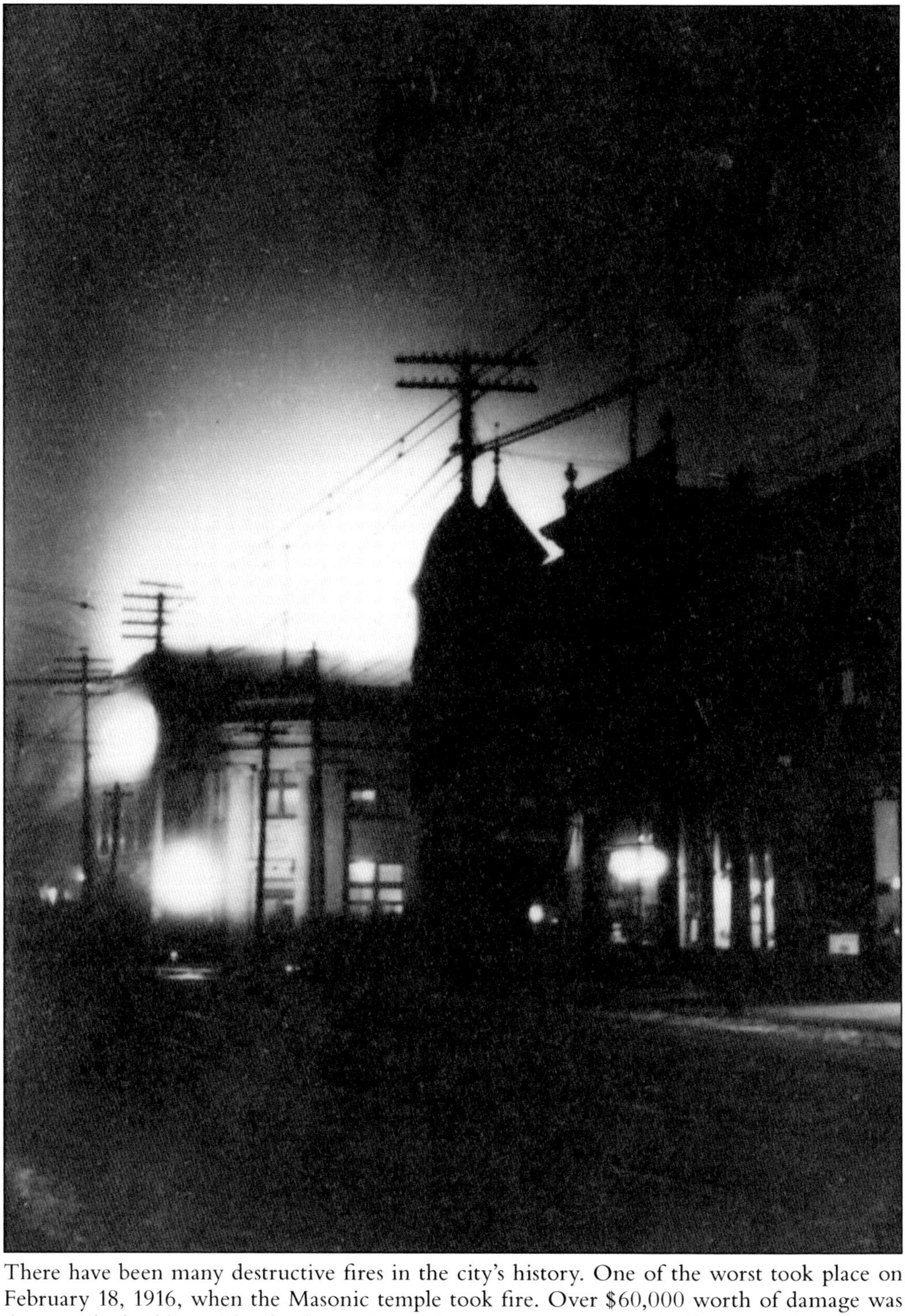

There have been many destructive fires in the city's history. One of the worst took place on February 18, 1916, when the Masonic temple took fire. Over $60,000 worth of damage was done to the building. The fire began in the basement, and it was finally extinguished when the roof of the building fell in. The call for help went out to Milwaukee, but they arrived too late to save the building. This dramatic postcard shows the glow of the fire at 6:15 p.m.

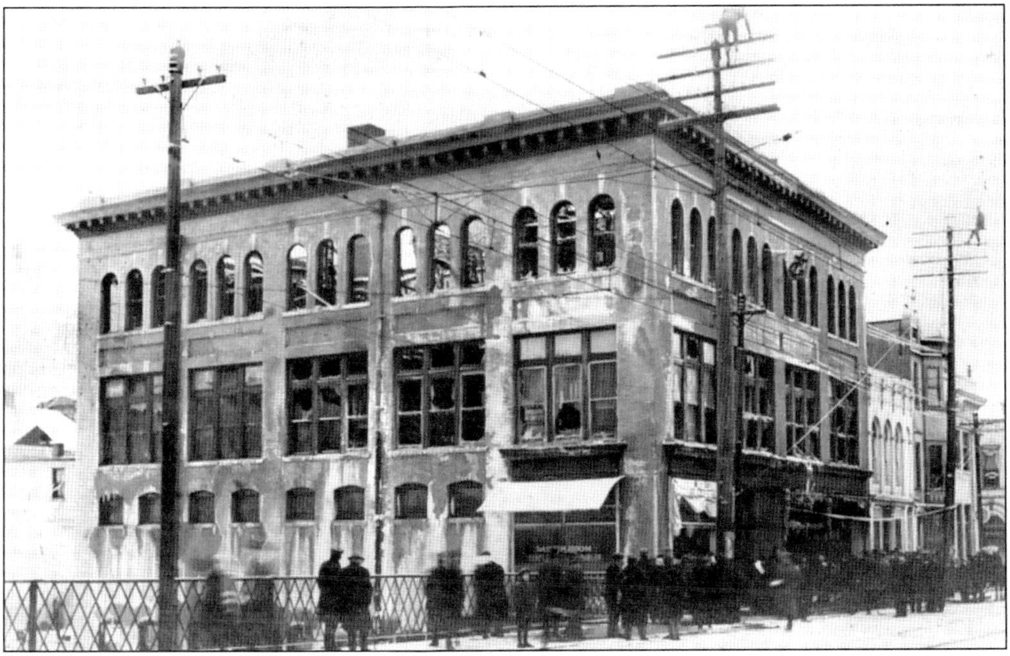

The Masonic temple housed the Watertown Daily Times and other businesses at the time of the fire, and they were displaced temporarily while the building was repaired.

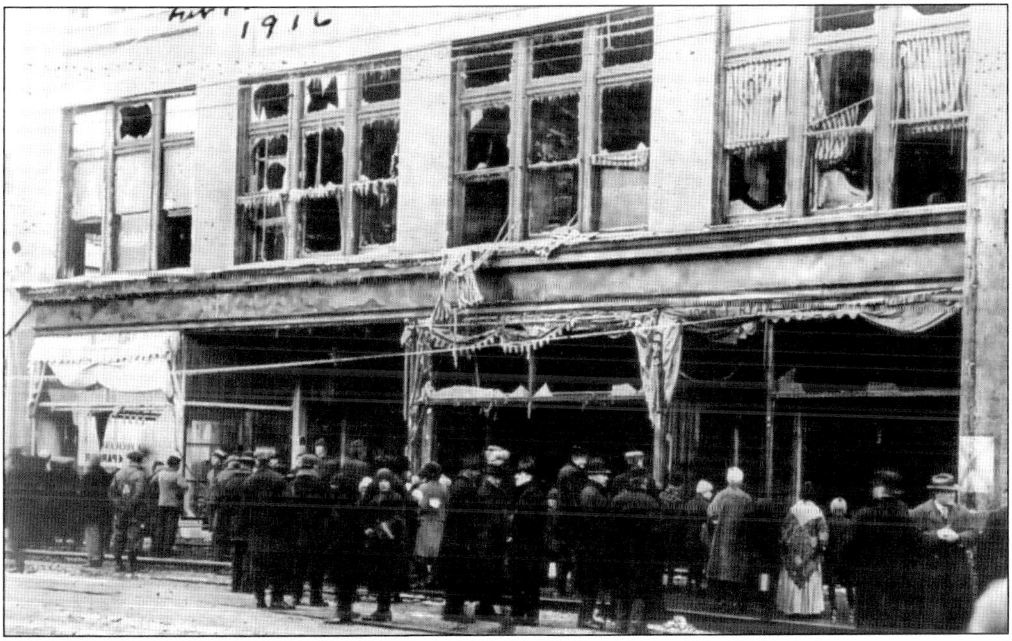

Fires have always brought out crowds, and here a group is seen milling in front of the ruined Masonic temple. (Kreitzman Collection.)

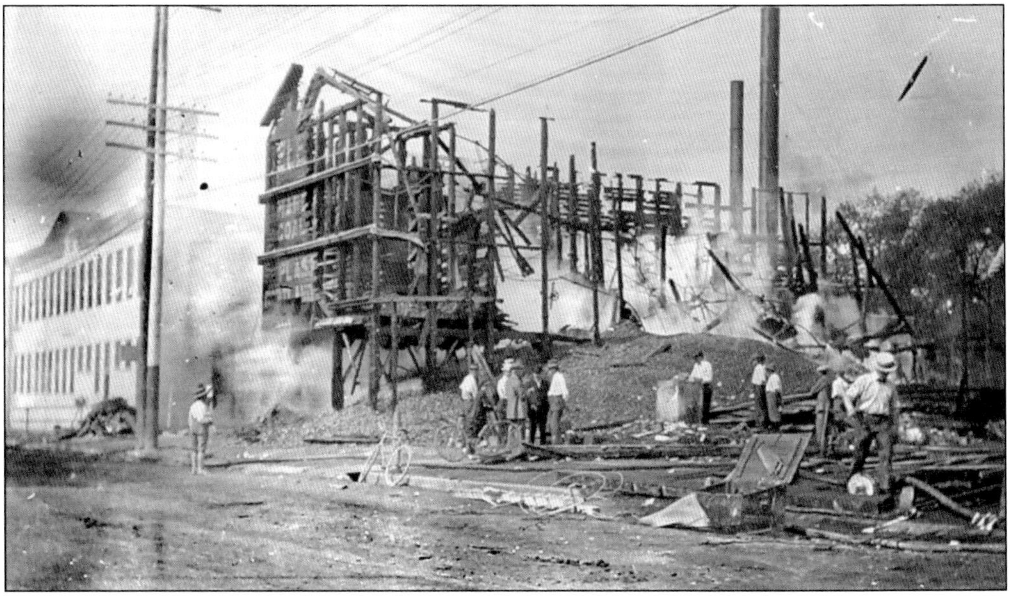

A year earlier, on June 29, 1915, another fire broke out in the city, this time at the Barker Lumber Company on South First Street. The fire began shortly after 3:00 a.m., and it destroyed the offices of the company, the coal elevator, and lumberyard. It also damaged the nearby New Method Laundry. Over $30,000 worth of damage resulted from this fire, which had flames that rose 40 feet high.

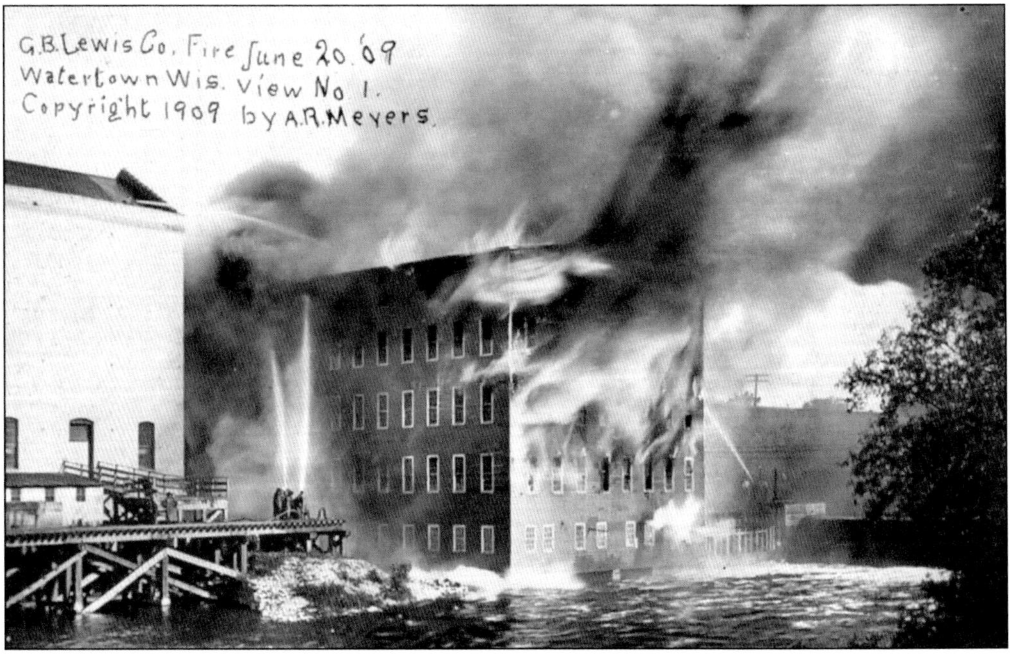

Perhaps the most dramatic fire in the city's history was the G. B. Lewis Company fire, which took place on June 20, 1909. The fire began early in the morning, its exact cause unknown. It caused about $80,000 worth of damage. This is one of 11 views of the fire taken by local photographer A. H. Meyers.

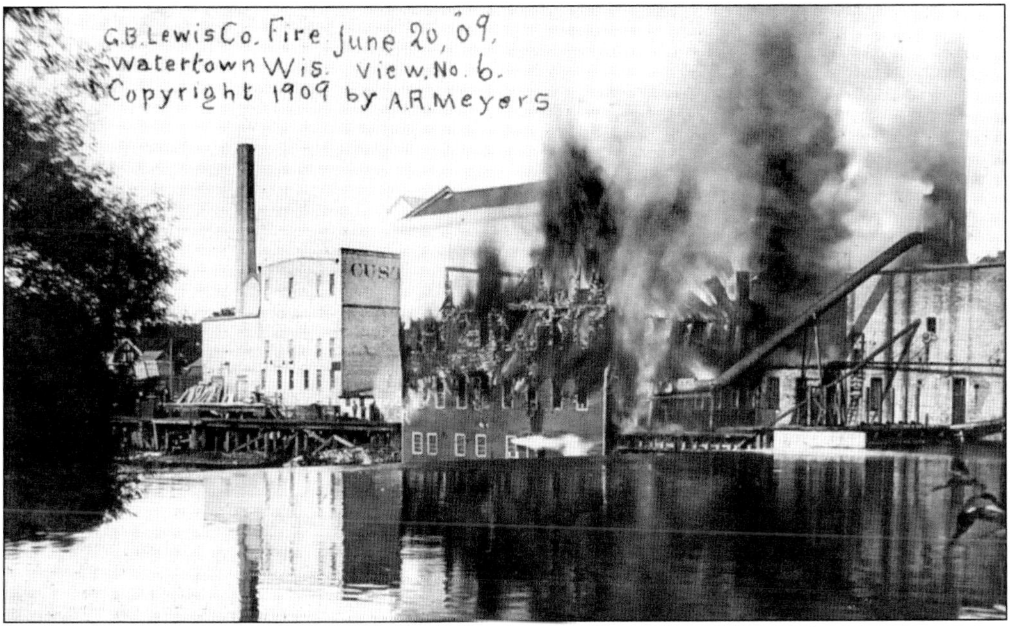

Taken from the east side of the river, this photograph offers a clear view of the conflagration. In addition to the Lewis plant, which was a total loss, the fire also destroyed the Watertown Woolen Mills (right) and scorched the Globe Mill (left).

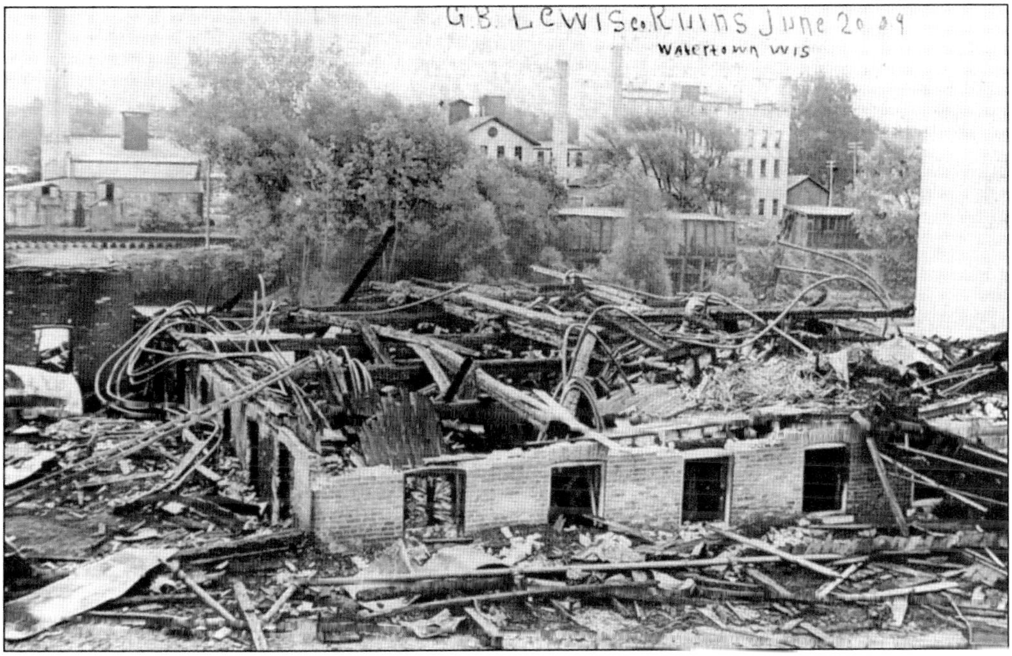

Here are the ruins of the Lewis Company. It was a total loss. The company moved over to South Montgomery Street and began anew shortly after the fire. The business continued on successfully until the company ceased to exist in 2000. Ironically, this was the second time the Lewis plant burned down. The first time was on April 19, 1890, when the company was set on fire by a disturbed youth who told authorities he set it ablaze because he "wanted to see a really good fire."

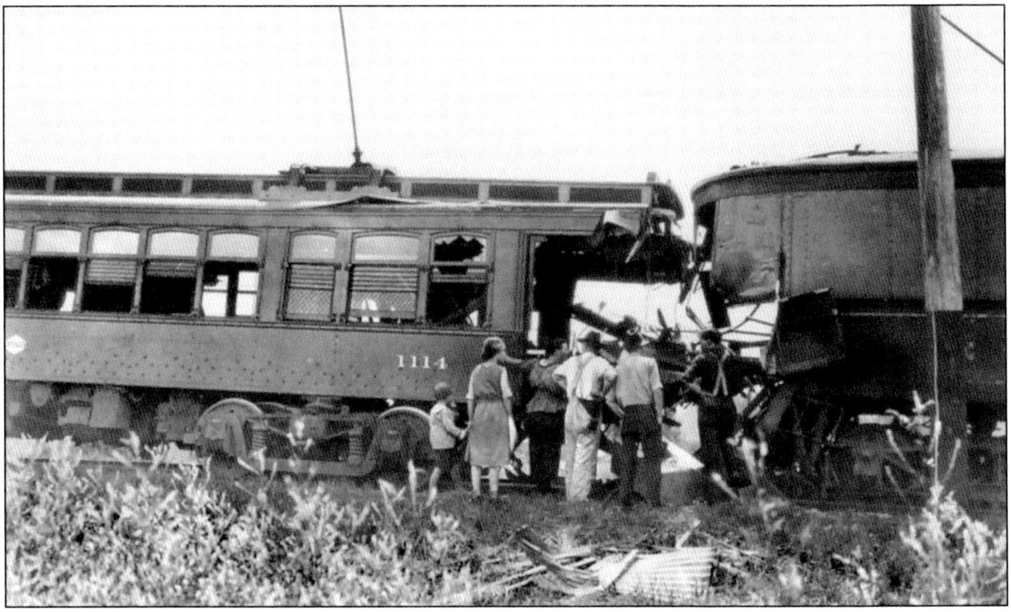

On July 14, 1923, a freight car and a trolley train with two cars crashed just north of Richards' Hill, on the east side of the city. More than two score of passengers escaped the crash, which completely wrecked the front ends of the two cars. Miraculously, neither car left the track. The collision occurred at 2:05 p.m. The car coming into the city was 20 minutes late, and the express car was given orders to leave Watertown. Shortly thereafter, they met head on. (Krietzman Collection.)

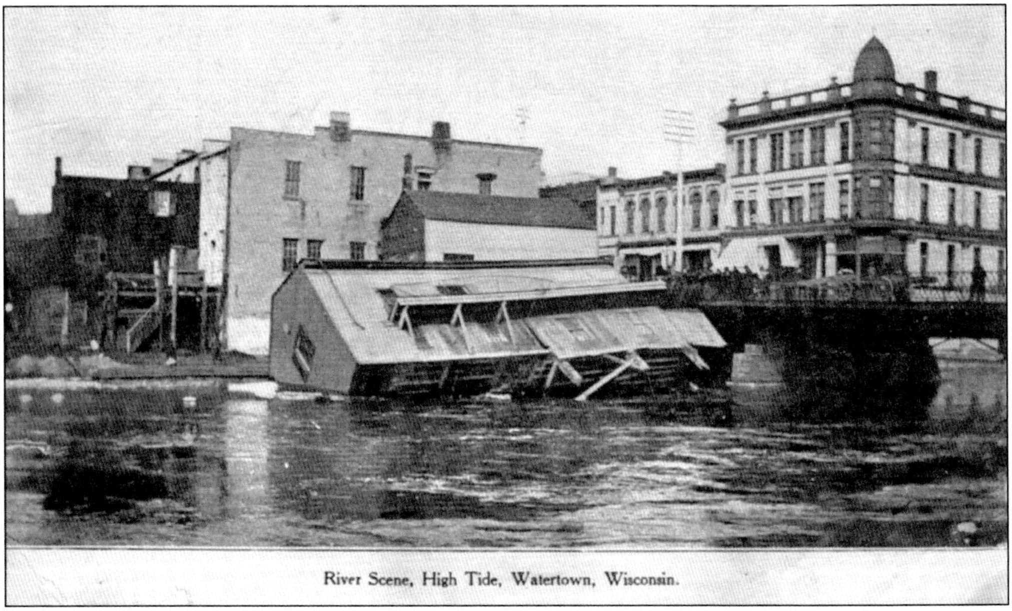

Mother Nature has tried unsuccessfully to do away with man for years, but so far she has been thwarted. Take this image, for example. On March 26, 1904, this small shanty, built on pilings off the south side of the Main Street bridge, was knocked over by ice breaking up on the river, and it floated away. The building, operated for many years as a barbershop, was built in the 1850s as a confectionary store by Henry Maes.

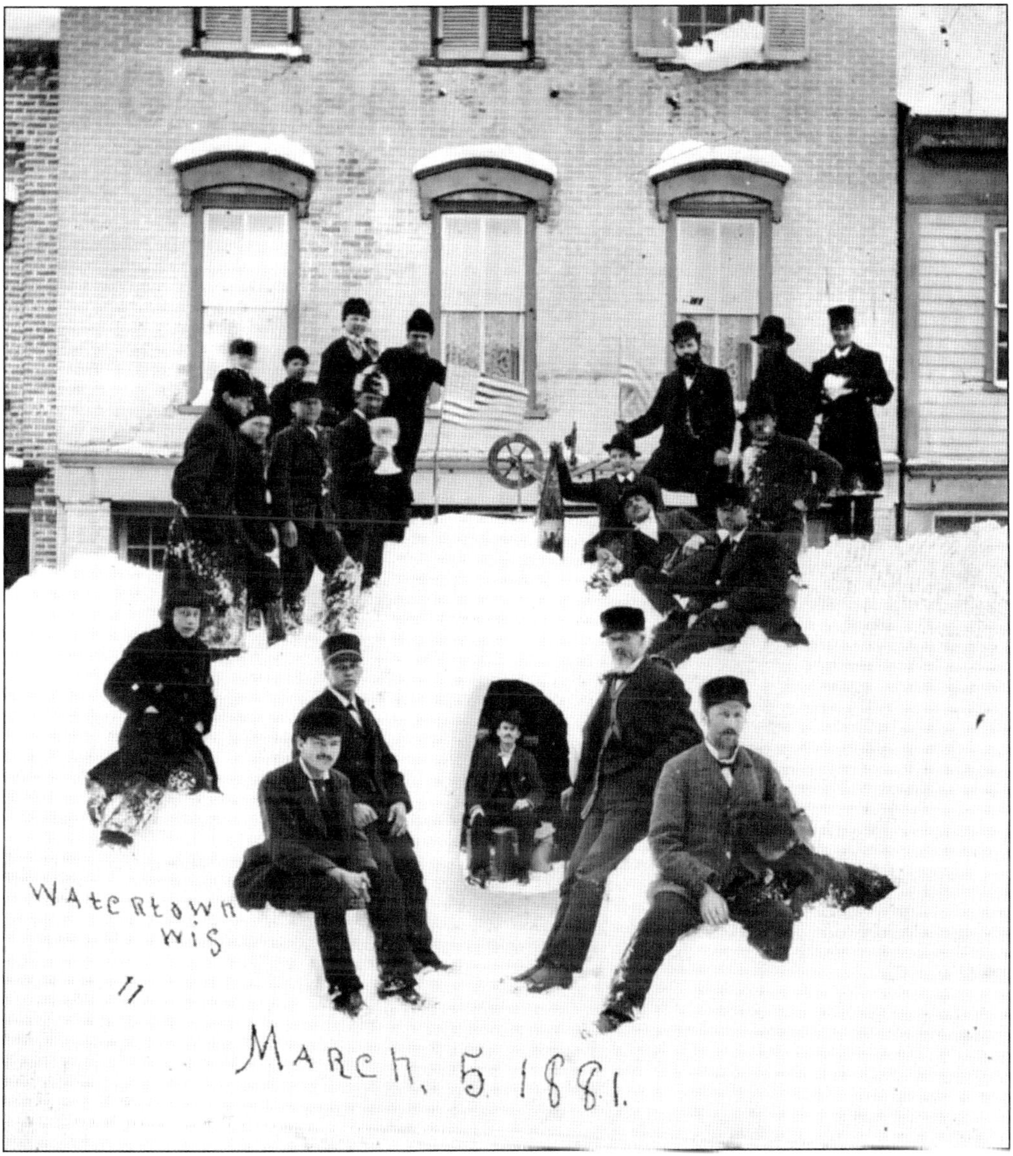

In March 1881, possibly the worst snowstorm to ever hit the Midwest struck Watertown and dumped over 11 feet of snow in some places. This postcard, made from a series of images taken at the time of the storm, shows one of the many tunnels that were dug on Main Street to allow for access to businesses.

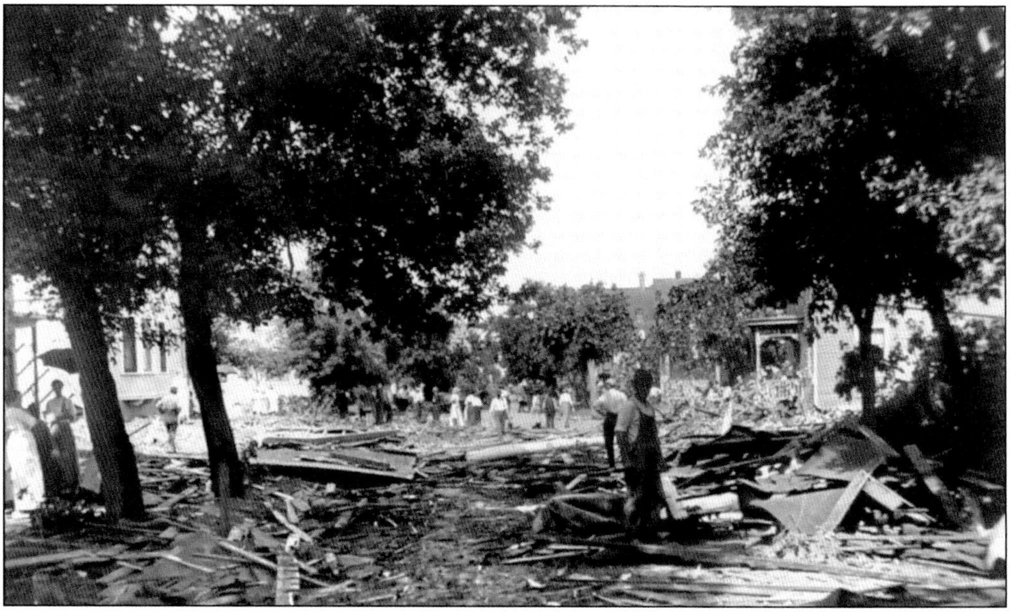

One of the most destructive tornados to ever strike the city, the Great Cyclone arrived on June 24, 1914. Here the aftermath of the storm that struck several homes and businesses in the north central part of the city can be seen.

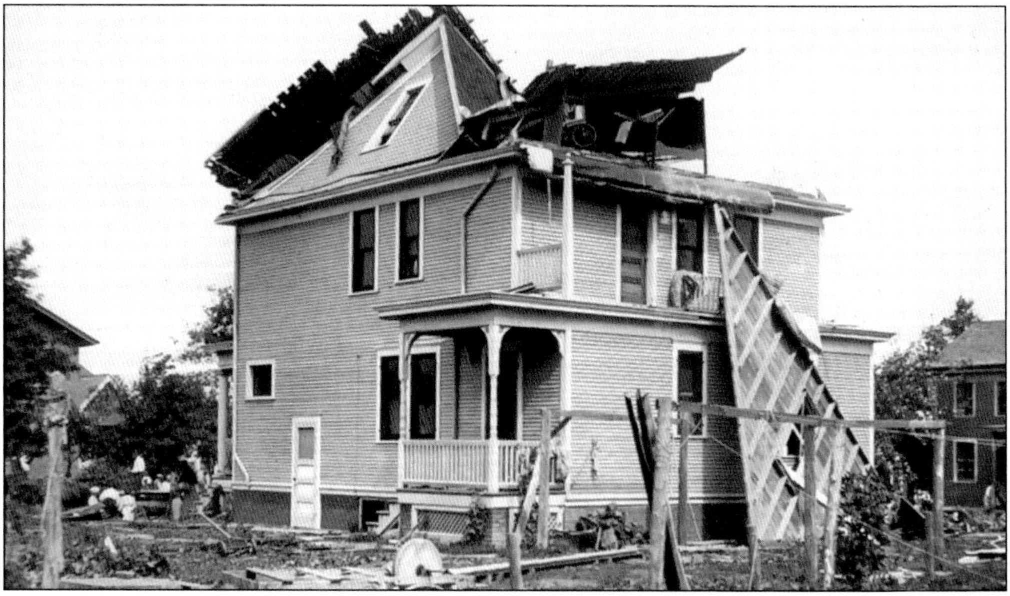

The Edward Else home, on the corner of North Second and Lynn Streets, was just one of several homes to be destroyed by the winds of the cyclone.

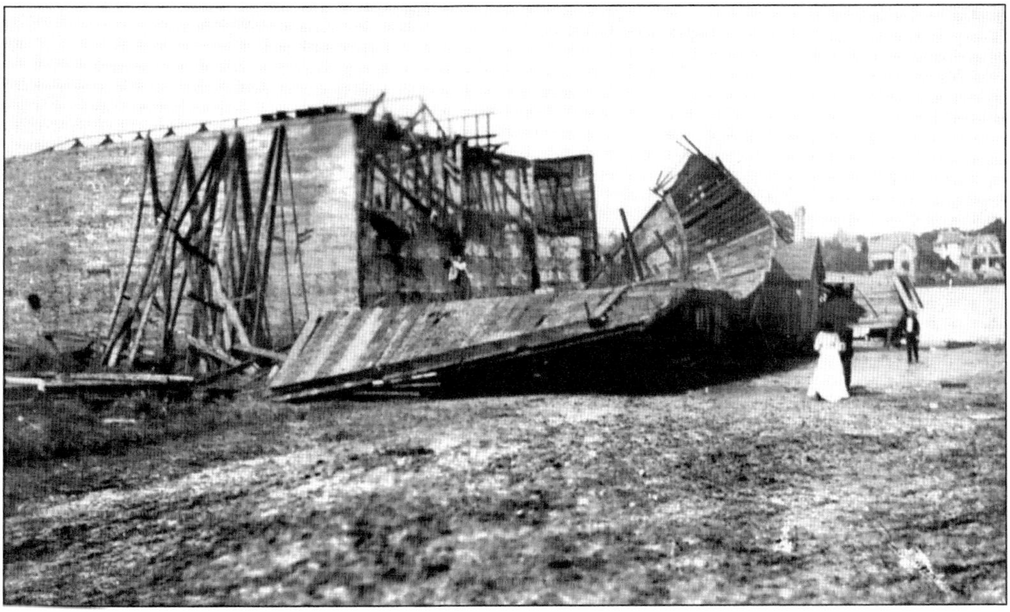

It was not just homes that were damaged. Several businesses were thrown out of commission, such as the John Knispel Ice House, shown here. The icehouse was located at the end of Cole Street.

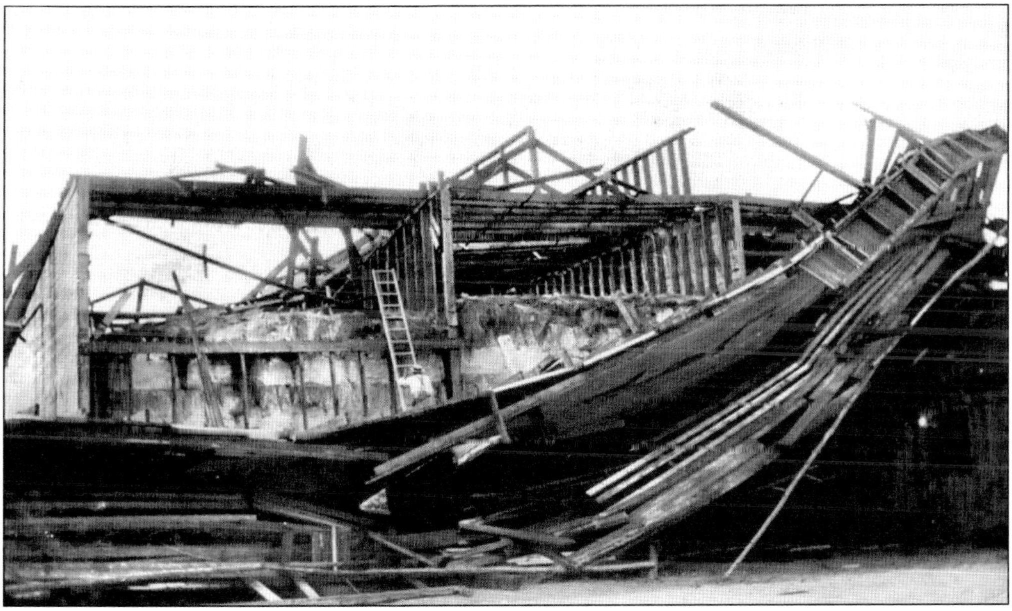

Here is another view of the icehouse wreckage in 1914.

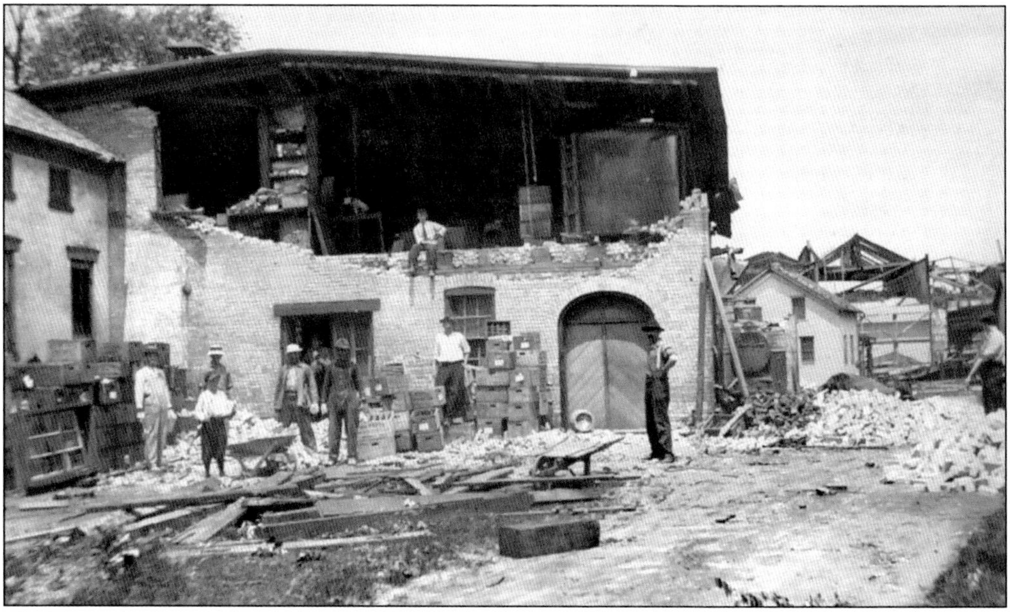

This is the bottling plant of the William Hartig Brewing Company on Division Street, along the river. This plant was originally the Cech Tanning Factory before being purchased by Paul Hoppe in the 1880s to use as a bottling plant. Note the wreckage of the Knispel Ice House, which can be seen in the distance on the right of the image.

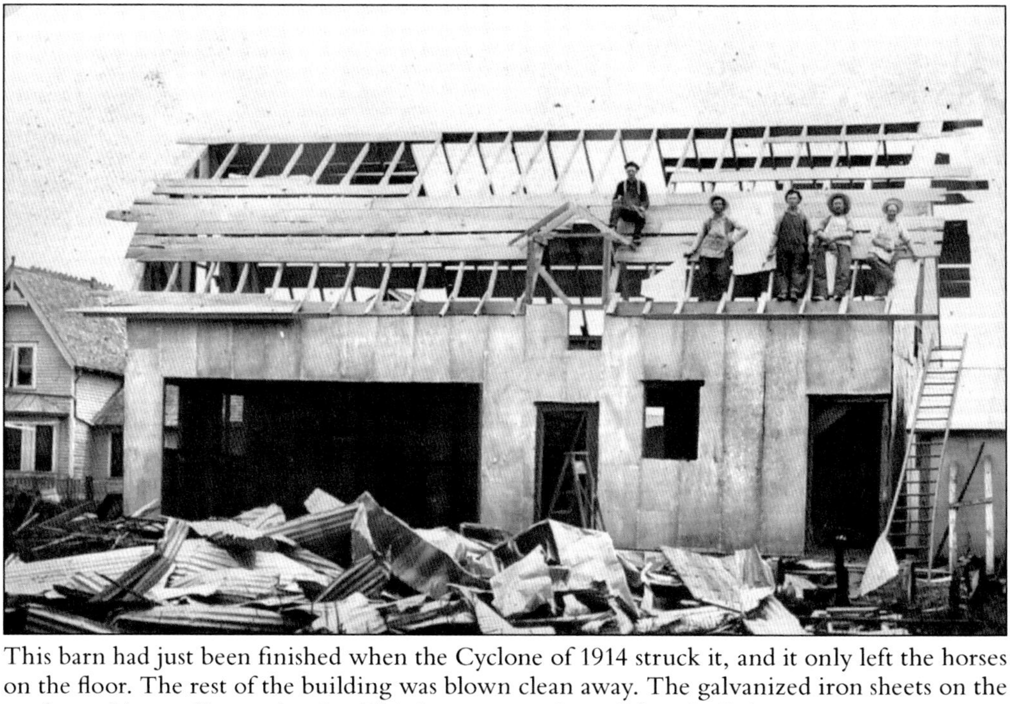

This barn had just been finished when the Cyclone of 1914 struck it, and it only left the horses on the floor. The rest of the building was blown clean away. The galvanized iron sheets on the roof were blown all over the city. This image was taken of the rebuilt barn.

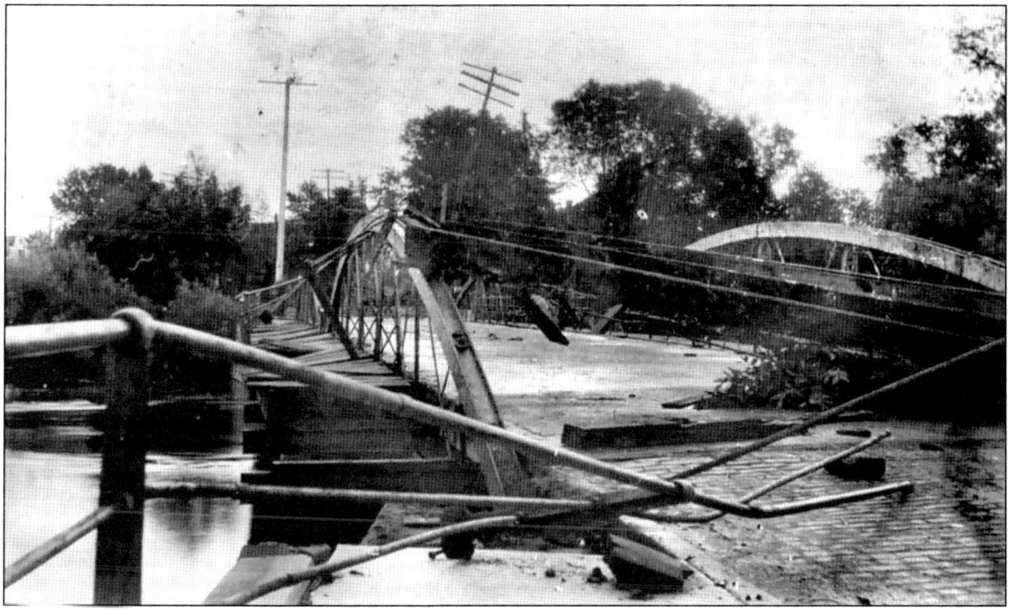

It was not only buildings that were destroyed in the cyclone. Here Laberee Bridge, otherwise known as North Fourth Street bridge, is shown after the storm struck. Note that this bridge was a bow-span bridge, just like the one leading to Tivoli Island.

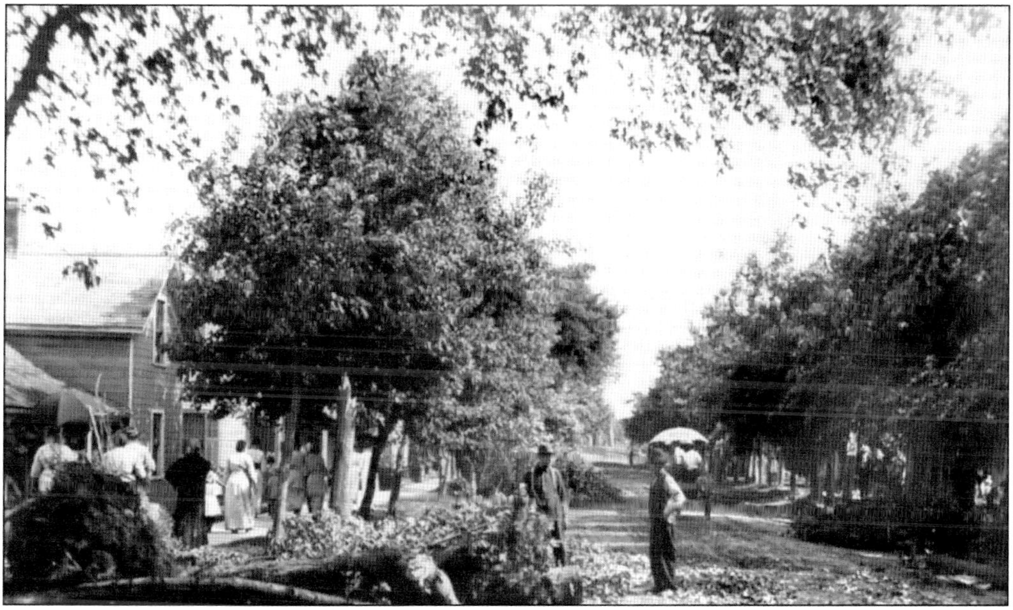

Here is the wreckage along North Second Street. Despite this setback, by the fall things were back in running order. Watertown would experience other windstorms, but none quite like the Cyclone of 1914.

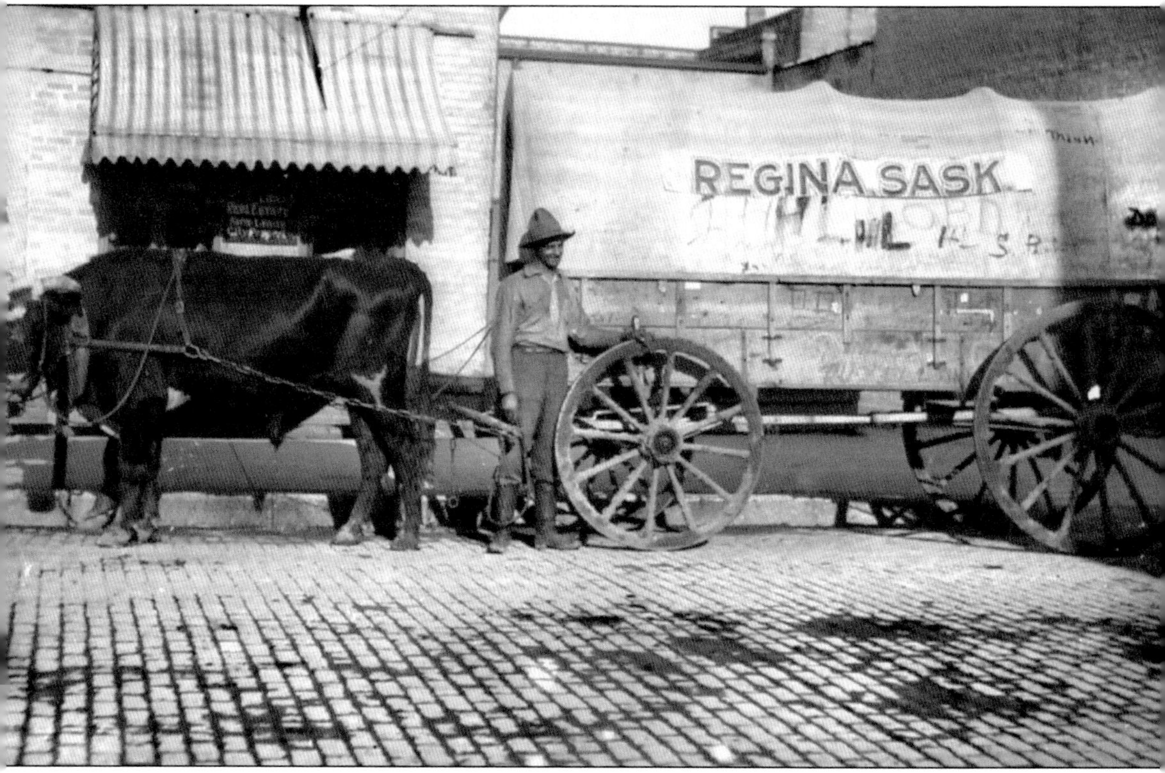

One of the more humorous (if that is the correct term) incidents of the cyclone was the arrival of Charles Wassam of Saskatchewan, Canada. He was driving a wagon pulled by oxen on his way to celebrate the centennial of his hometown, Belleville, Illinois, and arrived in Watertown just as the storm struck. Talk about bad timing!

Nine

NOTABLE BUILDINGS AND PEOPLE

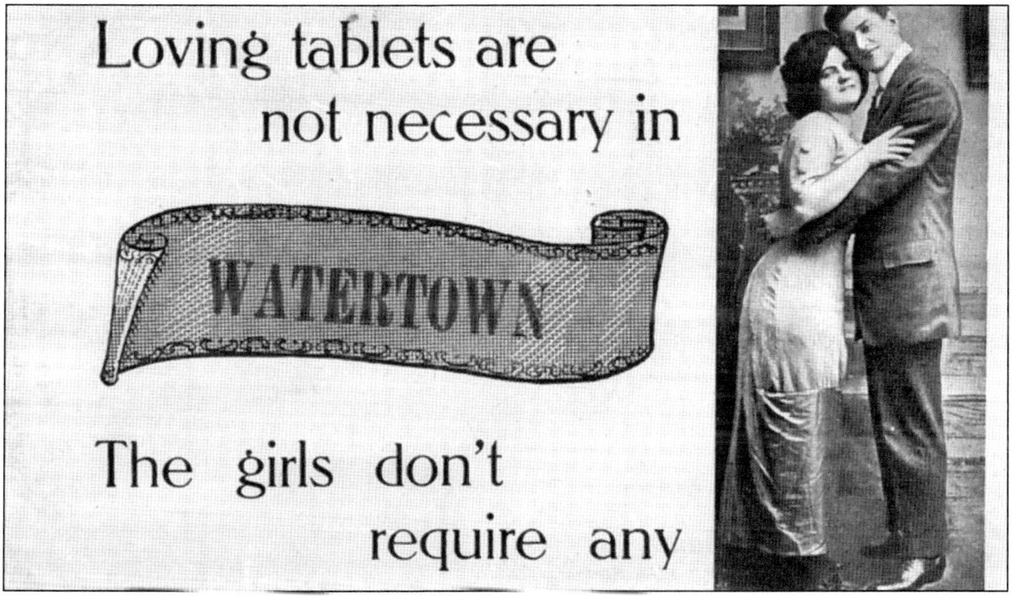

Watertown can be very proud of its many beautiful homes, the most notable examples being found on South and North Washington Streets and along Clyman Street. Perhaps the finest historic home in the city is the famed Octagon House, which is Watertown's museum, built in 1854. The homes run the gamut of architectural styles from Greek Revival to Queen Anne. But for every historic home that still stands, there are at least three historic homes that have been demolished, most for parking lots or banks. Likewise, Watertown can be proud of its many citizens. Watertown can claim to be the birthplace of such notables as Joseph E. Davies, ambassador to Russia during the time of Franklin Delano Roosevelt; Ralph David Blumenfeld, who rose from obscurity as the son of a local newspaper editor to become the editor of the *London Daily Express*; and of Daniel Brandenstein, a local boy who was a NASA astronaut and for whom a city park is named. On the next few pages are images of some of Watertown's famous people and some of the city's historic architecture. The pictures do not really do them justice, however. One should really visit the city to see the homes in all their glory. The author is not sure what message this postcard is trying to express, but, suffice it to say, the citizens of Watertown are a genial lot, to say the least.

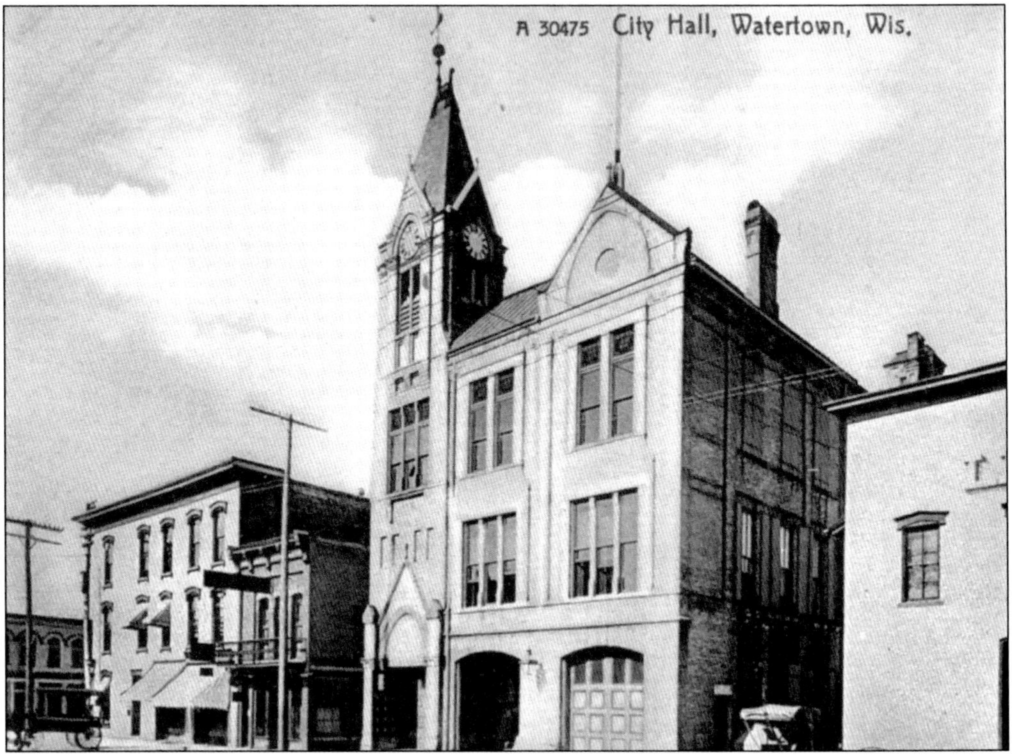

The first few images are of buildings no longer extant. The first image, from about 1905, shows Watertown's city hall, which was erected in 1885 and located at one time along North First Street. In addition to the city offices, this building also housed the police department and the fire department. This building was abandoned in 1965, when a new and more spacious municipal building was constructed. Shortly thereafter, it was demolished, and in its place there grew a parking lot.

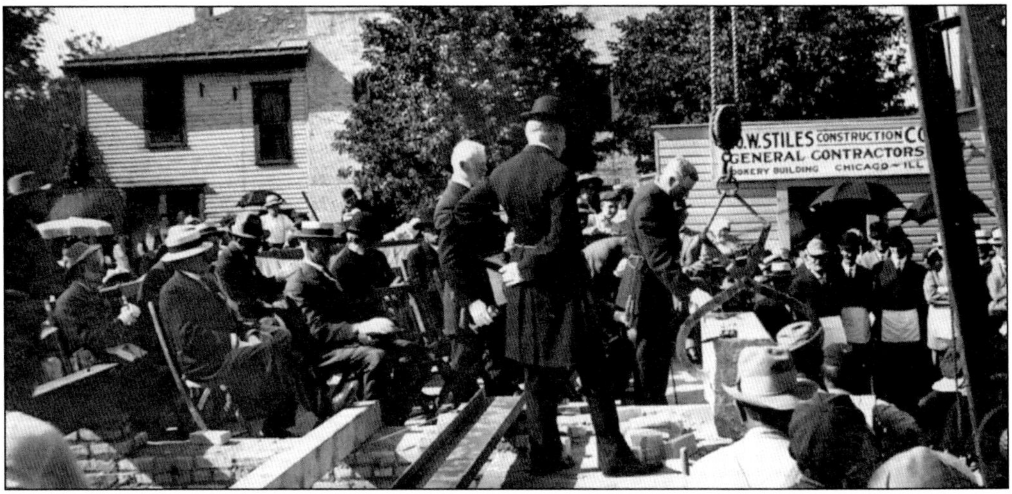

This postcard shows the laying of the cornerstone for the new post office in 1912. The first post office opened in the city in 1837, and pioneer settler William M. Dennis was the first postmaster. He carried the mail around in his hat. Over the years, the post office was housed in various buildings along Main Street, and then in 1912, it moved to North Second and Madison Streets.

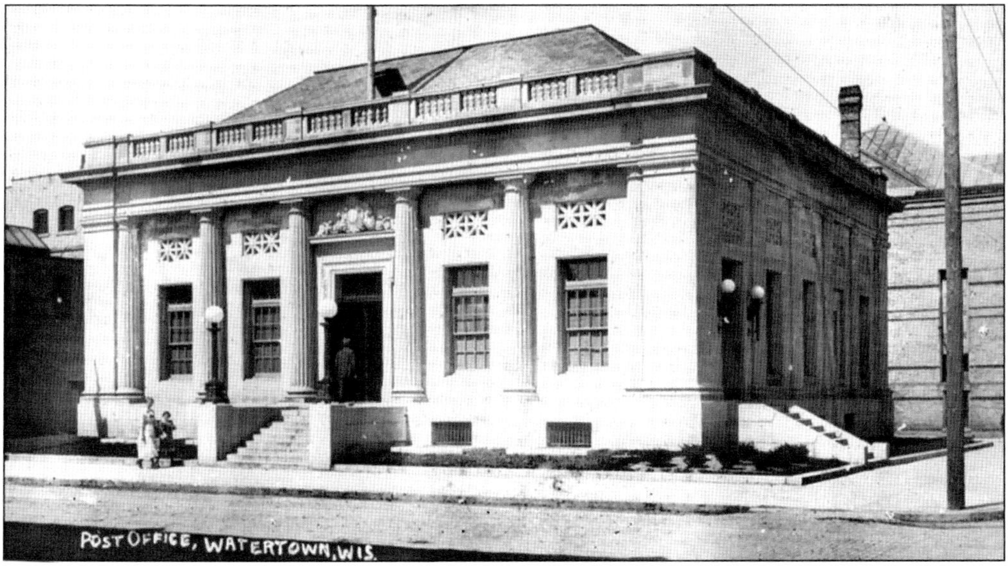

The completed post office is pictured around 1915. It served the city well until 1962, when a new office was erected along Dodge Street in the southern part of the city. At that time, the old post office was taken over by the Moose Lodge until 1972, when the building was torn down to make way for (what else?) a parking lot.

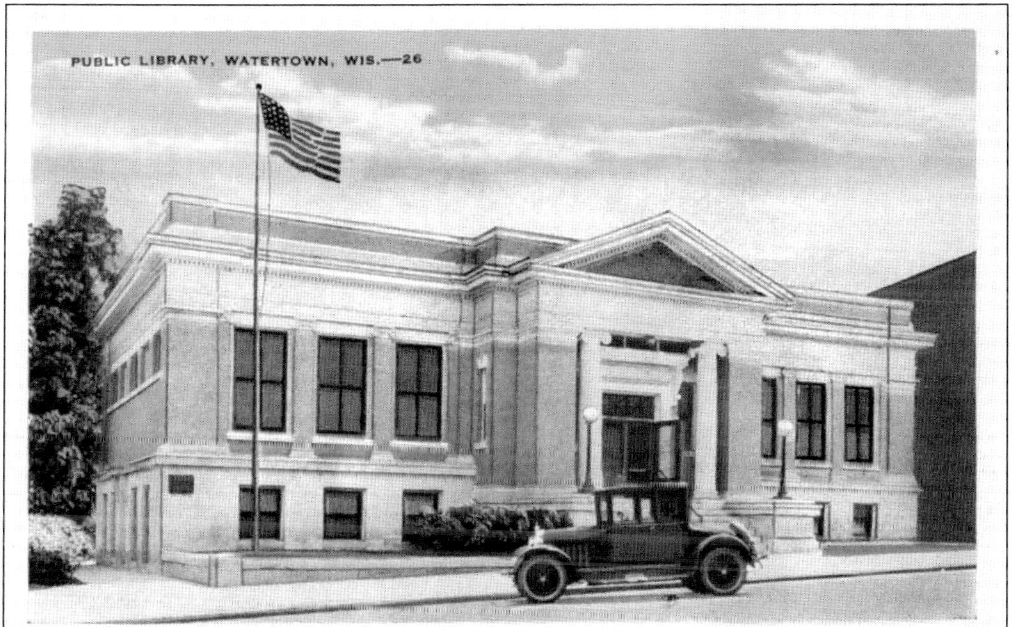

In 1903, a public library was opened in Watertown. At first, it was located on the upper floor of a millinery shop on Main Street, but then in 1907, it moved to the corner of Main and South Water Streets. The library building, shown here about 1910, was designed by the architectural firm of Claude and Starke and was paid for in part by a generous grant from the capitalist Andrew Carnegie. In 1984, the library experienced a major remodeling and updating, and a brand-new addition was added onto the back of the old 1907 building. This library is one of the largest in the two counties that encompass Watertown, Dodge, and Jefferson.

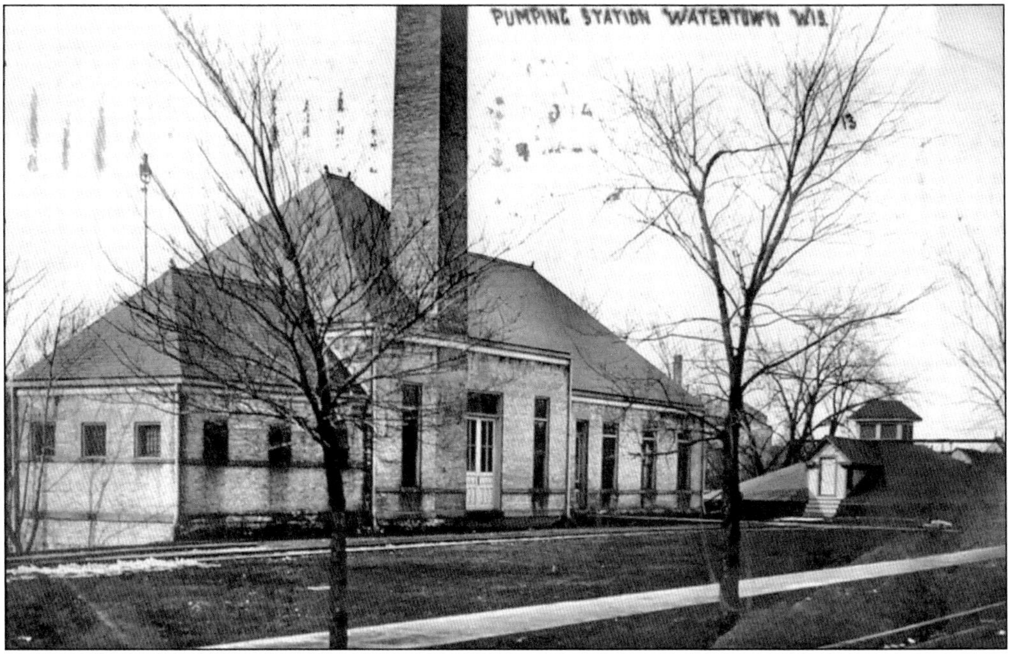

In 1895, the citizens of Watertown got their first taste of water from a tap when the city waterworks was created. This postcard from about 1910 shows the water department offices located along South First Street and the old pumping station. Today the water department is based south of town at the wastewater treatment plant.

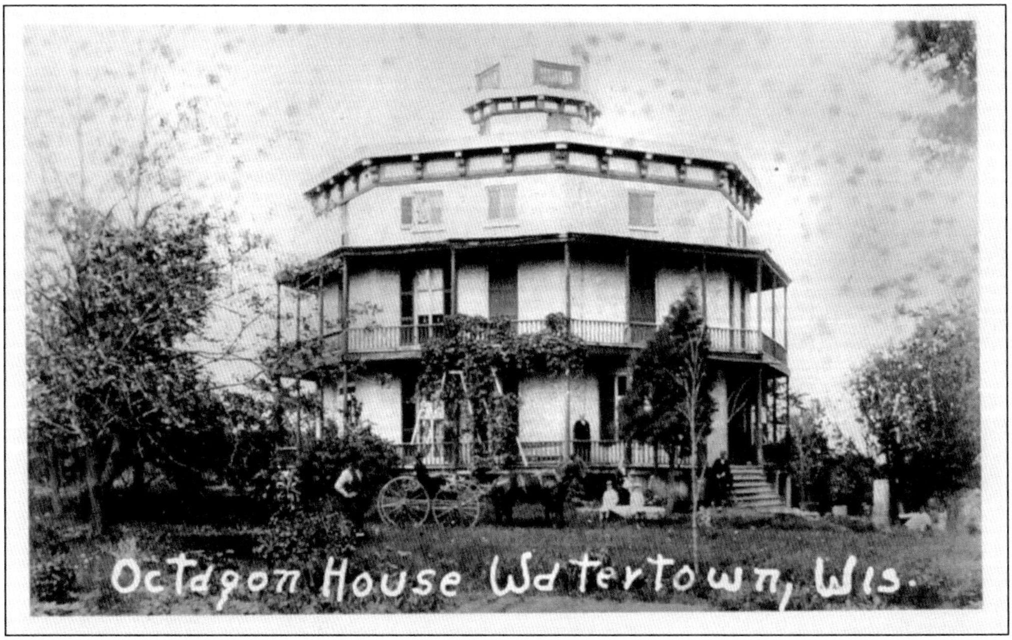

Of all the historic homes in the city, surely the most revered is the famous Octagon House, built in 1854. This postcard reprints an 1870 view of the home, which is located at 919 Charles Street on the east side of the city.

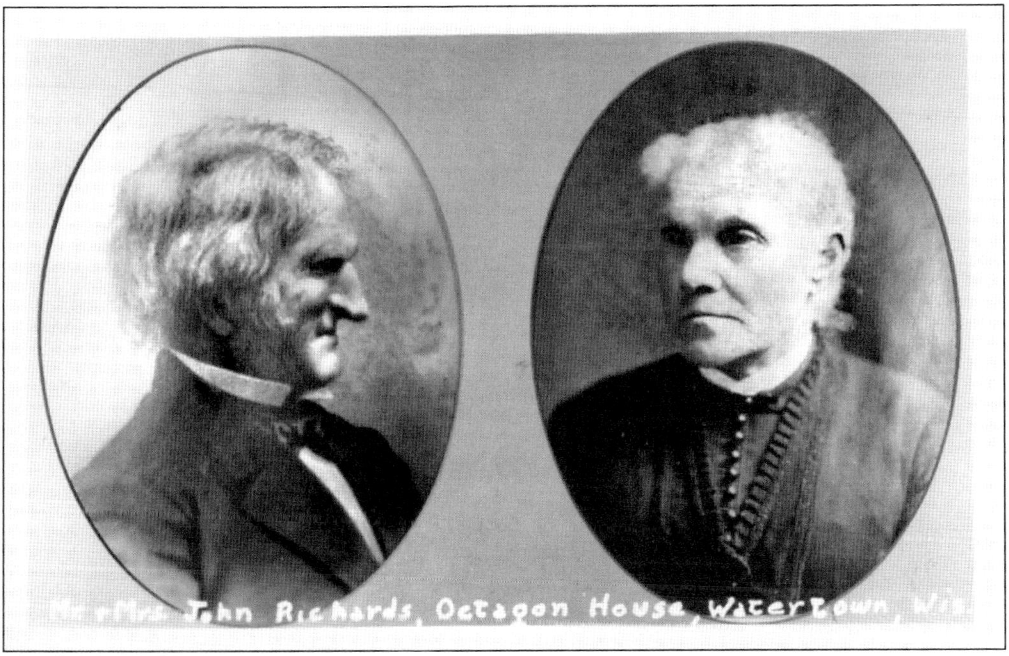

The Octagon House was built by pioneer settler John Richards, shown on the left, as a belated wedding present for his wife, Eliza, shown on the right, in 1854. Richards, a former lawyer and schoolteacher, spared no expense when it came to his home and had built into it rudimentary forms of running water, central air-conditioning, and central heating.

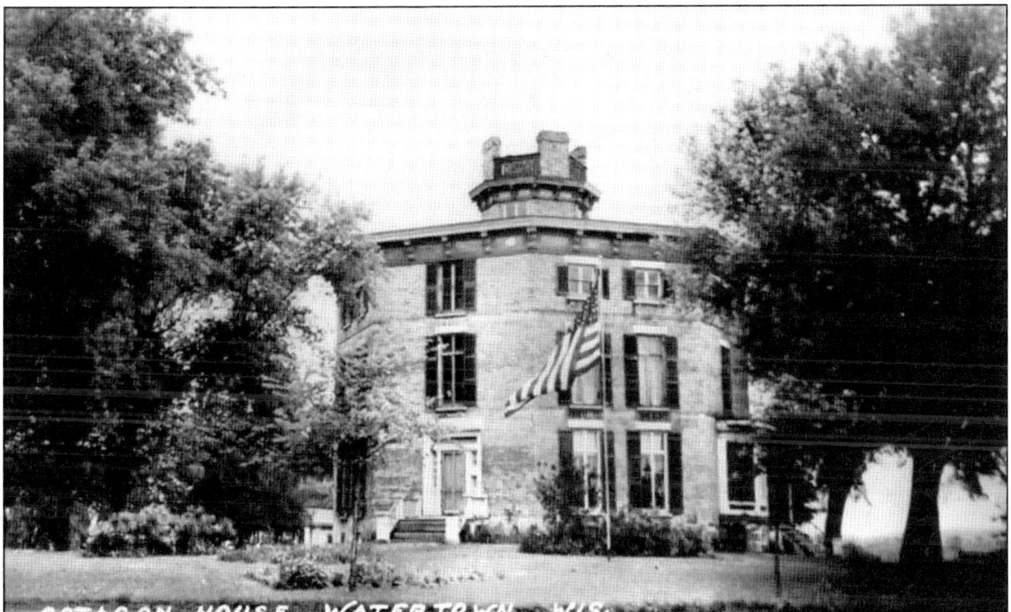

Originally, porches ringed the Octagon House, but by 1924, they had rotted away and were unsafe, so the family had them removed. This card shows the Octagon House as it appeared for over 60 years until 1982, when the porches were restored.

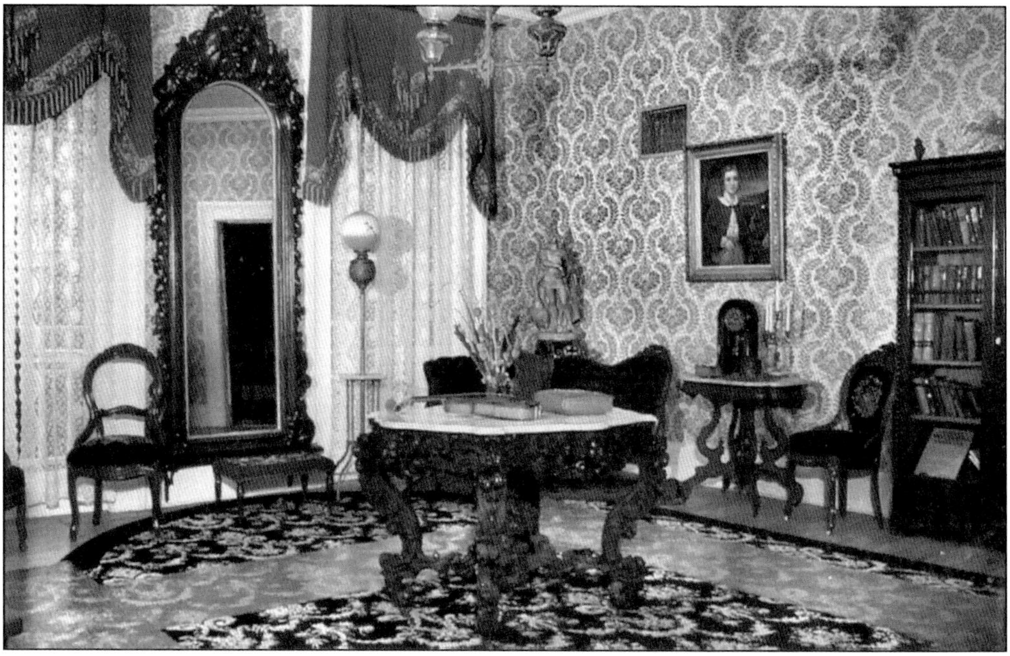

In 1937, the last descendant of the Richards family still living in the home passed away, and the remaining family members decided to deed the house over to the Watertown Historical Society, which has operated it as a public museum since that time. Here the music room in the Octagon House, the first room one sees when taking a tour, is shown.

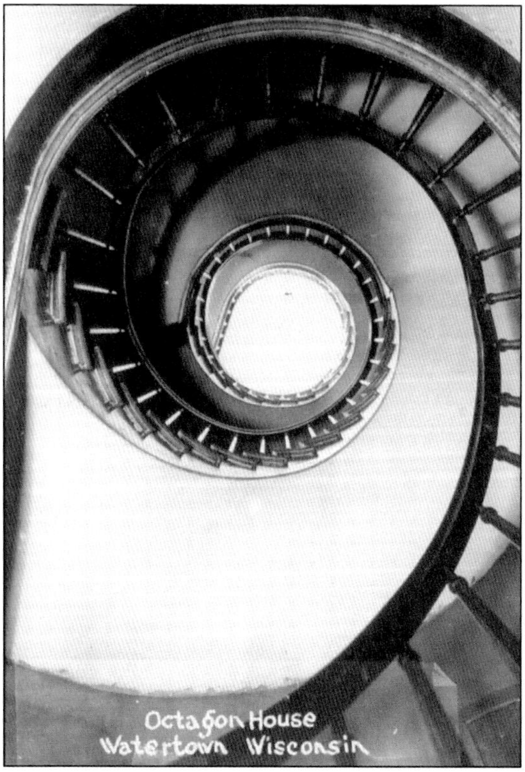

Perhaps the most spectacular feature of the Octagon House is the central spiral staircase that rises 40 feet through the house. Interestingly, there are 54 steps to this staircase, which coincides with the year the home was built, 1854.

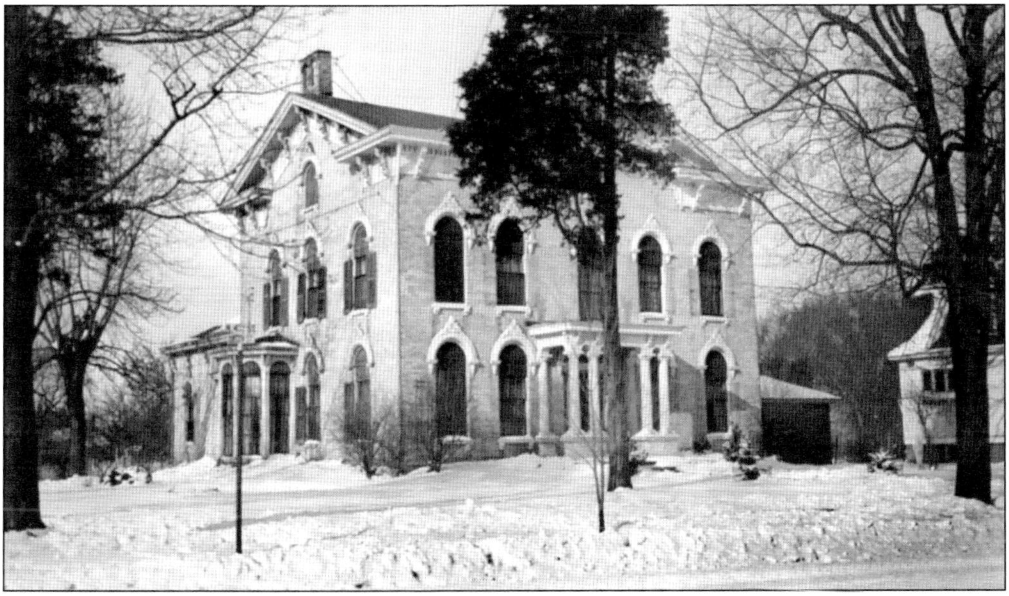

On equal footing as far as beauty and age is the John W. Cole home at 802 North Fourth Street, shown here in a 1937 postcard. Built about 1854 in the Italianate style, the Cole home at one time could boast of having a ballroom and cloakroom on the second floor. For many years, this was cut up into apartments, but since the late 1990s, the home has been restored to a single-family home once again.

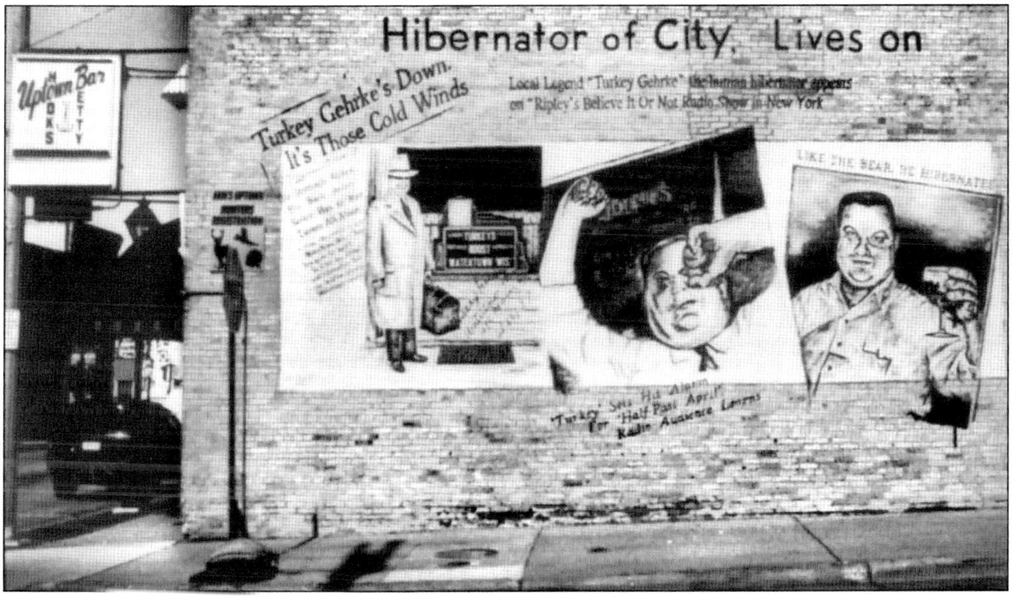

Perhaps the most celebrated figure in Watertown's history was local tavern owner Arthur "Turkey" Gehrke. What set him apart from others? His claim to fame was that he felt the cold winds of Wisconsin winters caused him stomach and leg pains, and the only cure was complete bed rest. So at the first sign of winter, he would retire to his bed and not leave it until the spring. He was famous for this quirk, and people came from near and far to meet him. He was even featured on *Ripley's Believe It or Not* radio program in the 1930s. This mural highlighting his storied career is painted on the side of his former bar, located on Main and Fifth Streets.

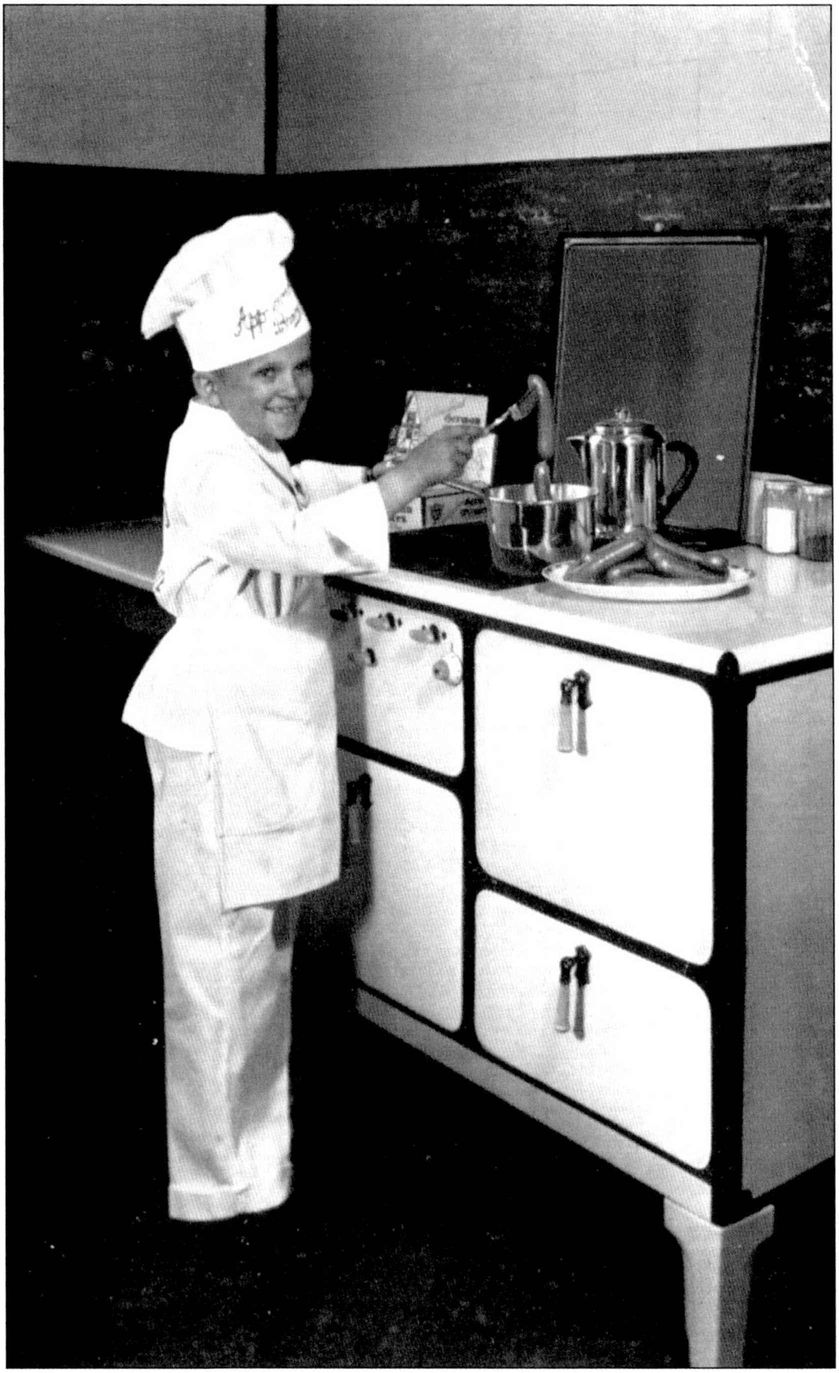

Ever wonder where Munchkins come from? If one were to say Oz, they would only be half right. Some of them come from Watertown. Well, nearby Johnson Creek to be exact, but this fellow, Meinhardt Raabe, shown here about 1938, went to school at Northwestern College in Watertown. One might recognize him as the Munchkinland coroner who pronounced the Wicked Witch of the East "really most sincerely dead" in the classic 1939 film *The Wizard of Oz*. He was also the first person to portray "Little Oscar" for the Oscar Meyer Company.

Ten

PARADES AND CELEBRATIONS

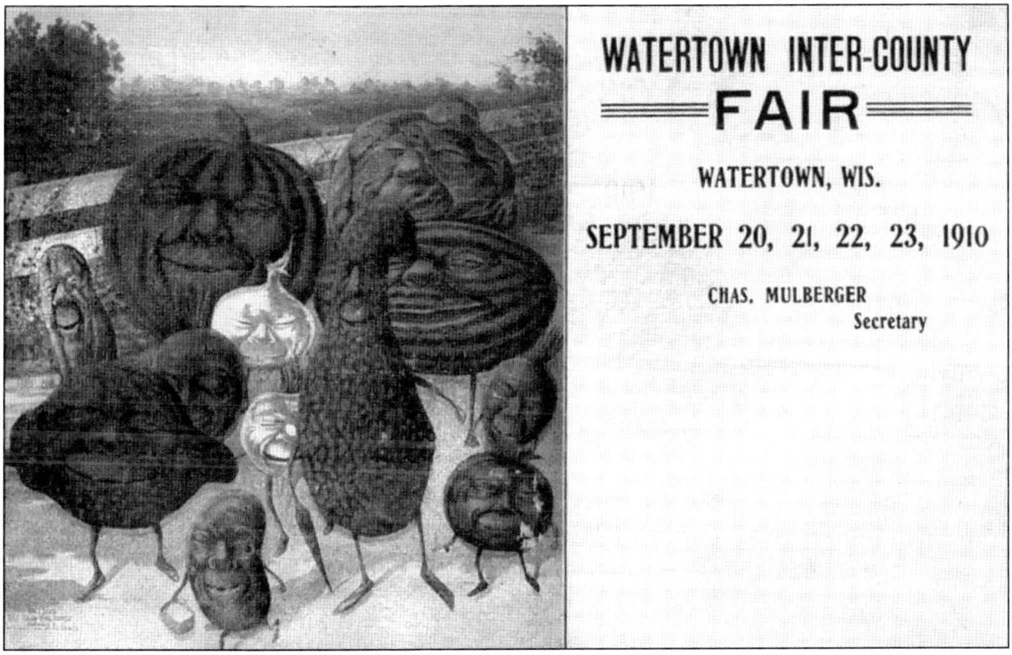

What better way to end a book than with a celebration? The following images show some of the many parades, celebrations, and musical groups that provided music to trip the light fantastic to. Watertown loves a parade and good music and fellowship. Even the vegetables wanted to attend the annual Watertown Inter-County Fair, as this postcard suggests.

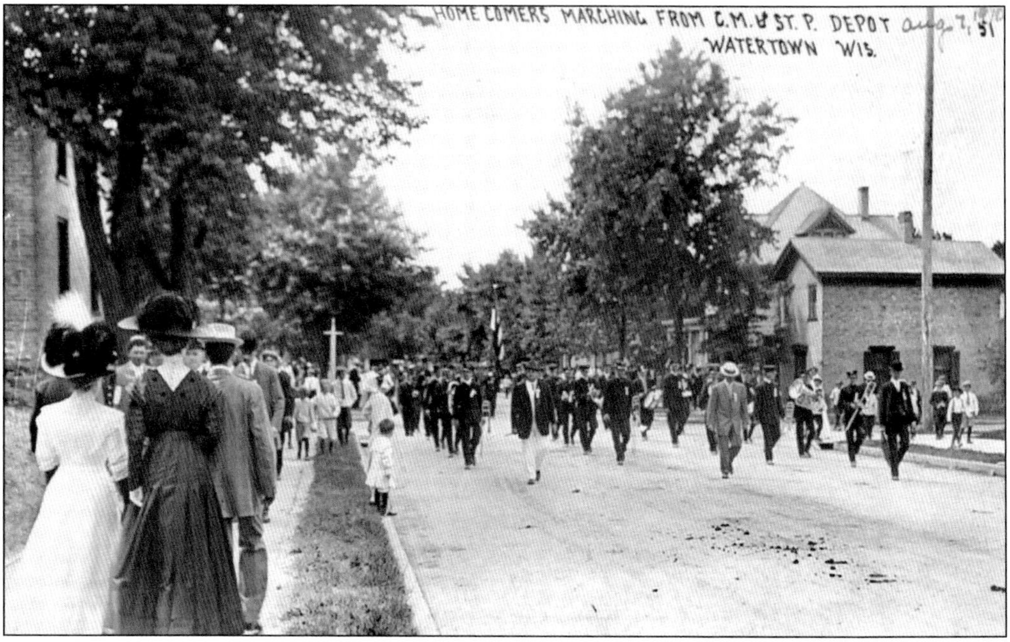

From 1903 to 1912, Watertown was host to an annual event known as the Homecoming. People who once called the city home but had left it to pursue careers and so on would make time to come back one weekend a year for a grand reunion, complete with a parade and speakers. Here Homecoming visitors march from the Chicago, Milwaukee and St. Paul depot in 1912.

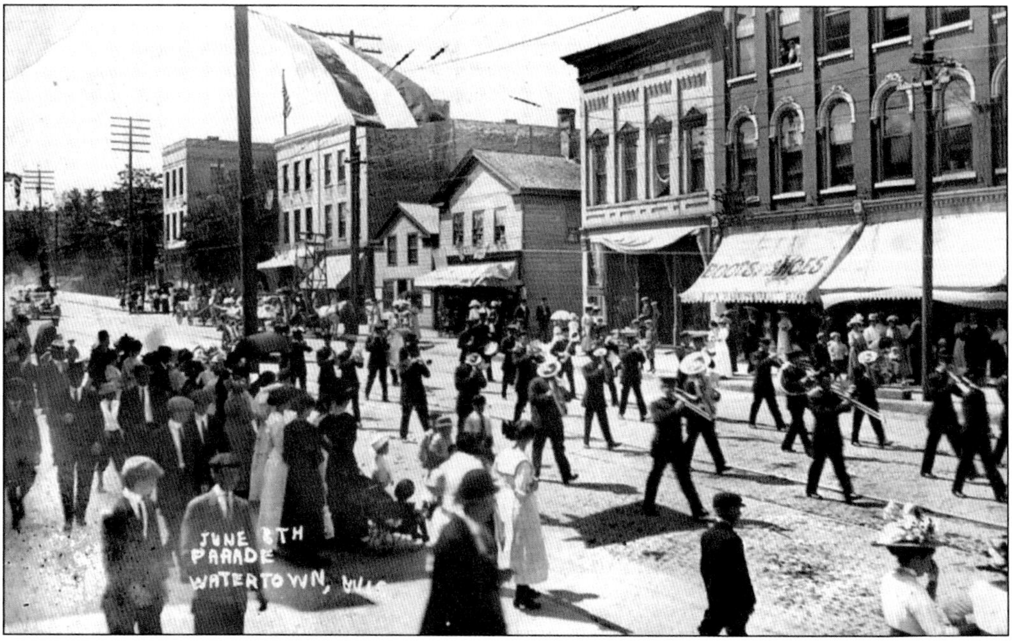

One of the Homecoming parades in 1912 along Main Street is shown here. Most of the buildings pictured still stand along the street.

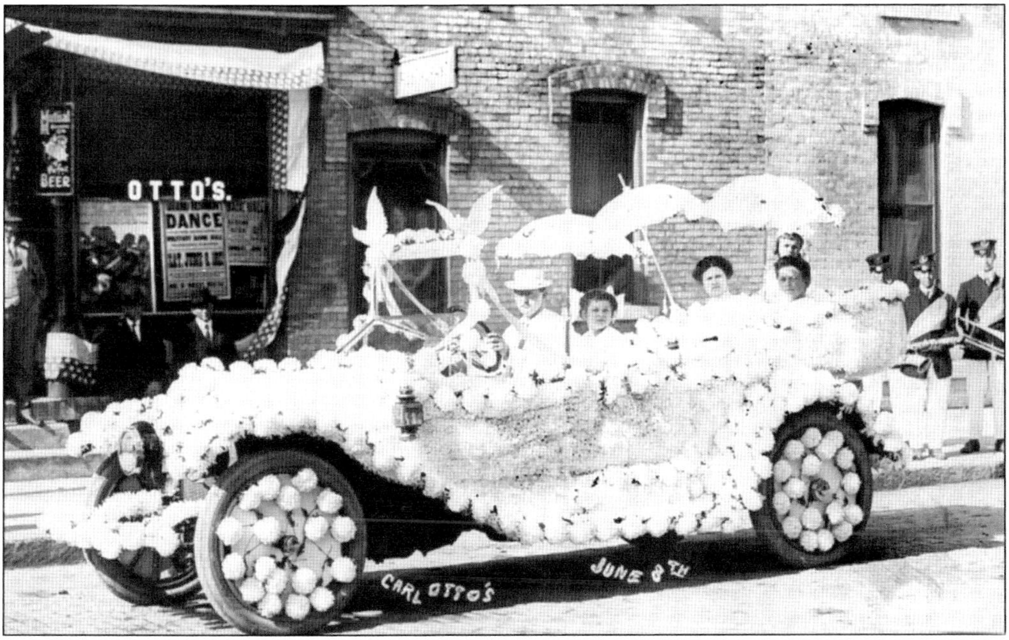

Carl Otto's decorated car parks in front of his saloon on East Madison Street in 1912. They do not decorate cars quite that way anymore.

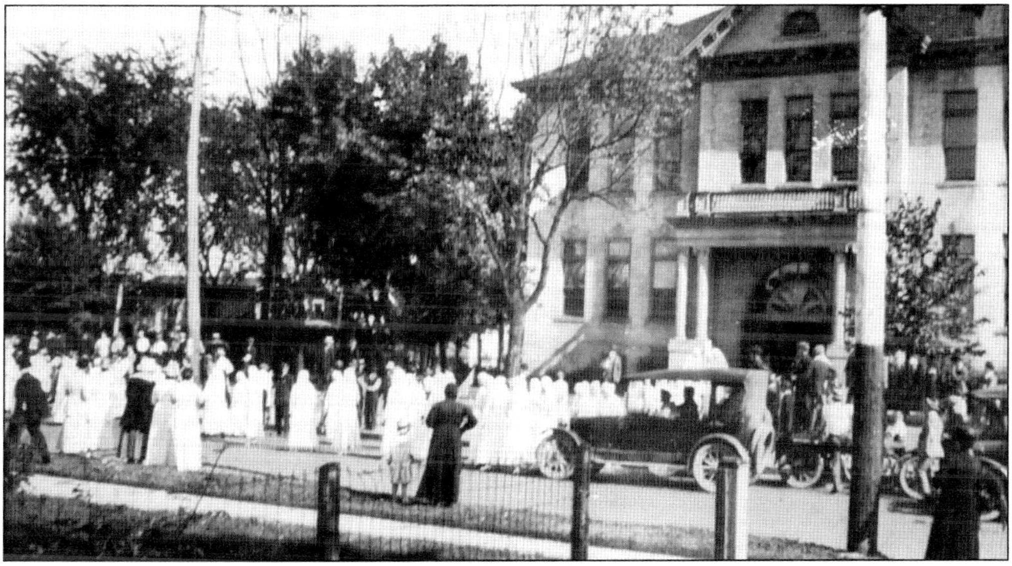

This image shows a patriotic parade about 1918, taken along East Main Street in front of the old city armory, formerly the high school, which can be seen on the right. The ends of World War I and World War II were celebrated in high fashion in Watertown.

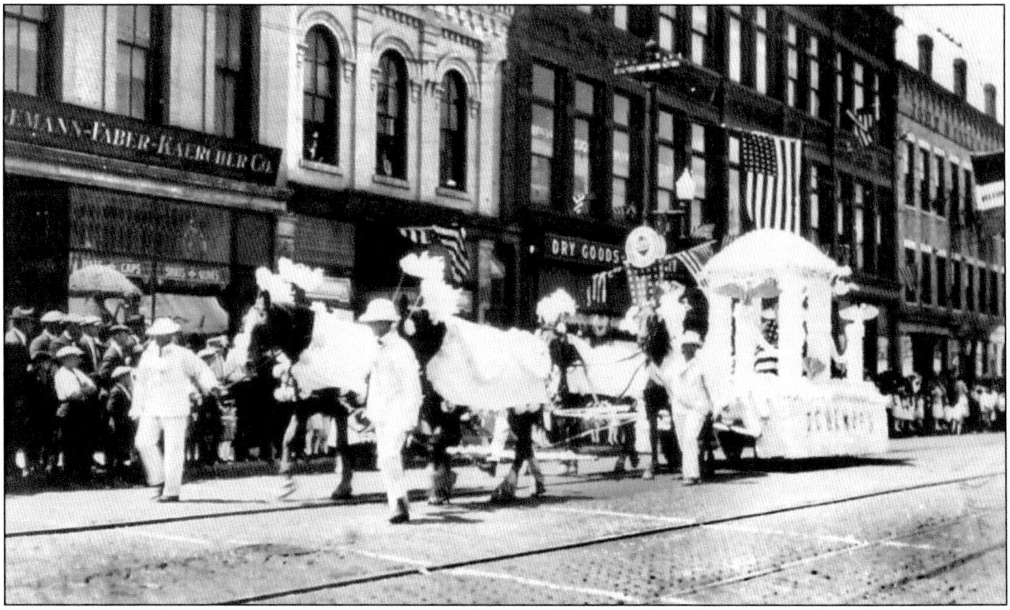

Here is a Fourth of July parade on Main Street in 1921. The first Fourth of July celebration in the city was held in 1840, and the parades keep on getting better and better. (Kreitzman Collection.)

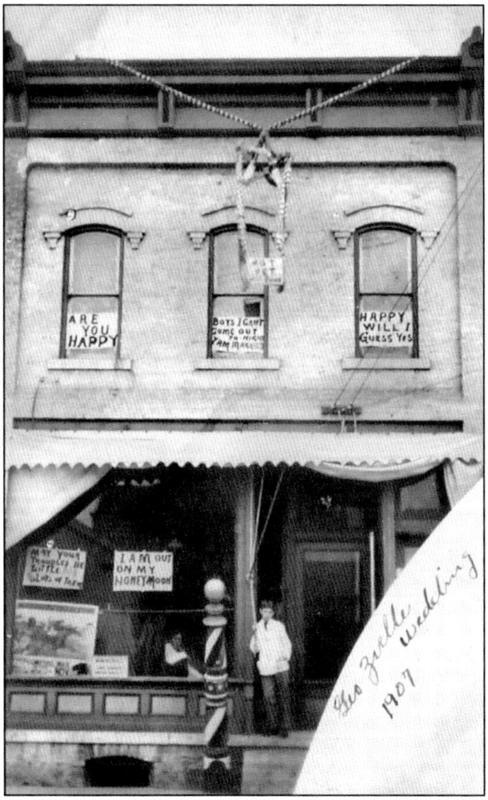

Weddings are times of great joy and always have been. George Zoelle's barbershop, located at 117 North Second Street, can be seen here. The year is 1907, and he has just been married. This is how he (or his friends?) decorated his shop to let everyone know of his new matrimonial status. (Kreitzman Collection.)

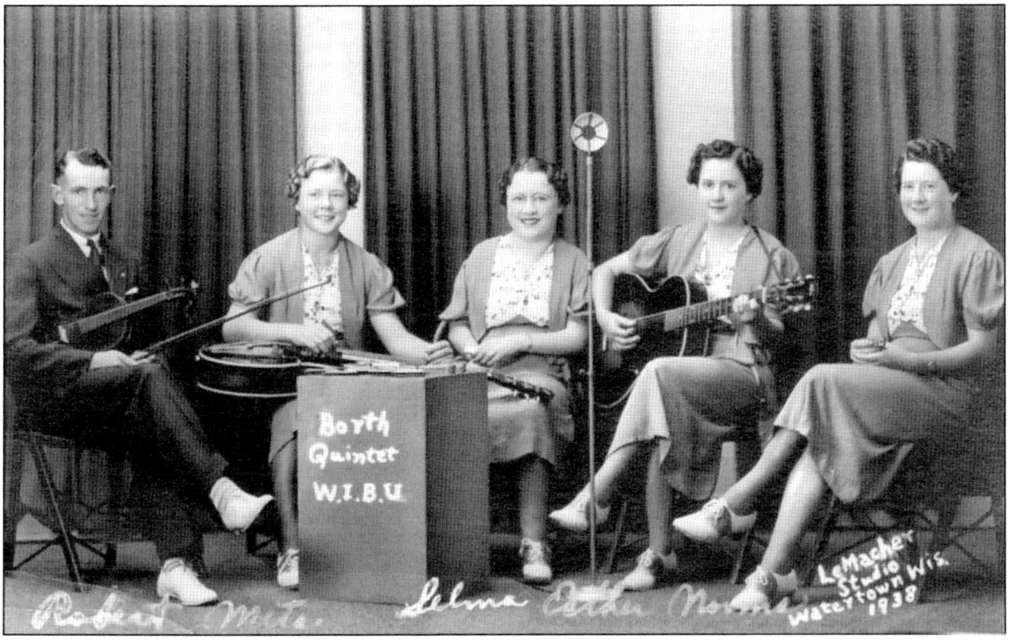

What is a celebration without music? Watertown has had many fine musical groups, and here is one of them, the Borth Quintette, shown in 1938. These siblings—from left to right, Robert, Meta, Selma, Esther, and Norma Borth—were heard each week over radio station WIBU in Poynette, Wisconsin, from the 1930s through the 1940s. They were popular singers, and one of their biggest hits was their rendition of the classic *Winter Wonderland*.

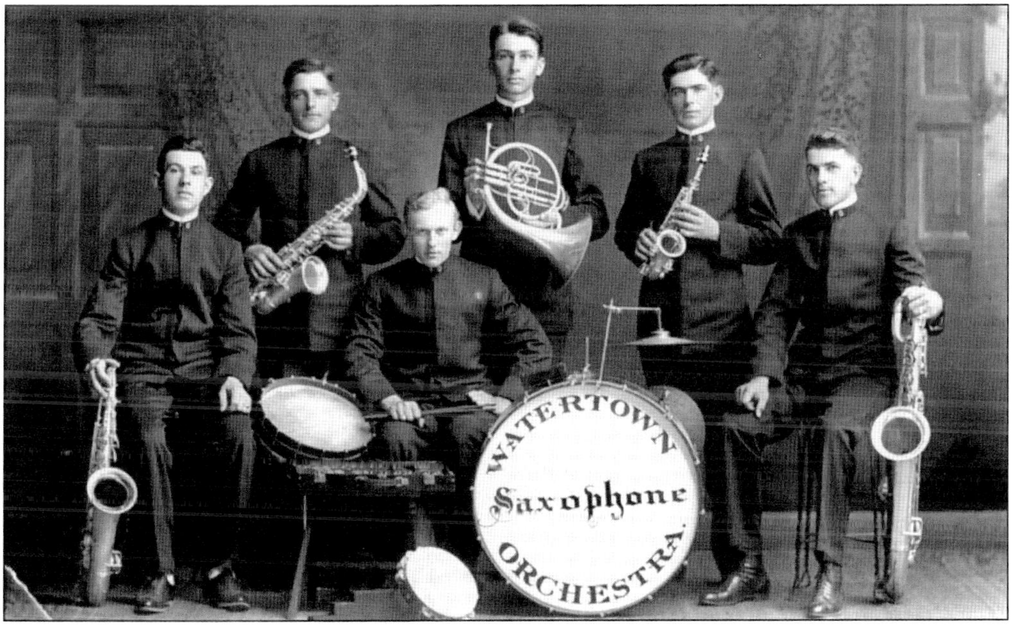

Another popular group that had their heyday in the 1920s was the Watertown Saxophone Orchestra, seen here. Other groups included the Pat Neitzel Orchestra, the White-Kuhns Orchestra, Babe Schoenath and his Orchestra, and Bob Strege and His Goosetown Dutchmen.

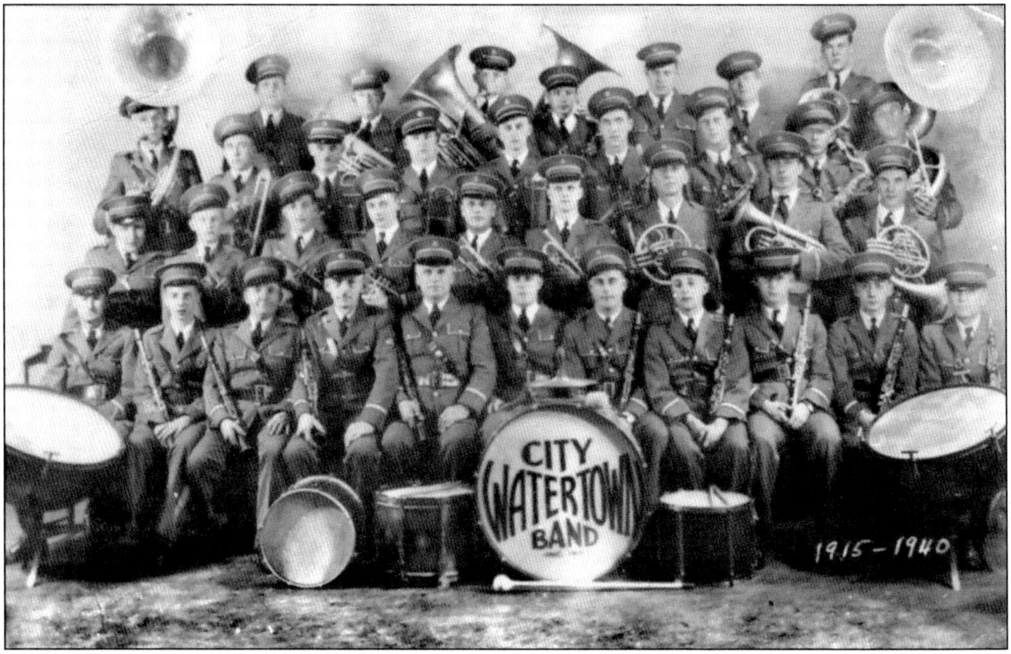

The Watertown Municipal Band, shown here on its 25th anniversary in 1940, was founded in 1915. The band plays for special events, parades, and Thursday night band concerts through the summer months, which are very popular.

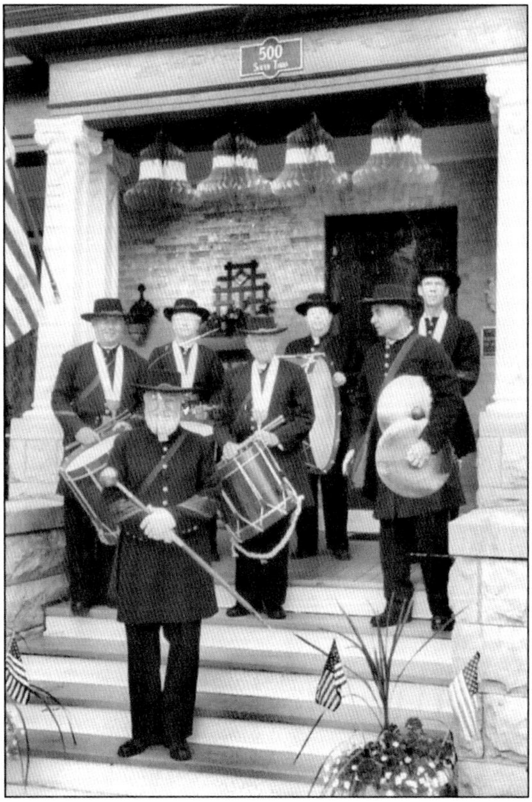

Since 1994, Watertown has been the headquarters of the 1st Brigade Band, a nationally recognized historical music group that re-creates Civil War–era music on original vintage instruments. Seen here are several of the band members on the steps of the Albert Fuermann home at 500 South Third Street. This home is on the National Register of Historic Places.

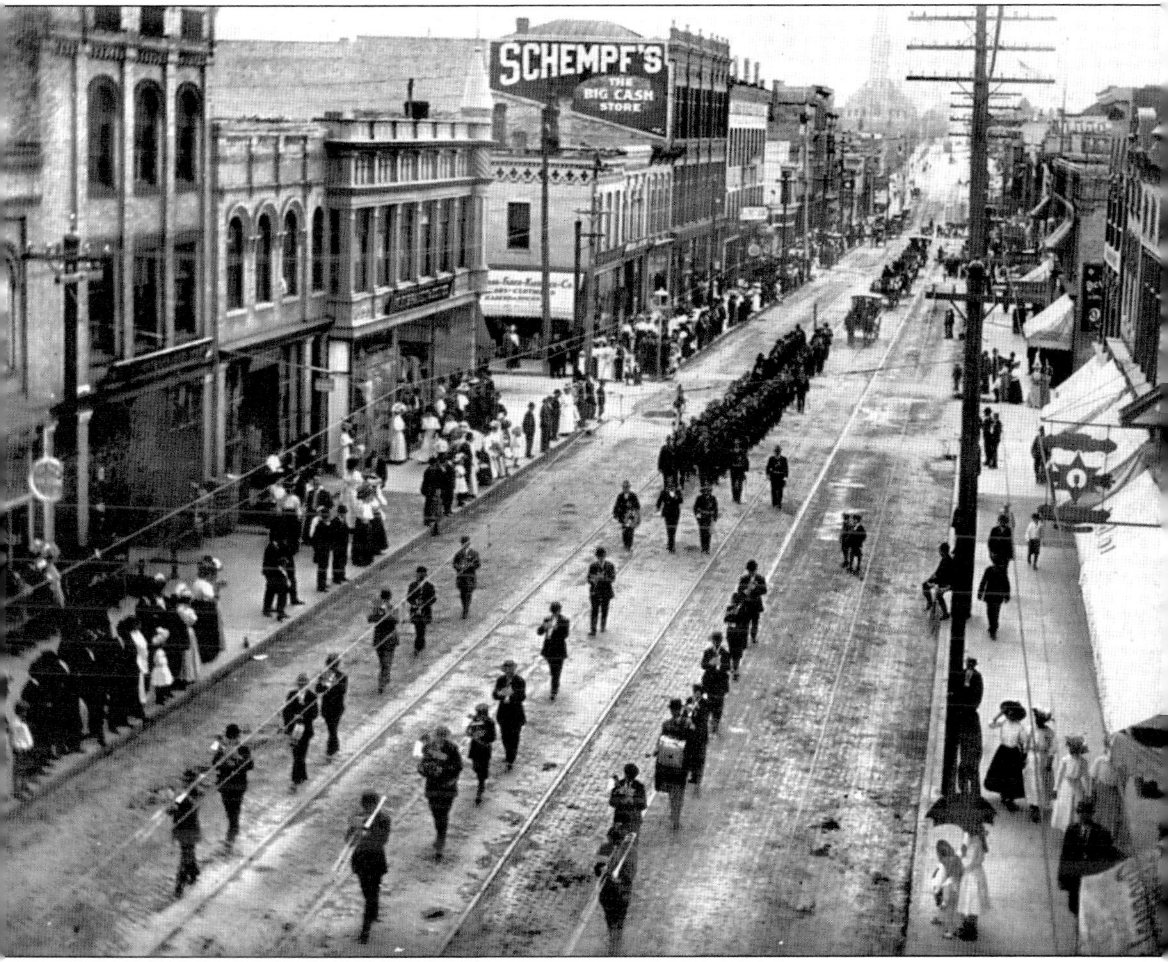

As mentioned earlier, Watertown loves a parade, and here is the Fourth of July parade of 1912. Watertown has always been very supportive of its veterans of the armed forces at these parades. Celebrations may come and go, but the features that always stay constant and bring the people out year after year are the bands, the floats, and the veterans. These make the parade.

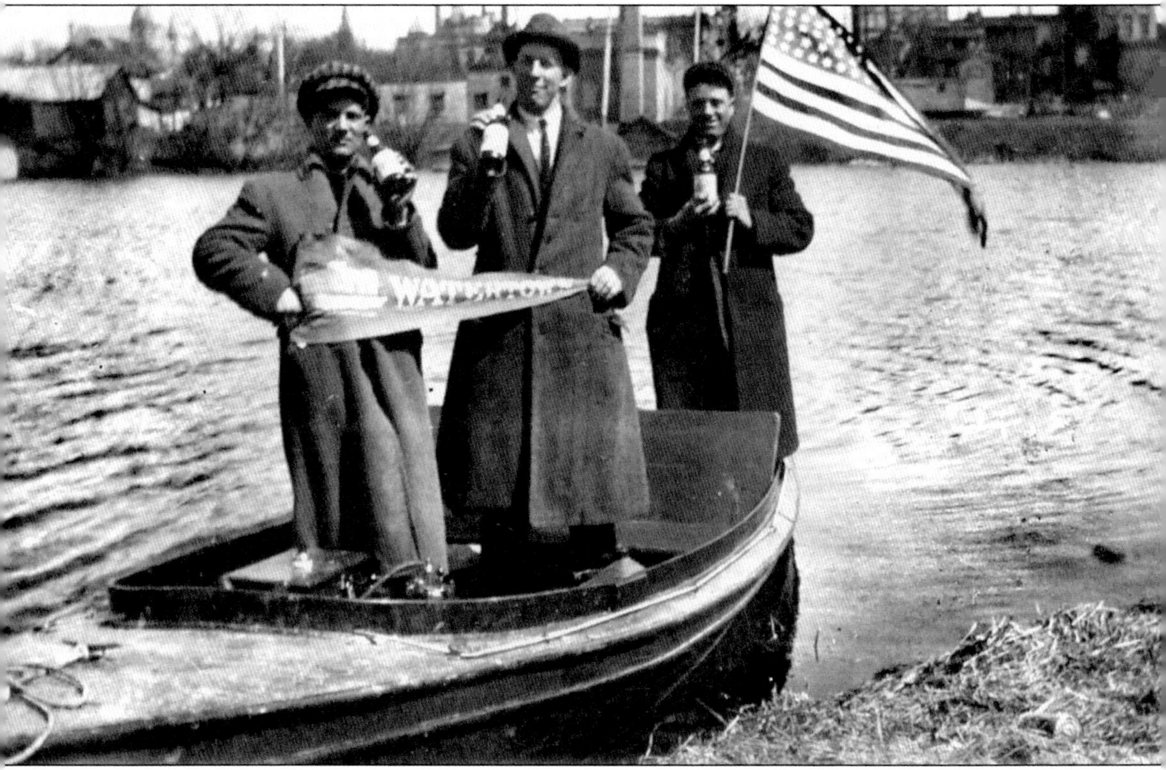

So, as the sun sinks slowly in the west, a goodbye is bid to Watertown, Wisconsin, and its quirky charms. Be it ever so humble, there is no place quite like Watertown.